Praise for *Personal Score*

"Ellen van Neerven's remarkable memoir *Personal Score* seduces with its synthesis of poetry and political critique, grounded in a strong sense of place. It is essential reading for its insights into settler colonial violence, gender and sexuality, climate justice and—of course—football. And it is also a reflection on family, friendship, love, pride, and the joy of kicking goals. Van Neerven describes *Personal Score* as 'an ugly book that was born of the ugly language that I grew up hearing in this country.' Yet it is a pleasure to read their account of the years during which 'I am the parts of me that don't know what I know now'—and to learn from them what it is they now know."

—Judges' report: Victorian Premier's Literary Awards 2024 - Non-Fiction, Winner

"In this ground breaking work of creative nonfiction, Mununjali writer Ellen van Neerven extends an invitation to readers to enter a cultural space. Within this space van Neerven candidly explores gender politics, trauma and resilience while fearlessly challenging the pernicious settler myth that 'sport and politics don't mix,' and asking poignant questions like: can a nation really separate identity politics from sport; and is sport really the great leveller that the nation claims it to be?"

—Judges' report: Victorian Premier's Literary Awards 2024 - Indigenous Writing, Shortlisted

"*Personal Score* is at once an analysis of the coloniality of sport and the Indigeneity of sport. Its scope is breathtakingly vast—Ellen van Neerven weaves together the autobiographical, the historical, and the sociopolitical so expertly, and, in doing so, demonstrates a new way to write toward Indigenous freedom. *Personal Score* hums with the vitality and intelligence of a definitive text."

'THOR OF *A HISTORY OF MY BRIEF*

"This work lays bare the many unspoken threads tangled up in modern Australian sport, from relationships with bodies to relationships with land, and highlights the paradox of sport as both a liberator and exterminator of difference, as told from the perspective of a queer First Nations writer—of which this space contains so few. Splicing together personal memoir with history, journalism, and throbbing poetry, this is a crucial interjection into the myths we tell about ourselves as a sporting nation, coalescing in a new and necessary kind of sports writing."
—**SAMANTHA LEWIS, SPORTS JOURNALIST, ABC NEWS**

"Ellen van Neerven's *Personal Score* is many stories, fragments, memories, anecdotes and poems interleaved with meticulously researched and beautifully written histories of First Nations sport in so-called Australia. This book is a night walk, a football bouncing deftly, bodies pushed and pushing—so intricately woven it reads like a root system. Read it. Then read it again. This work is exquisite."
—**QUINN EADES, AUTHOR OF ALL *THE BEGINNINGS: A QUEER AUTOBIOGRAPHY OF THE BODY* AND *RALLYING***

"Van Neerven brings their untameable voice and critical eyes to a tour de force that captures the complex, passionate relationship First Nations people have with sport, reminding us that we fight colonisation on every front, assert sovereignty with every act, and it's family and connection to country that keep us grounded, especially when the playing field isn't even."
—**LARISSA BEHRENDT, DIRECTOR OF RESEARCH AT THE JUMBUNNA INDIGENOUS HOUSE OF LEARNING AT THE UNIVERSITY OF TECHNOLOGY SYDNEY**

"Weaving together race, Indigeneity, sports, sexuality, gender, class and Country, they offer something no sport historian has. a beautiful story of Blackfulla love—for sport, for Country."
—**CHELSEA WATEGO, *THE CONVERSATION***

"Weaving memoir, poetry and polemic, Ellen van Neerven digs up some fascinating nuggets about sports played by First Nations people on this continent pre-invasion, returning through millennia to all the thorny present-day issues of how race, gender and sexual orientation play out in sport. With their trademark vernacular ease, van Neerven coasts between elite competition and community-run sport, their love for family, country and 'the beautiful game' shining through."

—**FIONA KELLY MCGREGOR, AUTHOR OF *IRIS, BURIED NOT DEAD,* AND *INDELIBLE INK***

"Van Neerven's prose is intimate and alive, their sentences arc like a fluid pass, linking complex insights with biographical reflections... An eloquent statement and a reminder that whatever is written about sport on these lands should be built on the recognition of what came before and still survives."

—**JACKIE TANG, *READINGS***

"Ellen van Neerven asks a direct and profound question: 'What does it mean to play sport on First Nations land?'... Van Neerven, through their own experiences as player and spectator, asks us to consider what we value most about sport and how we can nurture and protect it."

—**TONY BIRCH, *THE SATURDAY PAPER***

"Ellen van Neerven cleverly recalls their lived experience, touching upon the connections between sport, culture and identity... *Personal Score* succeeds in its depiction of van Neerven's holistic personal evolution, in their yearning for something that can be attained only if the playing field is level. Further, the offering challenges the reader to view their position on the field of life while interrogating their role within the game—because life is a team sport."

—**DORCAS MAPHAKELA, *ARTS HUB***

"Powerfully refutes any suggestion that athletes should avoid activism and instead 'shut up and play,' while also offering a wonderfully complex and thought-provoking account of the joy and pain of a sporting life from a vital, incisive voice that asserts a perspective too often neglected in discussions of the topic."
—**GEMMA NISBET, *THE WEST AUSTRALIAN***

"Soccer and non-fiction sit parallel as two of life's mysteries: I admire and consume both, increasingly when they're more than fields of men, but I'm certainly not a natural. Ellen van Neerven's *Personal Score* unmasks these forms through an intimate exploration of what it means to play and be on First Nations land."
—**LAURA JEAN MCKAY, AUTHOR OF *THE ANIMALS IN THAT COUNTRY***

"Van Neerven's ability to challenge and expand politics is thrilling, their flair for language exhilaratingly intimate."
—**NAKKIAH LUI**

"I'm a footballphobe whatever the shape of the ball, but I was riveted by Ellen van Neerven's shapeshifting *Personal Score*. It effortlessly warps the conventions of the sports memoir, deflecting attention from the individual to the collective, and replacing triumphalism with a thinking-through of what it means to play sport on stolen land. And its narrative voice is a marvel: direct, poetic, inquiring, intimate and frank."
—**MICHELLE DE KRETSER, AUTHOR OF *SCARY MONSTERS, ON SHIRLEY HAZZARD*, AMONG OTHERS**

"Interspersed with poetry, autobiographical writing, interview, history and sporting advice… we are always wandering, tracing, sometimes circling back, growing familiar or seeking out whatever is not, and all the while learning this lesson: not to be afraid."
—**DECLAN FRY, *THE AGE***

PERSONAL SCORE

Sport, Culture, Identity

Essays by
Ellen van Neerven

Two Dollar Radio
Books Too Loud To Ignore

Two Dollar Radio
Books too loud to Ignore

WHO WE ARE Two Dollar Radio is a family-run outfit dedicated to reaffirming the cultural and artistic spirit of the publishing industry. We aim to do this by presenting bold works of literary merit, each book, individually and collectively, providing a sonic progression that we believe to be too loud to ignore.

TwoDollarRadio.com

🐦 @TwoDollarRadio

Proudly based in
Ohio
TURTLE ISLAND

📷 @TwoDollarRadio

f /TwoDollarRadio

Love the
PLANET?
So do we.

Printed on Rolland Enviro®.
This paper contains 100% sustainable recycled fiber, is manufactured using renewable energy - Biogas and processed chlorine free.

100% **PCF** BIO GAS *ENERGY* ∞ PERMANENT

Printed in Canada

SOME RECOMMENDED LOCATIONS FOR READING: Pretty much anywhere because books are portable and the perfect technology!

First published 2023 by University of Queensland Press, Australia

AUTHOR PHOTO→ Anna Jacobson; **COVER DESIGN**→ Eric Obenauf;
COVER PHOTOS→ **Flowers, Mushrooms, Butterflies, Bugs, Seashells, Kookaburra:** Biodiversity Heritage Library/Flickr; **Starfish, Australian Salmon:** Tasmanian Archives and State Library (Commons)/Flickr; **Bicycle:** "Advertisement, Union Crackajack [front]," courtesy, California Historical Society, MS 197_003.jpg./Flickr; **Player:** "Sam Kerr playing against USWNT 2012," Thewomensgame/English Wikipedia, https://commons.wikimedia.org/wiki/File:Sam_Kerr_playing_against_USWNT_2012.jpg.

Two Dollar Radio would like to acknowledge that the land where we live and work is the contemporary territory of multiple Indigenous Nations.

CONTENTS

AUTHOR'S NOTE

I am not to scalpel you with details but sing to you in poetry, and that is where these memories will rest.

PERSONAL SCORE

Sport, Culture, Identity

Pregame

Kombu-merri (Yugambeh) Elder Dr Mary Graham explains that at the center of First Nations beliefs are two things: "Land is the law" and "You are not alone in this world." Put simply, only two relationships matter in the world: relationship with land and relationship with people.

Between these pages, I am asking myself, and in turn I want to ask you, what does it mean to play sport on First Nations land? Land that includes animals, birds, insects, plants, water, sky and everything underground. Country that is rich in story. Do we need to know the truth of land before we can play on it? Indeed, should we do *anything* on Country without knowing the truth? Can we participate in the broad spectrum of sport and fitness while following First Nations protocols? These protocols have an essential role to play in the present and future.

I want sport to return to its origins of inclusion and care for land.

In the media, racism in women's sport rarely gets mentioned, as if it does not happen. The faces of equal pay struggles in sport are white women. The faces of LGBTIQSB+ inclusivity in sport are white people. In the same system, successes are masculinized. The faces of racial equity in sport are Black men.

Are these really the only faces of the civil rights movement in sport? This is precisely why Kimberlé Crenshaw inaugurated the term "intersectionality" in 1989.

I am an armchair enthusiast of the sport we call "the world game": football, sometimes called soccer in Australia. I used to be an amateur player and spent most of my waking life at football grounds across so-called South East Queensland.

During my formative football years at The Gap (named for the gap that is the valley between Mt Coot-tha and Enoggera Hill, but also easily symbolizing "the gap" between how the men's and women's games were treated at the time) there was ambition. I was around motivated people who wanted to take the game to the next level. These people believed football could be the biggest game for female participation. They believed in the power of women's sport. They believed Australian women's football could be the best in the world.

During this time, many of the things we now take for granted in our game hadn't happened yet, but it was like we could see them in the distance. The A-League Women. An international star (Sam Kerr). Equal pay for the national team. Full stadiums. The FIFA Women's World Cup on home soil. My coaches shared that vision. My teammates shared that vision. My parents shared that vision. It was part of the reason we showed up to every game and every training session. We believed we were part of something that was bigger than us, and it would only get bigger.

The leaps and strides our game has taken since then are amazing to see. In 2021 I chatted to professional players at the hundred-year milestone game at the Gabba to hear their reflections. I heard stories of the first A-League Women's (then the W-League) final in 2009, told to me in detail through the scrapes, scraps and micro-stories as if it happened yesterday. As someone who struggles to remember what they had for breakfast but remembers their spectacular-leaning goals without a worry (the venue, the placement, the celebration), this doesn't surprise me. There's something about the way we play. We remember the narrative, beyond the stats. Who was there and who wasn't. The underdog moments. The missed sitters. The painful substitutions. The elation when a training move goes right.

There are many more stories yet to be told, and on the eve of the biggest-ever global women's sport event to be held here, the soil is especially potent for story. The historic 2023 Australia and Aotearoa New Zealand Women's World Cup is the first-ever World Cup to feature Indigenous language throughout its branding and designs, created by Kalkadoon artist Chern'ee Sutton and Māori artist Fiona Collis, and it will include dual names for the nine playing locations: Adelaide (Tarntanya), Brisbane (Meaanjin), Melbourne (Naarm), Perth (Boorloo), Sydney (Gadigal), Auckland (Tāmaki Makaurau), Dunedin (Ōtepoti), Hamilton (Kirikiriroa) and Wellington (Te Whanganui-a-Tara).

A football pitch is a hundred meters long. You run this field over and over again across your lifetime. A football pitch is seventy meters wide, and it will break your heart a few times. My own memories of and musings about the Country I've played on circle me.

This is not a beautifully written book about decolonizing Australian sport. This is an ugly book that was born of the ugly language I grew up hearing in this country. This book is me scratching my way out of the scrap of the schoolyard, just trying to stay alive. This book is reflective of the fact violence does not exist as a binary and we are all capable of causing harm as well as receiving it.

In this book, I am the parts of me that don't know what I know now. I am becoming and I am belonging.

I have a score to settle.

PART ONE

NORTH STAR

My first home backed onto the North Star football fields in Geebung. I was only a few months old when my dad started coaching there. He often got home late with wet grass blades stuck to his legs, bringing the grounds inside. One night he brought me a ball back from the club. That was the start of football for me. I grew and took my first steps on that ground. There was a camp between the trees, between where the railway was now and the old waterholes. I was scared of the creek. There was something that had happened down there. Much older, I thought about it and cried, for how every club ground and stadium I'd known had history, and for all that time in those places feeling things I did not know how to name. And for what had happened. What had happened.

I Want to Play

What we love makes us whole. What makes us whole is how we survive.
adrienne maree brown

"I want to play," I say to my parents. It is as close to a demand as it can be. An insistence. No extra words required.

I am eleven years old. My brother, Ben (three years and three days younger), has already been a signed, registered player for four seasons at our local club, Albany Creek Excelsior (ACE). Every day we match each other in the backyard. I attend his games jealously, playing around with a ball on the sideline and, yes, maybe showboating my juggling a little at half-time in the hope someone will notice. I don't feel like I fit in with the mums who try to coax me away from the field to come sit with them on their deckchairs on the hill to listen to their conversations about things other than football.

No thanks.

I don't remember when I first kicked a ball. I just do it. Oh, the things I can do with a ball! My ball is always there, at foot's length, ready to attach itself to me. The charge I feel between me and the ball is electromagnetic and irresistible.

More than this, I am a football academic-in-training who can watch football on TV all afternoon, who does watch football all afternoon on Sundays with Dad during SBS's *The World Game* specials. And Monday nights: English Premier League highlights. We fold the washing on the couch and Mum cooks dinner.

I know most of the players' names by heart. I have huge posters of Dutch stars Ruud van Nistelrooy (Manchester United) and Dennis Bergkamp (Arsenal) on my bedroom walls

I talk and strategize football all day. When I need to zone out of something unpleasant (in the dentist chair, for example), I recall the formations of Barcelona or Arsenal or Man U I've memorized. Starting with the forwards, all the way to the back line and the goalkeeper. Little football webs creep over my mind and keep me balanced.

Our backyard is our church of football, spilling out into the park outside our house and into the nearby cricket batting net we use as a goal.

The protagonists:

my bro, Ben—light-footed, tricky, quick

my dad, Wilhelmus "Wim"—dogged Dutch football fanatic

me, Ellen "Eff" (family nickname)—two-footed, tries hard

our dog, Max—always up for piggy in the middle

my mum, Maria—occasional cameo player,

though always upstairs to nurse scrapes and injuries, cut up fruit to eat later. Truth is I never remember being tired—I never remember anything that stopped me playing.

"I want to play." To play, to actually play, beyond the backyard, is the first desire that I have expressed out loud. When I name this desire, it stirs something in me, and something in my family and the people around us as well.

Reflecting on it much later, I realize growing up AFAB and growing up First Nations in a racist nation-state, I was not meant to have desires that were outside those of the colony. Everything around me was telling me I needed to know my place.

There is a perceived difference between Ben and me. He is a "boy," and I am a "girl." For me to play, as a "girl," it's not simple.

ACE has numerous boys' teams—so many that they're named after all thirty-two clubs in the English Premier League; my brother's team is Everton—but no girls' team. And there are no girls playing in the boys' teams.

I am a child who rarely speaks, whose words and confidence come later in life. Of my dad and me, my mum says, "You're scared of your own shadows." She tells me I have inherited my dad's shyness, and I'm also told I am like my dad's mother. I'm proud to be compared to her. Oma was a beautiful, kind, gentle soul, incredibly intelligent. She lived through war and famine, and raised, fed and cared for nine children. She had the best marks at school but did not go further with her education, cos gender. She had twisted toes, which I've inherited. "Oma's feet," my parents say whenever I spend money at the podiatrist. When I think of Mierlo, the town my Dutch family belong to, I remember being four years old in a new country on a visit with my parents. Oma sensed the frightened child in me, she sensed we were alike. She comforted me in her home, and I felt better.

It is clear to my parents I need a soft and supported introduction to team sport, so my dad drives around the local area with me, looking for a club that has a dedicated girls' team. They are hard to come by at the time, and we almost give up.

But one day, Dad tells me we are going for a drive. We drive north, along Old Northern Road. We cross Cash's Crossing. We turn left at our church in Eatons Hill. We drive west, on the scenic Eatons Crossing Road. We drive over Clear Mountain. We drive another fifteen minutes on the mountain range, before descending on farming area and a small township called Samford. Driving through Samford, we turn right at the service station and pass bush and farms for another five minutes. There, on a nondescript road, down a hill and next to a horse club, is the ground of the Samford Rangers. All up it is a thirty-minute drive.

It is 2002. My dad signs up to be my first coach.

A week later, Dad takes me to Amart All Sports in Stafford near his work to buy my first pair of football boots, also known as soccer cleats. This remains one of the most joyous days of my life. I still remember ripping open the paper in the shoebox when I got home and touching the soft black leather. Italian. Sexy. Shoelaces on the side. They don't make football boots like that anymore. They are somehow on sale too, so they don't break the bank.

"At least you'll look good," Dad tells me, as I walk out of the house with my boots, socks and shinnies on, ready to play our first match. I'm number eight. Our strip, or uniform, is a baby blue with black shorts and blue socks that fade quickly (mine turn white by the end of two seasons).

Years of playing in the backyard have given me a soft touch, and although I favor my left, I am conveniently two-footed. (Dad, chronically only right-footed, told me I needed to learn to kick with both feet, that it was important for footballers today. It didn't used to be. Take Maradona, for instance; he was notoriously only left-footed!) But I have to learn stamina, match fitness. My dad likes to tell people I tried to come off after just five minutes during my first game, a game at Wynnum that required us all to play a full match as we only had ten players. "I'm hot," I said, apparently (insert whiny eleven-year-old voice). I tried to sit down, but Dad didn't let me. I was, though! It was a stinking hot day.

Physicality was/is not easy for me. I was born with a neurological developmental coordination disorder called dyspraxia, or weak muscle tone, as my mum calls it, and I received physio for the first six years of my life to do simple things such as tie my shoelaces, sit upright and write my name. All these things make my brain hurt.

It's something that continues into adulthood, kinda slightly invisibly (though physios always pick it up: "You were a floppy baby," they tell me), and I am really happy when *Harry Potter* star Daniel Radcliffe talks about it in 2008, how he has a mild form of dyspraxia and how it sometimes prevents him from doing simple activities, such as writing or tying his shoelaces. Everyday things that make my brain hurt and my hands slightly tremble still today include putting on jewelry, cutting slices of bread, opening packaging and learning any kind of new skill, except if it has to do with football. The thought of doing anything complicated with my hands in front of others can make me feel panicked.

When I was a baby, my mother was told by the physio to enroll me in ballet as this would help my coordination. The classes were expensive for my single-income family, and in my first-ever production as a Christmas pudding I danced the wrong way in the opening. I maintain that all the other ballerinas went the wrong way and I was the one who was right! So it's safe to say my ballet career didn't stick. At least my costumes got worn—by my brother, who enjoyed dressing up more than I did. I was always a bit butch like that.

In all the ways ballet is difficult, football is joyous. I can't put into words how much I love going to training and playing games in my first season at Samford. I feel useful, proud. I think I love training even a little bit more than games. I love small-sided games the most, trying things out when I have the opportunity to learn, to grow, to play.

In some ways it is miraculous to my mother that I can play football. And play well. Even during my first season I am getting rave reviews and awards. It is an immediate confidence boost. I am a striker. I am fast. I am skillful. I score goals. It is the ultimate affirmation. My mother notices the difference between my on-field and off-field personalities.

"When I first saw you play," she says, "I was surprised at how aggressive you were."

It is where I can express myself. On the field I am determined and proud. I am finding faith in myself.

My first season draws to an end. Around the time of my first club presentation night, I subscribe to popular music for the first time through the irresistibility of teen rockish ballad "Complicated" by eighteen-year-old French-Canadian singer-songwriter Avril Lavigne. When I was younger, we didn't listen to the latest music. My parents listened to radio stations that played 1960s and 1970s easy listening. Mum sang 1980s Tracy Chapman to me when I was in the womb. I'm grateful Bob Dylan, Fleetwood Mac, Van Morrison et al. are the foundation for my music DNA, but at some point, for better or worse, I was going to enter the big bad world of noughties pop and be totally engrossed.

At the club presentation night, activities outside are interrupted by a massive electrical storm that flashes against the field. We watch the storm play out from our retreat in the clubhouse, the wind pushing against the glass. I am annoyed. I want to muck around with the football; parties bore me. When lightning strikes, grass gets greener.

Water washes over the green. The sounds get softer as the storm passes. We can hear ourselves talking once more. The speakers are switched on, and I recognize Lavigne's song. It's been playing on the radio.

Now, "Complicated" and the other songs on Lavigne's debut *Let Go* are like pages of my teen diary. I feel them deeply in my soul. Like I'm living my emo teenage fantasy.

I learn how to tape her songs on the radio so I can play them again. She wears ties over tank tops with oversized cargo pants. Baseball cap backwards and Cons firmly planted on skateboard.

I want to skate in an Avril Lavigne film clip. I love skateboarding. I'm not very good on a board, at least in real life, but I do smash it at Tony Hawk's Pro Skater on our family's PC. I am too scared to approach the local Albany Creek skate park across the road. It's not really the practice park I would like it to be. My brother and I went once cos I wanted to watch, and we didn't feel welcome. Years later I will indulge my skateboarding fantasy by longboarding with my first girlfriend along the back streets of East Brisbane.

I manage to convince my mum to let me buy an item of skateboarding clothing on sale at City Beach once a year, so after a few years I have an outfit I can wear to our annual free dress day at school: an Element T-shirt, paint-spattered khakis, logo trucker cap and coffee-colored skate shoes several sizes too big that my physio said were the worst shoes I could ever wear for my body. Cool, right?

I sit in the Samford clubhouse beside my parents, watching the field, singing the lyrics to "Complicated" in my head. The song feels so fresh, so different. I feel different to the other people around me; this is my soundtrack. A beautiful rainbow begins to paint itself onto the sky. Next week is my twelfth birthday. I'm growing up in years and height. In a few months I will graduate from primary school and attend my local high school.

Very Athletic People

Aboriginal bodies speak to sovereignty. I am the embodiment of my country. I am an uncomfortable truth reminding you of your forefather's past deeds.

Fiona Foley

Australian sport did not begin in 1788. On the contrary, sport of many kinds was played on this continent by blackfellas for thousands of years before whitefellas arrived with their supposed expertise and prowess.

The word "sport" comes from the Old French "desport," meaning "leisure." The oldest definition in English, circa 1300, describes sport as "anything humans find amusing or entertaining." *Roget's Thesaurus* defines the noun "sport" as an "activity engaged in for relaxation and amusement."

Unlike whitefellas, First Nations people don't necessarily subscribe to the binary of work and leisure. These two activities are intrinsically linked and can't be separated. For First Nations people, sport is part of life, part of work, part of education and part of looking after Country. First Nations cultures are highly sophisticated and embedded in care for natural resources and deep knowledge of fire, flood, stars, aquaculture, agriculture and architecture as part of life.

The division between work and leisure was severe for Europeans. Opportunities for leisure came with money or organization and less working time, rising dramatically in the mid-to-late nineteenth century, starting in Great Britain and spreading to other wealthy nations in Europe. The British brought this attitude here. For example, up until the mid 1930s sport was banned on Sundays in all states, and sport on Sunday wasn't made legal in South Australia until 1967. It was also an elitist pursuit, reserved only for men and the ruling class. First Nations sporting arenas, in the form of camps, corroboree grounds and sacred ceremonial sites, were grabbed by the Europeans and made into public parks for leisure. As the eight-hour working day took shape, sport and leisure by 1900 had become a profitable industry, one that the working class could also enjoy.

As First Nations people from Australia are the oldest surviving living culture in the world, we are also the oldest living sporting culture and the oldest sportspeople in the world. First Nations people have beautiful words adjacent to sport in our own languages, rooted in land and culture and relations. Sport, for us, is umbilical to the land.

For example, "yulunga" means "playing," in the language of the Gamilaroi (Gamori) people of north-western New South Wales.

"Moogahlin" is a Yuin/Bundjalung word meaning "to play" or "to fool about," and has been adopted by a First Nations-owned theatre company.

"Woggabaliri" is the Ngunnawal or Gundungurra word for "play."

"Nabei" is the Yugambeh word for "play," while "na'bulela," as Jenny Fraser tells me, is our Yugambeh word for "fighting."

And countless other words exist.

Each individual nation (Australia has over 500) has its own sports, though many are shared between cultures. First Nations sporting traditions include various types of games using balls made of possum, kangaroo or wallaby skin, as well as wrestling, spear-throwing, spinning discs and stick games. Some sports are linked to tracking and hunting. Many saltwater First Nations peoples played sports that involved swimming, diving, fishing, surfing and canoeing.

These are some examples of the traditional sports belonging to First Nations peoples.

1. Weme

The Walbiri people of Central Australia created this stone bowling game. One player throws or rolls a stone that is then used as a target by the second player. Players take turns, with each aiming at the other's stone. In Eastern Arrernte language, "weme" refers to "throwing something at something else and hitting it."

This reminds me of a similar game my brother and I used to play with glass marbles on the concrete outside my house. We played a lot of games to amuse ourselves when we were growing up. I loved creating a new game with rules and scoring, then inviting our neighbors and cousins to come test it out with us. I enjoyed that time, before mobile phones and computers, as I could become fully absorbed in a game for hours without distraction. I was always the jarjahm ("child"), who tired of games the slowest. I'd be the last one standing.

2. Kokan

The hockey game called kokan comes from Mabuiag Island and is one of many varieties of hockey games played in the Torres Strait. Played on a long stretch of beach by all genders, the game involves striking the kokan (ball) with a rough bat, called a baiwain or dabi. The bat is made from a piece of bamboo with a cut-out grip.

I loved playing hockey during primary school. I wanted to continue playing, but it wasn't offered at my high school. For me, football and hockey are very similar: one you use your feet to keep possession of the ball, and one you use a hockey stick. Hockey goalkeepers can even use their feet.

3. Edor

Edor is also known as eda and by other similar names. It's a running game commonly found in North Queensland and Torres Strait. It involves chasing and tagging with a large group of players.

In the Aurukun community the game has been played for as long as the local Elders can remember and is still played in the streets and at school.

In the Torres Strait it is played on the beach using two trees up to fifty meters apart. One selected player starts by running towards one tree to try to touch it. If they are touched by another player this player calls out loudly "Eda" (signaling that they are now the runner) and starts running towards the tree that is the furthest away.

In the Tiwi Islands children collect grass seed heads growing on the sandhills and toss them in the wind to chase at full speed.

I loved running games when I was small. I was pretty good at sprinting. I was always saying to my brother, "Race you to that tree!" Running along the beach was my favorite. I loved the feeling of powering through that heavy sand, feeling like I was not going anywhere fast. But after a few good strides, I would feel like I was flying. Lucky for me, my brother hates sand, so I always had an advantage.

4. Woggabaliri

Wiradjuri people from the Bogan and Kalari rivers area of New South Wales, as well as neighboring peoples, played a kind of football with a ball made of possum fur and bulrush roots. The fur was typically spun by women. The ball is just slightly smaller than a tennis ball. Woggabaliri is recognized by the Australian Sports Commission as one of the oldest Indigenous ball games. The name for this game is taken from the Wiradjuri word for "play."

This is a kicking volley game. The players do not take sides, instead using teamwork, technical ability and agility to keep the ball from hitting the ground. One player kicks the ball up in the air to start. All kicks are made with the feet or knees.

Juggling circles were a staple of my childhood. We used juggling to improve our skills, readiness and touch, all of which were vital to be able to ping the ball back to the other members of a group. It does involve teamwork; you're only as good as your weakest link. It's not a game that promotes showboating. Instead, you need to be there for the other players, anticipating their kicks, ready for anything.

Possum-skin balls sewn together with ochre, ash, resin and binder are a staple of First Nations sporting cultures and our cultures in general. First Nations artist and possum-skin-cloak revivalist Carol McGregor says that possum-skin cloaks "were important cultural items and affirmations of [our] identity."

A traditional possum-skin ball was used as a symbol for Australia's failed 2022 Men's World Cup bid, as a roundabout way of saying, "Never mind the British, the first codes of football were invented here."

"We were in essence playing with a football 'for possibly thousands of years," says Worimi man John Maynard, who wrote *The Aboriginal Soccer Tribe: A history of Aboriginal involvement with the world game* (2011), which honors the legacy and largely untold story of Aboriginal footballers past and present.

I have never made my own ball with possum skin or other natural materials, but I have juggled a toilet paper roll, a balloon, a tennis ball and a hacky sack. My dad said when he was growing up it was a tin or a bundle of rags, "nothing special, as long as you could kick it around."

When I traveled abroad, I could not take my eyes off the talent displayed in the Vietnamese street game da cau, played with a shuttlecock. It's known as sipa in the Philippines, jianzi in China and featherball in English.

I joined in on a few games in Hanoi, which remains one of my favorite cities. My friend's seven-year-old son was a keen player. I let my teammates down with my reflexes, not used to kicking something that wasn't round. My friend's son offered to teach me a few secrets to keep the da cau up. When I next played with him, a few years later in Berlin, we were both impressed with each other's improvement.

On the streets it's non-scoring, "just for fun," but at the same time wildly serious. It's a game that requires concentration and cooperation.

Many First Nations sports are non-competitive, whereas European sports are almost exclusively competitive. First Nations sporting traditions promote wellness and social bonds, whereas European sporting traditions can further social divides. This puts the racial vilification of Adam Goodes and countless others into social context. European sport is set up to prey on the "othered."

A key difference emerges: First Nations sport is about working with the environment and animals and plants, whereas non-Indigenous sport is in direct opposition with the environment and sees the environment as part of the conquering.

Before Captain Cook set off on his journey, before the ships had even sailed, the racist imagery of First Nations Australians had already been seeded. Through scientific racism and the codes of white supremacy, a white/black and civilized/savage binary had already been set. From the arrival of the Invasion in Botany Bay, armies of mass destruction descended on the east coast of Australia.

Queensland Badtjala artist Fiona Foley writes in *Biting the Clouds* (2020) about the legacy of the "violent pathology" of British colonial racial hierarchy. She writes, "it was considered sheer sport to hunt down Aboriginal men, women and children on horseback. Not to consider them as human but as vermin made it easy to shoot to kill, rape and pillage."

Blood sports, a category of sport that involves bloodshed, were traditionally practiced by aristocracy—some historians say the name relates to the "royal blood" of those who practiced them. It relates to power and excess. In Australia, the term has uglier connotations of a squattocracy spilling blood for dispossession. And, like the English aristocracy knowing they could get away with it, settler-invaders were versed in blood sports. Europeans brought blood sports here—killing for fun, for trophies and conquest, not food.

There's a powerful link between sport and killing in Australia, with bloodthirsty British on horseback going on rampages, egging each other on to kill as many of my people as possible, as though it was a game. What was the scoring they used? Ten points for a man, six points for a woman, three points for a child?

While writing this I am watching Peter Morgan's *The Crown*. In season four, an entire episode is dedicated to the hunting of a wounded grand stag. At the start of the episode, the royals declare the stag's head must be placed on the dining room wall. All engagements are canceled as it is stalked. The shot stag lingers, holding on to life, but by the end of the episode its head is mounted in Balmoral Castle.

I can't help but think: forty pairs of Aboriginal ears were nailed to a homestead wall by station manager Jack Watson as a trophy after orchestrating a massacre with accomplice Jack Hann in north-western Queensland. The house, called Lawn Hill Station, in Waanyi Country, still remains.

I can't help but think of Mounted Native Police Lieutenant Frederick Wheeler, a notorious figure, openly murdering First Nations people in Queensland for over twenty years.

"To the European eye, Brisbane or Moreton Bay as it was known then, was virgin land. Like the rest of Queensland they assumed it was available for the taking," Foley writes.

In 1827, settler botanist Allan Cunningham wrote in his diary on passing the Great Dividing Range and entering Turrbal, Yuggera and Yugambeh Country that the First Nations people he had seen were "tall, well-formed persons of rather athletic features." It was reported that First Nations people on average were twenty centimeters taller than the British.

South East Queensland First Nations people had carefully built roads into extensive networks throughout the continent, allowing for transport, trading, hunting and ceremony. These "served as thoroughfares for people on the move, bearing trading items or new songs, dances, information and ideas," says historian Raymond

Evans. The invading Europeans used these roads to gain the land and resources they needed to prosper.

Very quickly, the campfires burned out in Meaanjin (which refers to the bend of the river where the city of Brisbane now sits) and surrounding areas.

Dr Mary Graham says that land "recognizes the sweat of people," and when the Europeans arrived, land recognized another type of sweat. Evans states that the frontier wars caused a decline in the Queensland Aboriginal population of "95 percent," indicating that the intended genocide of First Nations peoples in Queensland was almost completed. But it was not completed.

As Foley says, "the decimation of tree species is interchangeable with the decimation of human life." They killed our peoples while they milled our trees, like the red cedar and the bunya pine, and we lost our food sources and burning practices. Construction, even in its simplest form, meant the destruction of Aboriginal country and culture. The materiality lives on; it is repurposed. Its spirit remains. Shell middens and sand and trees are in the new architecture. And our old camps are the sites of sporting fields. They chose campsites to build football fields because they were already cleared. But the original custodians were erased.

Receiving information from a book or the historical record is different to what I feel and know when the blood courses hot in my veins. No book will ever compete with what I have already been given by my ancestors: the gifts of learning, of love and of belief.

Jenny Fraser writes, "we were there on The Frontier when our land was taken and our tribes were decimated." You might correct our grammar here, or question the use of hyperbole, and say, how could we possibly have been there, for we were not yet born? However, my cousin, in her own words, is a "direct descendant of a murderous English police officer and an enslaved Aboriginal woman." This puts her in the center of a matrix of past, present, future; a physical, metaphorical, emotional enmeshment.

Jenny goes on to say her matriarchal ancestor Jidda was given to Frederick Wheeler as a "thank you" for Wheeler committing a massacre at the request of other local pastoralists. Although Jenny and her family are living proof this massacre happened, she writes, "when I search for information on this massacre, nothing much comes up … so much history has been covered over, unheard, untold." Until much is done to free the true stories of the past, we will be "there" without end.

Conversations about sport are not honest if they don't reference dispossession and displacement. Land is an archive, saturated with information. When I think about First Nations children's sports like the ones I listed earlier—chasing grass seed heads, rolling stones; sports that have a sensitive engagement with Country—they sit in stark contrast to the yelling I hear when I pass a school. Children as young as five are encouraged to be aggressive to their fellow students, using the language of war and blood sports: beat, flog, smash, attack, defend, destroy. The lexicon of violence shapes a language of movement at a young age. Children are told to push through discomfort, toughen up, fight, and to harden themselves into weapons to win at all costs, humiliating another person or group of people.

But sport can exist without contest and conquer. It is not about destroying. Let's see what we create when we are not attempting to destroy something in each other.

Sugar Fields

There's the inner game and the outer game.

At twelve years old, it's my first time going away by myself. To say I am excited is an understatement. I am flying with my Brisbane North Rep team to Mackay for the state championships after just over one year of playing football for a club.

It's my second time on a plane. The first was with Mum the previous year, when we traveled further north. We spent two weeks in Cairns and we got to go on a boat and see the Great Barrier Reef.

I carry a tracksuit and sports bag in the Brisbane North colors—red, white and navy—with my initials on them into Brisbane Domestic Airport. I had almost forgotten to pack my boots, which resulted in a quick dash back home to retrieve them. Mum is teary when my family drop me off.

"Look at you. You're all grown up," she says. "Sorry we can't come, darling. We'll miss you."

"Bye, Mum. Bye, everyone."

It's the first time I will be away from my dog, my brother and my three cousins who have been living with us. Us five kids are between the ages of nine and twelve and attracted to anything with the *Parental Advisory* sticker on it. I am allowed to take the Walkman with me to Mackay so I can play all my tunes, especially my rap rock favorites, Linkin Park and Eminem.

Mackay is 970 kilometers north of Brisbane, or an hour and a half by plane, but still not even half the length of the Queensland coast. The flight is just long enough to play most of a bootlegged copy of Eminem's *The Eminem Show*. My cousins are obsessed with this album and the soundtrack to the movie *8 Mile*. We want to be Eminem even though we Blak. We watch the movie under the house when my parents aren't around and play the album low so they don't hear the cussing. We make up our own raps, challenging each other to battles in the backyard, just like in the movie. My cousins shriek at the beginning of the sex scene in *8 Mile* when Eminem leads Brittany Murphy to the back of the car factory. My cousin says Eminem is hot. I don't know what the fuss is about.

The plane lowers onto beautiful Birri Gubba Country, rain clouds over the Coral Sea and the Pioneer River snaking through the town, which is called "the sugar capital of Australia."

Terror, violence and massacres were inflicted on the Birri Gubba people from the 1860s onwards with the arrival of the Europeans. So began a history of extractive colonialism, involving erasure, exploitation of land, exploitation of people and the artificial landscapes of colonization. In 1865 the first sugar crop was established, and tens of thousands of South Sea Islanders, many of them children, were "blackbirded" (kidnapped or taken through coercion) from their home islands to Central Queensland to work as slaves for white farmers in the sugar and cotton industries. Mackay is named after Scottish-born colonizer John Mackay, who led a group into Central Queensland in 1860 firing shots at Birri Gubba people and later commanded ships to complete regular human trafficking missions in the Pacific Islands, as well as personally traveling to China to kidnap labor for Queensland. Particularly close ties developed between the South Sea Islander and the Birri Gubba peoples, resulting in an interconnected community today. The Birri Gubba people hid and protected South Sea Islanders from the violence inflicted by the slavemasters.

By the mid 1880s there were over thirty sugar plantations and twenty-six sugar mills in the Mackay region. The government and employers knew that the South Sea Islanders' lack of immunity would fatally expose them to diseases such as the flu and measles. Over a quarter died prematurely, the vast majority buried in unmarked graves by the Pioneer River. The population were seen as expendable labor, to be discarded when they were no longer needed. The Pacific Island Labourers Act of 1901, enacted on the back of the White Australia policy, saw the deportation of around 10,000 Pacific Islanders, with over 7500 "press-ganged" onto ships. Migrant workers from Malta, Italy and elsewhere soon replaced the labor.

You could say this is a dark chapter in Australia's agriculture industry, but the whole of Australia's agriculture industry post 1770 is a dark chapter that is ongoing. Australia doesn't need an officially legislated White Australia policy anymore because it is so ingrained in our society.

Mackay Sugar, German-owned as of 2019, produces around 800,000 tons of raw sugar and 200,000 tons of molasses each year. Sugarcane remains in the soil all year long and is one of the world's thirstiest crops, making sugarcane farming perhaps the most environmentally destructive agricultural industry. Forests have been cleared for it and invasive species such as the cane toad have been introduced, destroying ecosystems. Sugarcane production pollutes freshwater with silt, fertilizers washed from farms, plant matter and chemical sludge from mills. These contaminants flow out to the Coral Sea and are killing the Great Barrier Reef.

The year before I arrived in this place for the first time, the Queensland government found the sugar industry had allowed five pesticides to enter the river, exceeding acceptable standards.

First Nations people care for sacred Country in the face of erasure and extraction. Uncle Jim Gaston, Birri Gubba Juru Elder, has set up a monitoring program to protect the Gungu—the green turtles who feed off the seagrass that's damaged by nutrient run-off. He was grown up with Sea Country knowledge passed down from Elders.

The team bus pulls in to the main football ground just off Sugarshed Road where we will be playing the tournament. The green of the grass is mixed in with the red-brown of the soil. I visualize curling a ball into the top right-hand corner of the goal closest to the clubhouse. Smack. The net bulging. I have set my sights on making the Queensland team, so I have to stand out and play my best. If I look at pictures of myself playing during the tournament I see total concentration on my face, my right thumb up indicating to my teammates where the ball is going, and a slight lean of my body to the left side. Our female coach is kind and caring and notices I have issues with my back cos I hold my hips sometimes at training.

"You better get it sorted, Ellen," she says, saying it could be more than just growing pains. "You don't want to have issues with your back long-term."

"Yeah yeah, I'll get onto it," I say.

When we arrive at the camp where we will be staying for the week, I suddenly get nervous. I've made a habit of getting out of school camps since the first one in Year 4, when I was eight or nine. But it seems like this might be okay. I'm in a different environment. I'm not at school. And two of my teammates who I've been playing with since last year at Samford, Harriet and Anita, have been assigned a dorm with me.

Harriet is a very good player. She's got better ball control than me. She plays in the midfield and has unbelievable vision and long passing. She can also shoot the ball from outside the eighteen-yard box and get it on target every time. She is a pretty laidback person. She is best friends with Anita, both white, rich parents. They go to the same school, a private girls' Catholic school in the eastern suburbs.

Anita is a pretty good player too, but not as good as me. She is very aggressive and fast and plays as a winger. She has a tendency to run the ball out because she forgets about the sidelines. She loses her temper on the field, and her loud British voice really carries. Dad had issues coaching her last year because she would sulk if he asked her to come off. She started calling me names in frustration. But since Dad's not our coach this year and the new coach doesn't take her off the field, she has lost interest in me lately.

Our cabin is furthest from the main building and inside is small and dark. Harriet and Anita put their bags on the beds they want,

Anita top, Harriet middle, leaving me with the bottom bunk. I don't mind.

We go to the shared bathroom block together and have showers. Mum has given me plastic flip-flops to wear so I don't get athlete's foot. I change into my PJs.

When I get back into our shared room, Anita and Harriet start laughing. Immediately I panic. What's wrong? Is it my hair? Is it my pajamas? What kind of PJs should I have brought with me?

"You look like you had some fun in there."

"What do you mean?"

They keep laughing and won't tell me why. I'm blushing and angry and anxious. Then they start calling me "cumface," and I ask why they are calling me that, but they won't tell me.

Eventually I go back to the bathroom, look at my reflection in the mirror and see a spot of dried toothpaste on the corner of my mouth. I go back and say, "It's just toothpaste, and I got it off," but they keep laughing at me.

It could be a lot worse, but I find being with them together in that room very hard. They are determined to pick on me, and I don't understand. Aren't they my teammates? Dad told me Anita is a bully, so I know that, but why is Harriet being just as bad?

I don't fully understand yet how packs of girls work and why no one is sticking up for me.

The first time we have dinner I enjoy it. For one, the food is plentiful. They let us grab seconds. Pasta, salads, curries, it seems we can have anything we want, and we are very hungry twelve-and thirteen-year-olds. It is also a chance to see all the players from the whole competition in one space. There is a girl called Aurora from South Brisbane who walks around in her sky-blue jersey with her name on the back, who claims she is going to be the best player Australia has ever seen. There are the North Queensland girls who wear green jerseys and are always smiling. There're ten teams and a hundred and sixty of us. We all love football, and we're all very happy to be there.

The second time we have dinner is just after our first match; we won the game and I played well and came very close to scoring a goal. I hear "Hey, cumface" across the table. Harriet and Anita again. Some of the other girls start laughing. Our coach is not around. Everyone's eyes are on me. Everyone's laughing now, even some of the other teams. I get so uncomfortable that I think I shouldn't be there.

After dinner, homesick as anything, I try to ring my parents using the payphone outside the games room, just to hear their voices. But no one picks up.

The remaining nights I don't go to dinner. I stay in my room, because this is the only time I get away from Harriet and Anita. They sneak out on the second last night and I have double time away from them, to just be alone with my thoughts. But then at 1:00 am they come and wake me up, throwing my clothes around, trying to get me to play a game, my hands above my head, fending them off. It's the night before the final and I am desperate to get some good sleep.

In that moment I realize it doesn't matter where I am, who I am with or what I do; kids are always going to come for me, because I am quiet, because I am different, because they are bored, because they know I am going to keep taking it and they are going to get away with it. I have to put barriers up cos they are always going to come for me.

That's the inner game and the outer game.

On the bus on the way to the game the next day I listen to Eminem's "Lose Yourself" loud, headphones a reprieve from the name-calling. These days, honestly, Marshall Bruce Mathers III just sounds like white fragility, misogyny and homophobia to me, but at the time it was the shit, it was motivational, it was the art of putting words together and being understood.

During camp, I always keep my Walkman on my body or hidden in a secret compartment in my dad's suitcase so Harriet and Anita can't steal it. It's a small victory that I get to keep this wonderful device of magic, power and defense.

This is what I am not thinking about: as we near the river, we are passing the Mackay cemetery, where in the "other" section, formerly known as the "heathen" section, is a field of unmarked graves. It will be more than a decade later, in 2017, when the souls who died while cutting cane will gain recognition through mother and daughter Marion and Imogen Healy. Researching family history will bring Marion and Imogen to the unmarked graves, and a team of thirty volunteers led by Starrett Vea Vea will look through cemetery records to add names to headstones.

"I used to ride across here for a shortcut and not realizing I was riding over my own ancestors," Starrett says of the discovery. "These were the ones that never went back to the islands."

This is what I will think about in the future: "Is it fair to have a town named after a man who treated us like slaves?" the question Marion asks *The New York Times* in light of her research.

At the football ground, about two kilometers from that resting place, we win our final against South Brisbane, two goals to us canceling out a single goal from Aurora on the other side. I am happy to be winners and to get the medal we all deserve, but deep down I am not happy with my performance. I know I should have scored and killed the game off earlier. I was too hesitant in the moment and I kick myself for it later.

After we receive our medals, we are told to go back to the field and wait for the announcement of which sixteen players have made the under-thirteen Queensland team to go to the national championships in Canberra in December. Names are called. Aurora from South Brisbane. Other names, some I recognize, some I don't. Harriet's name is called. A big smile creeps over her face. She is also named player of the tournament. Names continue to be called, and my heart sinks. I know deep down I have not done enough to deserve a call-up to the Queensland team, but it still hurts. I guess I realize that just because I want something doesn't mean I'm going to get it. There will be other times I don't make teams, but I will always remember how it feels this first time: like all my dreams have been quashed.

I call my parents that night from the payphone. I feel guilty because they have sacrificed so much to get me to Birri Gubba Country, so I hate letting them down. The good thing is, with the jubilation of the win, our last night here, and Harriet making the state team, I don't think Harriet and Anita will harass me too bad tonight. And I am coming home tomorrow.

"We can't wait to see you, Effie," Mum says.

"We'll pick you up at the airport at ten," Dad says.

Gender Police

To those who keep asking, I have no gender, no sexuality, and no fucks to give

Shamir

I love this quote ^
I wish I could have said it at eleven years old.
I grew up under a microscope, as a lot of us did.
Brown skin, dark hair, different features.
Always asked, from such a young age, "Are you a lesbian?"
"Are you a girl or a boy?"
Always interrogated about everything.
At eleven my primary school staged an intervention and got me to see a school counselor because I was too masculine-appearing. She gave me make-up tutorials and made me remove my body hair.

I started cutting my arm hair with scissors in class. I tried to cut everything off me.

It's taken a while to remember this and reflect on it. On the deep sense of shame and humiliation I felt all the time, that I was never enough.

The experience was a violation of my personhood.

I'm grateful to know this now and to be on a journey to healing.

Two years later, I was thirteen and at high school, and things got worse. While the teacher was out running an errand, two girls in my math class came and sat by my desk.

"You have to start shaving. Look here. Your moustache. Your bushy eyebrows. Your hairy legs. It's ugly. You're thirteen now. It's not right. You need to take care of yourself."

"I just want to play soccer," I remember saying. "I don't have time for those things."

"But you can play soccer and look like a girl and take care of yourself. My sister does."

"No." I refused to say anything more.

I grew even more afraid of anyone saying anything about my appearance. I hated being made an example of.

Part of the humiliation of having second-hand uniforms was that I had holes under my arms, which showed my thick, dark armpit hair, and holes in the torso, which showed my stomach hair.

My body hair wasn't like the white girls'.

It was thick, dark. It wasn't normal.

I began to feel monstrous.

I started shaving and waxing and made an effort to be more "feminine," but I found there was always something that stopped me from being accepted. That game I wasn't going to win.

But I won many others. Hat-trick hero.

"Who is the boy playing with the girls?" I overheard people say when I played for my club team.

"Who is the girl playing with the boys?" I overheard people say when I played at school.

"Who cares?" I wanted to say. "Can you just please let me play?"

If my identity makes you angry, jealous or sad, maybe you are the one you should be interrogating.

If I could, I would say to my old teachers, schoolmates and all the parents—what about my appearance makes you uncomfortable? Why do you think I'm the one who should change?

I'm Afraid of Women

After Vivek Shraya's I'm Afraid of Men

I'm afraid of women who tell me to shave my legs
I'm afraid of women who ask how much % Aboriginal my mum is
I'm afraid of women who talk about my grandmother
I'm afraid of women who move their seat further from mine
I'm afraid of women who stare me off in bathrooms
I'm afraid of women who get up and sit somewhere else
I'm afraid of women who ask me if I have a boyfriend
I'm afraid of women who lower their voices when I come closer
I'm afraid of women who say my hair was pretty longer
I'm afraid of women who tell me I'm too angry
I'm afraid of women who tell me I'm too quiet
I'm afraid of women who grab me by the shoulders
I'm afraid of women who tell me I don't believe in God
I'm afraid of women who tell me what to fear
I'm afraid of women because it was women who taught me fear
I'm afraid of women because women are afraid of me

Confidence Game

Did I tell you I was in the football class at high school? Twenty of us were picked for the Soccer School of Excellence in my year—mostly fellas, you know. I was one of only a few that weren't boys. Our coach was Greg Di Losa, a big, tall center-forward who played semi-pro for the Lions. Dad and I went to see his games a few times.

For football class we spent our mornings on the oval. I can't tell you how much football meant to me back then. It was who I was. On the oval I could fly. I loved feinting—they come rushing in and you just place a little touch beside them and you go speeding past and there's no one in front of you. I waited my turn in the wings to float in to cause damage. They didn't know I was there until I got the ball. Zip in, zip out. I showed my intent and went for the corners.

Di Losa told us when you're at a tight angle, coming from the wings, to hit it across the goal. Always go across the goal. And nine times out of ten it's too late for the keeper to intercept it—even if they do get their hands on it it's going in anyway. I got a lot of tips off him about psychology on the field. He taught me goalscorers are born, not made, but he also showed me how much of it is a confidence game.

Football was set up in a way I could understand. On the oval we didn't talk. It was teams, not groups, and you took your position on the field. I felt like an equal, but I also knew I was good—the boys didn't like it when I went past them. This was a way to communicate. Express myself with a defense-splitting pass. Get to know the patches of dirt on the halfway line.

Being in the football class gave me a lot of pride. It gave me more than being Aboriginal did at that time—gave me more pride than anything else.

I would sit in the afternoon class with the scent of morning sweat on me. Scraped knees, my joggers scuffed. This didn't go unnoticed. Different class now, more girls. In the afternoons there was a sense of making it through the day that hadn't been there on the oval in the sun. The girls would heckle me. Playing with the boys I had grown tougher physically, but underneath I had weak skin and their taunts pinched that skin. I had holes in my uniform, I had hairy legs, I had darker skin and darker features. I didn't brush my hair, I didn't have label shoes or make-up. I was more interested in the fields, in the trees. I was interested in listening, not speaking.

I didn't go to the bathrooms at school, as they were places where I could be ambushed by my fellow classmates. I held on to the point that my bladder hurt. I would run to the bathroom as soon as I got home.

Sometimes I could get through afternoon classes without being noticed, but that was rare. The girls would ask me questions and my answers always made them laugh. I didn't know why. I wasn't sure how to respond to their name-calling. I just wanted them to leave me alone so I could get through the day. Sometimes I couldn't.

One day the blackboard was blurry. I couldn't concentrate on the equations. I could only think of what was behind me—the giggles, the whispers, the wet balls of scrunched-up paper. I got up from my chair and asked the teacher if I could go to the sick bay. I think this was the first time he had noticed me, as he looked pretty surprised. Before then I must not have spoken. This day wasn't any worse than the others, but I could feel a sharp pain in my stomach growing, the feeling I couldn't keep it all in, not today. The teacher nodded and I walked quickly down the halls.

At the sick bay I went to lie down, thinking I was finally alone and maybe I could cry ... a girl on the next bed started talking to me. She was from an older grade—I hadn't seen her around before. This girl was asking questions. She wanted to know who I was.

"Where you from?"

"Dad's Dutch."

"No, you look ... there's something else."

"No, Dutch."

I didn't answer truthfully, thought she would be like the others, latch on to me, pull me down. But maybe that had been my chance to be heard by someone who may have just said—in response to my declaration of my culture and family—"That's cool, hey." I needed that, you know. Because words had begun to change me. Creep in on what used to be safe corners of the oval. I'd be in on goal and shoot straight at the keeper or wide or, even worse, way over the bar, and that feeling of humiliation and failure brought everything back to the surface. They whispered to me—"monkey girl," "Chewbacca," "vegemite"—and my head went down like it did in class and I couldn't look at my teammates.

I worried myself when I missed these easy chances. Stayed on my mind at night. Didn't want to lose "it," you know. The only thing I thought I had. I started practicing extra hours at home by myself, sometimes with Dad. I went back better and more prepared. I started slotting them in again and one weekend I scored four against the rival school and I was cartwheeling inside, but there was the feeling I couldn't get ahead of myself, not ever. As there was little I could do to prepare for those afternoon classes.

Sitting in that room with my head down, fingers interlaced, nothing meant more to me than three o'clock, running home, sometimes singing to myself—five minutes across the road, through the park, across the creek, between the trees and to the back gate of our house (I was home!) and my dog, Max, always there to greet me, his nose on my leg—take him out with a soccer ball until Dad got home—and we would watch the sports highlights on TV as we ate pasta at five o'clock and then we were off to training in the car—with the mountains in front, the sun setting and the sky fading and the feeling I'd escaped something for another day.

Every Goal and Every Miss

We lived in a house behind a patch of bush, and I remember the sounds of flying foxes at night, owls too, and sometimes koalas, comfortingly close to my bedroom. It used to help me wind down, but in my early teens I turned restless. I didn't sleepwalk, but sometimes I got up. I went down the back stairs and found company in Max, who I could see in the dark, feeling exactly where his head was, the cap-like part between his ears.

I stared into the dark mass of trees, ribboned by moonlight. I had a lot on my mind. I worried I would always feel the way I did, painfully shy. I wondered how it would affect my ability to go to university, to get and keep a job, to meet someone—a friend, or more than a friend. Max would sit next to me and take these thoughts from me. After a while all I felt were his matted paws and his forelimbs, skinny like mine.

In the breath of the trees, in the clearing of language, I had inherited a silence that made school life difficult. And home life safe. At home, I was deeply reliant on Max and my family to give me what I needed. We were a close-knit group. We had football in common. "Let's go to the park," we would say, and Max would follow, racing out as soon as we opened the back gate. We had a kick next to the cricket nets, the ball rolling over the long, rough grass. Max chasing, moving back and forth between the three of us, Dad, me and my little brother. Mum was part of the team too—the one who made us pasta before games and washed the jerseys after. Sometimes she took Max to our games with her and Dad. They sat on the hill behind the goals instead of in the cold metal stands alongside the field.

I remember a lot of my life at clubs. The twice-weekly drills. The lights, brighter on match days. The field so familiar. The grass and the gum trees beyond. The field epitomized for me "home ground"—I was home there, and if I were to go there again, I would probably feel tears.

I whispered to Max, told him I used to be scared of dogs before him. There had been a few incidents. The terrifying fox terrier that jumped at me on the way to school. And worse could be coming around the corner. Despite this, for so long, I wanted a puppy, and each year I wrote the word on the Christmas wish list I made for my parents. They made no promises. After a few years of trying, at the end of 1999, when I was nine years old, my brother and I decided to add in brackets "but it probably won't happen." That must have pulled some heartstrings because a few months later we were driving as a family to a faraway southside suburb called Kingston. It was quite the drive; we didn't drive that far for anything. At the Kingston home was a litter of nine from a beagle mum and an unknown father. All the pups were black and white except for the smallest, tan, with white paws and a star-shaped patterned chest. This one was the friendliest of the bunch, coming to us at the fence. He chose us, Mum and Dad said. Our millennium pup.

On the way home, my brother had him in a box on his knee. I was asked if I wanted to take turns, but I wasn't yet ready to hold this new, shivering, squirming animal-thing that I named.

In the days that followed, slowly I got used to him. Observing, looking down at him in his box, wrapped in a blanket. He was only a baby. Seven weeks old. He cried. And needed us. In what felt like no time, he became part of the family. His name felt right on my lips. My best friend. If I had been scared of him and now was not, I thought as I stroked his ears, could other things change? Could I overcome the big unknowns in my life?

Wasteful was how I felt most days when I got home from school and went straight to Max. There wasn't an easy way to make friends without talking, I knew. There were no jobs for people who didn't talk. Would I live in this house with the forest behind us forever? Part of me knew I would mind this. Part of me wanted more for myself, but I didn't quite know how to get there.

Like at school, I didn't talk to anyone at football. I just made sure when I turned up I was good at what I did and wasn't wasteful.

My teammates pointed out that I never celebrated a goal, just stood still and silent. Attention wasn't welcome, but scoring was always sweet. Strikers want to score in every game. I felt the burden of being a striker, but when it paid off, I enjoyed the responsibility. Part of me remembers every significant football moment.

I remember a big game, a final that I was gearing myself up for. Mum was going to miss her sewing class to come with Dad.

"And Maxy?" I asked.

"I don't think I'll bring Max. He was naughty last time."

Max, now five, still hadn't really gotten over "that puppy stage," according to Dad. He still got overexcited in crowds, and he didn't like to be separated from any of us. Mum couldn't go to the club-house and get a coffee without him making a fuss. Mum and Dad would have to spend the whole game trying to distract him from the fact that I was on the field. The few times he'd seen me he hadn't wanted to stop barking, a sharp bark followed by a high-pitched whine. Very distracting for me and for the others on the field. Not so cute anymore, Mum reckoned.

The day of the final I came home from school hiding the tears on my face from my parents, drying them on Max's fur as I lay my head on his. It was something the teacher had said. Or my classmates. I was not okay, it was a bad day, and many bad days together feel, well, shit. I slumped. The game was in front of me, but it wasn't really. I didn't want to play. I felt my silence in my whole body.

When the game started, things were happening without me. I was circling the dust in the opposition's half. Running every direction, trying to get on the end of a long ball. But of course my teammates didn't hear me. Who could? At one point I looked up to my parents on the hill for comfort. Mum had gone home.

The scores remained even into the second half. I repeated mistakes. I kept disappearing.

And then. Our central midfielder with a bit of space. I sensed the opposing defenders slacken. I began running in a straight line, running without looking behind me. There was no way the ball would come to me. But it did. Just in front of my right foot. I traveled with it, found only the goal and goalkeeper ahead. I crossed over the eighteen-yard box, put my best foot forward, lined it up … and fell. Before I could make the shot I had been clobbered from behind. The ref blew. It was a pen.

The crowd and my teammates were happy. I picked up the ball. Looked at the goal. Visualized a motion—the ball hitting the post and bouncing off. In my head I had convinced myself I would hit the post, that I would miss, so I put the ball down. I wanted someone else to have it.

And they would have, if it wasn't for Max. He was running onto the field, tail wagging, towards me. His legs were moving fast, his lead trailing behind. The pitch changed. My dog. I dropped to my knees and touched his panting, smiling face.

I was smiling too and feeling how strange a smile felt on my face.

"Is that your dog?" my teammates asked, gathering around. Max was enjoying the attention.

"Yeah," I said. I held his collar and patted the fur underneath it. I could see, in the distance, my mother rushing forward, my father looking on, unsure.

"We've got to get this dog off the pitch," the ref said. "And who's taking this spot kick?"

"I will," I said, standing up. The ball soft and ready at my feet, Max ushered off by the team and put in the safe hands of my mother on the sideline.

I want to say now that the outcome of that kick didn't matter. The feeling of conviction before was much more important. But I am a striker. And I remember every goal and every miss.

I stared down the goal and took those steps back. The kick was clean. Low and powerful to the right-hand corner. No post, all goal. The winning goal in the final. I felt a shout on my lips, and I ran out the movement of my kick, my heels floating off the ground. Max joined my sound with an excited bark—well before my teammates found me—and I heard my mum and dad in the crowd. We would not be quiet.

Protest in Sport
(A small selection, 1957–2023)

1957, The Gully, Katoomba

Aunty Rose Cooper refuses to leave her home

1

2

3   4

5   6

7

1. Before Invasion / the Gundugarra and Darug people used the Gully at the headwaters of the river as an important summer camp.

2. Land grab / In 1854 / settler-invaders at the foot of the mountains forced a large group of Gundugarra and Darug people to leave and relocate to the Gully / Flooding of the Burragorang Valley in 1950s made this permanent.

3. Group of businessmen / backed by council / searching for tourist attractions / contemplating development on the western slopes of Katoomba. / A good idea: turn the area below into a racecourse for cars (and a flying boat).

4. The local people could have told you it was a terrible place for a racecourse.

5. Evictions began in 1956 / Grandmother Rose's cottage was directly in the path of the track / she and others refused to leave / the night before she was to be evicted and her cottage destroyed / she suddenly passed away of a heart attack. / The bulldozer operator was asked to hold off so the family could lay her to rest.

6. Thick fog / mist / racecourse disused by 1970 / see the shape from the plane.

7. 2002 / the Gully finally recognized for its Aboriginal cultural significance / managed by mob for the future.

1971, Turrbal and Yagera dhagun, Brisbane

Sisters Aunty Lilla Watson and Aunty Maureen Watson
are two of many First Nations people that take to the streets
to protest the Springbok match
to Say No to Apartheid
at the Exhibition Grounds.
Not safe to walk the streets while Aboriginal
riot squad police enacted
immense police line.
White people couldn't see
the racism hiding in plain sight
in their own backyard.
Premier Joh says
don't mix politics with sport
catchphrase at the time.
For First Nations people this was never ever
a choice. Politics was never a luxury
neither sport
It's taken a while—for these White Australians—
for their feet to touch the ground

1971, Gadigal land, Sydney

Lyn Thompson (nee Craigie) wears a Springbok jersey
outside her and her husband's residence during
the Springbok tour. Unlike her brother Billy and friend Gary
she does not wear shorts, socks and football boots.
Is barefooted instead. Wears the jersey as a dress,
falling above her knees, is pregnant with daughter Yeena,
both defiantly wrapped in this jersey.
A proud Gamilaroi woman from Moree
makes an anti-Apartheid statement with her body.
A Black man will never wear a Springbok jersey,
Vorster said. Well, a Black woman wore a Springbok jersey,
a Gamilaroi woman wore a Springbok jersey and she wore it well.

1971, Gadigal land, Sydney

Verity Burgmann storms the pitch
The young white Australian woman disguises herself as
red-headed South African older female fascist
to be unassuming in crowd at SCG
waits for the right time to infiltrate then storms
pitch with her sister, Meredith
what do I do, sis?
get the ball!
so she grabs the loose ball
all eyes on her, stands tall
kicks it high
        direct lob through the posts
the best kick of the game. The best kick of the series for sure.

1994, Camosack, Coast Salish Country

Cathy Freeman runs with the Aboriginal flag
Before she leaves Australia
the twenty-one-year-old
carefully folds up a black, red and yellow flag
designed by Luritja artist Harold Thomas
in her kit bag
When she wins the 400 m
she celebrates by wearing both flags
around her neck in a victory lap
Australia's chef de mission Arthur Tunstall
explodes with rage
orders the Australian team to inform Freeman
not to display the Aboriginal flag in future events
otherwise she will not compete
she will be sent home.

1   3

            2

---

1. If there are two flags / only one is illegal and / should be banned
2. Her shoulders
3. When you lose you're Aboriginal / when you win you're Australian

2015, Wurundjeri Kulin Country, Naarm

Deborah Cheetham does not sing the national anthem
Deborah does not sing tonight
at the MCG
cos she ain't young and free
and we ain't *young and free*
she feels it's an honor to be chosen
but can't get her mouth 'round the words
she says hey, let's make it
in peace and harmony
we'll get back to you, and please
do remember, you'll be turning down
the chance to sing live to 90,000 people
and countless more
on primetime TV
well, we can't change the lyric, Deb
but will you still sing?
I can't, that's not who we are
no worries, I think
Kate Ceberano's free
I won't leave it at that
I won't keep it under wraps
70,000 years won't be erased or silenced
the Ancestors sing so powerfully

2015, Gadigal land, Sydney

The Matildas withdraw from US tour
This is the first time
an Australian sports team has gone on strike
60,000 tickets already sold
Only months after being quarter-finalists
of the 2015 World Cup
contracts expired and no future mentioned
train full-time on part-time wages
and many need second jobs.
Players on full-time contracts
are paid $21,000 a year
compared to a full-time Socceroo
who made $200,000 that year
the men are ranked 58th in the world
and the women are 9th.
"This was an extremely difficult decision to make,"
says goalkeeper Lydia Williams
"However it's simply unfair to continue to expect us
to make enormous sacrifices to play for Australia."
The team doesn't board the plane to the USA.
As a result of the strike, the PFA
sign a new agreement with the FFA.
The top Matildas receive $41,000 a year
with a second tier set at $30,000
in addition to match fees.
Further to this
in 2020 the Matildas receive pay on par

with the Australian men's team
in a world first.
The 2015 strike paved the way for this decision.

THE GAP

Fourteen at a club all about performance. Dad's pressure, and pressure from the club and the coach. My role was to be the team's big center striker—to hold up the ball like Viduka. I ate to be taller, gulping down extra serves of Mum's pasta before and after training, determined to fit into Dad's boots, but I stopped growing sometime that year. Deep royal-purple strip—colors are colors, but somehow this made it feel even more like a femme club. It was an elite women's club and we were all treated with respect. Kept it about the football. No parties after. Desire on the pitch and training ground. Head down in the changing room. Dad hurrying them to training on Tuesdays and Thursdays because if you were late you didn't play on the weekend. Sprinting out of the car and sprinting around the oval. Trying to be as fast as the other players. My legs were flogged in preseason—long depleting runs beyond the field's boundaries into the bush.

One year, deep into winter, reports came in of a prowler stalking the area. Everyone on high alert. The team stopped going out of the club's grounds. The creek and bush around the fields were out of bounds. I missed the water, missed standing at what had been a meeting place at the junction of the creeks. All of the fields had a source of water, and I felt that source, needed it before I could understand it. No longer did I chase balls down the creek and feel that power. Shadows fell and the field seemed darker when there was a "don't leave anyone behind" rule. Fear and rape and land-rape just outside the gate.

The Bike Path

While I was playing at Samford, Dad found out that there were trials at The Gap Pastime, on the other side of the mountain range, and asked me if I wanted to go check it out.

This was a chance to test myself against the best. I joined their Premier Youth team, the under-sixteens, changing my colors from sky blue to purple and gold. The club culture was very strict, and there was a level of professionalism I was not used to. The discipline was useful, but it did make me feel nervous. At the time, we were the best women's football team in Queensland. We were the team to beat.

The girls' and women's teams trained at The Gap High School. Behind the football field was bushland and a creek. In that bushland was a bike path that was part of a complex matrix of bikeways in Brisbane's west.

In 2006, a serial sexual predator who was known at the time as "the Bikeway Rapist" attacked women while they were exercising along these bikeways in the The Gap and nearby suburbs of Ashgrove, McDowall, Ferny Hills and Stafford, my neighboring suburbs. These women were riding bikes, walking, jogging and taking in the beauty of the forest and parklands in the evening or early morning when they were attacked by this predator. It was a systematic series of attacks that went on for two years, with eleven victims. The proximity of the bike path to our football club had the adults on high alert, and as young people we picked up on the anxiety.

The adults told us we would start earlier and finish earlier. Our parents were asked to make sure strictly car transport was arranged to and from training. There was always an adult who would stay behind to make sure everyone had a lift. I would tell Dad to come early, embarrassed at the idea of being the last one left and having the coach wait for me.

Perhaps this was the first time I was made aware of how our conditions of play were gendered, as the boys did not have these rules. It seemed the fear had to rest on us. It didn't feel fair that we could no longer play in the creek, walk or run freely while they could.

This bushland is important to me, because it is where I grew up. It's my meditation place. It's the place where I learned to be still and to listen, to properly listen. It's a place that koalas, potoroos, kangaroos, echidnas, platypuses, lizards, birds, insects and many other living beings share.

Perhaps what I could not put into words at the time was the correlation I felt between the threatening stranger on the bike path and the erasure of First Nations presence and the exploitation of the environment. The suburbs I grew up in were haunted by absence, and this fueled toxic race relations between us and them. I remember a school trip to The Gap bushlands. The tour guide showed us a bora ring, a sacred men's gathering site marked with stones, as evidence of previous occupation, but there was no talk of current occupation. "This is what the Aboriginals *used* to do. But then they were all killed off." My schoolmates and teachers accepted this as truth, but I noticed they looked sideways at me.

Few bora rings exist intact today in South East Queensland. Many have been purposely destroyed or effaced, notably large bora rings on private property at the nearby Keperra, and north of us at Kippa-Ring (meaning "bora ring" in the local language) and Redcliffe. The Gabba stadium in the city is an example of a bora ring turned modern-day sporting arena. The evidence of First Nations significance is ignored, but the energy of the place remains. The bora ring in Samford we were shown when were young people is one of the best-preserved rings in South East Queensland.

The Bikeway Rapist created an atmosphere of fear around outdoor places. Many women and girls no longer jogged or walked alone. Their relationships with nature and the environment had changed.

Such was the palpability of the communal fear, the first short story I wrote, part psychological thriller, part gothic horror (somehow I was channeling Barbara Baynton), was about a young girl waiting to be picked up at football training, left alone in the rain. Relieved to finally see a car approaching, she notices that the eyes in the car are "carmine and sharp but not familiar." I wrote this short story for a school assignment and was well graded on it. I ended up using it in the writing portfolio I submitted to be accepted into a Bachelor of Fine Arts in creative writing at QUT.

Looking back at the story, I see how I was influenced by the socio-bio-psyche of the times. In my story, trees I had once seen as familiars were twisted into dark shapes. What drives a fifteen-year-old to be fearful of the bush? Was it natural fear? I don't think I knew what I had been taught to be afraid of.

The police had a hard time apprehending the serial rapist. The mainstream news was on a constant loop, speculating who he might be and when he might attack next. Finally, he was caught by an astute citizen who noticed his car speed away suspiciously. "They caught him" was all I thought at the time. We could go back to before. We all breathed a sigh of relief and went about our business.

The cold hard fact is that, as young people in a sporting team environment, we were far more likely to be sexually abused inside the gate rather than outside. A study of Australian athletes found that 31 percent of female and 21 percent of male athletes reported experiencing sexual abuse at some time in their lives. Of these, 41 percent of females and 29 percent of males had been sexually abused within the sports environment. It was also found that almost half, 46.4 percent, of the elite group reporting sexual abuse had been sexually abused by sports personnel. These rates only increase, sadly, when athletes are non-white, identify as LGBTIQSB+ and/ or are elite athletes. Sexual abuse can be accompanied by emotional abuse, physical abuse and bullying masquerading as coaching necessary to "push" an athlete to be their best. Disturbingly, many opportunistic abusers thrive in these sorts of "high-stakes, competitive" environments where systems are corrupt. This abuse has ruined many lives and many sporting careers.

A Gymnastics Australia inquiry by the Human Rights Commission in 2020 revealed a "spectrum" of abuse. After the *Athlete A* documentary in the United States (reporters from *The Indianapolis Star* exposed Dr Larry Nassar's sexual abuse of young gymnasts and USA Gymnastics' cover-up) put a spotlight on the sport, an anonymous hotline was established in Australia for former and current athletes. The lawyer Adair Donaldson who represents forty current and former gymnasts says what they want most of all is systemic change, "so those who come next are not left with the same psychological burden as those who came before." I light a candle for all those who have been affected. We are not safe until we are all safe.

Skills

I am on Taribelang Country, what's known as Bundaberg, for my brother's state tournament. My brother is staying somewhere else with his team, and I'm sharing a motel room with Mum and Dad. We've woken up in the middle of the night to watch the Italy vs France 2006 World Cup Men's Final—and we are completely shocked because my favorite player, Zinedine Zidane ("Zizou"), has been red-carded for a headbutt on Materazzi. We have no idea what we have just witnessed.

The 2006 World Cup has been an exciting one. The Socceroos have taken part for the first time since 1974 and it feels like the whole of Australia has been on the journey with them. It has only been a few nights since they were controversially dismissed from the tournament in the round of sixteen by this Italy outfit through a Totti penalty. We've been looking forward to the decider of the tournament. With so many great players at their peak, the quality of the matches has been very high. A few months prior to the tournament, France's Zidane announced his retirement from football, saying his playing career in all formats would end after the World Cup.

It has been an electric start to the game, 1–1 in the first twenty minutes. France got a soft penalty off Italian center-back Materazzi, who made contact with French player Malouda in the seventh minute. Zidane stepped up to convert a sizzling Panenka, which hit the crossbar and bounced over the line, leaving Buffon, the best goalkeeper in the world at that time, no chance.

A Panenka penalty is a particularly brazen move in a World Cup final where there is a lot at stake. It was named after Czech player

Antonín Panenka, who introduced it to the world in the UEFA Euro 1976 final. He was called "a poet" and, by Pelé, "either a genius or a madman." A Panenka is a literal stroke of luck. It relies on successful deceit of the goalkeeper to dive low to either side, and the ball is scooped into the empty net. Zidane's was executed perfectly. You could argue that it wasn't clean as it hit the woodwork and could have bounced out. But the drama of it hitting the crossbar made the result even sweeter.

Only about ten minutes later, Materazzi has redeemed himself for conceding the penalty by leaping high to score a strong header from a Pirlo corner, and it's game on.

It's 1–1 and we are all still waking up in Australia. Even with the Italy goal, I feel like France has the edge. More than twice the number of shots as Italy. But the Italians are digging in their heels in the way they know best.

As the match enters extra time, I am still convinced France are most likely to take it. Everything comes through the middle with Zidane. At the 103rd minute Zidane slips the ball out wide to his winger, makes a perfect run into the box, leaps up high and heads the ball. We are all convinced that he has scored the winning goal, but Buffon makes a spectacular save to deny a spectacular goal. Zidane can't quite believe it.

At 105 minutes, halfway into extra time, Dad puts the water on for tea. As my first coach Dad gave me many different football lessons so I'd have an advantage on the pitch, from heading, giving a free kick top spin, lobbing and controlling the ball with my chest, to going past a player with the Cruyff turn. I then applied these skills to life more broadly, to repel racism and protect myself from what I would go through: things that my dad may not have anticipated, things that I didn't understand at the time.

Mum tells me stories of my dad's playing years, when she met him. He was a central midfielder, an engine with a powerful header. Mum got to see him play competitive matches several times for his local club, Mifano, before his body gave way. Not hesitating to put his head to those hard, rock-like balls, as they were in those days, and in icy conditions, he wonders to me now what pressure that put on his brain over time. My brother and I only saw my dad play with us, and while he coached. We were particularly impressed with his heading technique and balance. He used to juggle with his head as easily as he juggled with his feet, his eye not wavering from the ball.

Dad takes me to the cricket pitch outside our house and kicks balls at my face until it gets dark. He aims to desensitize me from my reflex to flinch when the ball comes towards me. *This is how you hit the ball with your head so you don't hurt yourself. If the ball comes off the wrong way, like on the top of your head, or if hits you in the nose, it's gonna hurt. You have to put your sweet spot, your forehead, on it, and it has to come off clean.* The subtext reads: this is how you give yourself an advantage on the field. This is how you protect yourself.

My older cousin Michael comes over. "Show us your skills," he says, knowing I'm a little football fanatic. But I hide away, too shame. There is a time and a place for this.

This is how you head the ball
Stand on the penalty spot
Take four steps sideways, four steps back
Tense your body as you wait
Keep your eye on the ball
as you run towards it
Leap and nod
chin down
forehead first
Use all the power from your arms
Direct the ball down
to the corner of the goal
Don't be scared of the ball
Don't be scared of the ball
Repeat until you are not scared of the ball

This is how you head a player
If they slander your sister
If they slander your parents
If they slander your people
chin down
forehead first
all the power from your waist

This is how you control the ball with your chest
Watch the flight of the ball
Get under it, lean back, arms off your sides
Cushion the weight in the soft firm space
the hollow of your thorax
the second biggest hollow
in your body
It's a good feeling

This is how you bind your chest
Watch the rhythm of your breath
Lean back, arms off your sides
Wrap the soft firm space
to match your pace
as tightly
When you breathe again it will
come from the same place

This is how you chip the keeper
Sense where the space is
It's just you, the ball, the keeper and the goal
It's purely mathematical
It's a measure of control: not too early, not too late
not too little, not too much
Lean back and take a dig
Give them a question
they can't answer

This is how you chip away at self-doubt
It's mathematical, it's an equation
You put in what comes out
If they say shit on the sidelines
If your opponent adds a word with a shove in the back
maybe just for now, take it as a compliment
Tell yourself: I was born to do this
Give them a question
they can't answer

This is how you take on a player with the Cruyff turn
Make the defender think you're taking a shot
but stop the foot just as it goes past the ball
Angle your foot so the inside faces flat against the ball
In the same movement
scoop the ball backwards
in your path
as you turn 180 degrees

This is how you take on the world with the Cruyff turn
Feint a shot at the white establishment
Let your foot drag
Scoop the ball backwards
as you turn 180 degrees
Go your own way

When it happens, it happens offscreen. The camera doesn't capture everything. Five minutes to go of extra time.

"There's another player down injured," the commentator says, "so play won't be restarted." The camera moves to Materazzi face first on the ground. Zidane grabs at his captain armband nervously, like he will soon be taking it off.

"Well, what's going on here?" the commentator continues, incredulously. "Something's happening out here."

Then they show the replay.

"Well, there's Zidane. Oh. He's just headed Materazzi in the middle of the chest."

The referee consults the official on the sideline and issues Zidane with the red card. Zidane pleads his case but knows he has to trudge off.

"But what had gone on before?" the commentator wonders. "Zidane has been sent off and that's the final game of his career."

Zidane's dismissal is a symbolic and psychological loss for his team at this late stage of the game—you feel like the match has been thrown. When penalties are taken, Italy win.

"That's ridiculous, completely inexcusable. What a way to throw your career," my dad muses. But I'm with Zidane and will not speak a bad word about him. Even not knowing what Materazzi said to him (this will come after, and there're still conflicting reports from those who were there), I feel very sad for him. And I feel sad for a long time afterwards. There will never be another Zizou on the pitch, and I wish that the match had not had the outcome that it did. But that's football.

I was fifteen then and will learn more later: how Zizou, at age fifteen, went to the Cannes academy. "His feet spoke with the ball," said Jean Varraud, who discovered him. It was at Cannes that Zidane's coaches described him as raw and sensitive, prone to attack spectators who insulted his race or family. Zidane's family are of Kabyle Algerian heritage, living in France where racism is ingrained. His coaches encouraged him to "focus on his own game." Zidane was publicly punished for his occasional violent outbursts, but there was no punishment for those who racially abused him or his family. Doesn't that still happen now—Nicky Winmar, Adam Goodes, Nathan Blacklock? They react to racism and get called divisive, or worse.

I'm imagining that these coaches, all white in the 1980s, didn't get it. Didn't get how comments slowly wear you down and are heavy in your heart. How there's no escape. How this happens not just on the pitch but off the pitch too. It was something that Zidane, one of the most decorated players in the world, could not escape, even in the last game of his career.

These days, my friend Laila reminds me of Zizou's headbutt at least once a year. This final motion, a fourteenth red card, is what he is remembered for, along with the dancer-like qualities of his game, the trophies, the accolades. All are him.

I guess this piece is about my father, and everything my parents taught me. I don't blame them for what they could not protect me from. I know they did the best they could and they did a very good job.

I didn't tell my parents about the racism I experienced at school. I would pretend everything was okay. I didn't want to disappoint them. I think my mum thought that because I had lighter skin it wouldn't happen to me. I wanted to pretend that it was just words and I had the power to ignore it. But often I couldn't. I felt so much internalized shame and guilt. I lacked self-worth. I couldn't even walk a few meters without dropping my head. I dissociated for most of my schooling years, putting myself into fantasy worlds: fanfiction, reading, music, writing in the margins of my school books.

I hated the way it made me feel inside. Like I was worth nothing. I hated the attention it brought. How people would stare. How people would feel sorry for me when they witnessed the attacks. How I learned years later my best friend would break down and cry after school, feeling powerless to stop it. I hated how, when I found out that my mum struggled with post-partum depression after she had me, I wrote to my best friend that I felt guilty for existing. I just wanted to disappear, slip inside the crawl space.

The morning after the final, we have been primed by the World Cup to rise before dawn, without an alarm clock. We go watch turtles hatching on the beach. It's the most incredible thing. The cold sand. The half-light. The baby turtles coming up out of the sand in their hundreds. Stumbling then running out to the sea where the tide is waiting.

WESTSIDE

My new coach was surprised I could smash in a half-volley with my right foot. "Aren't you a leftie?" "Dad taught me to play with both feet." I shrug. "It's easy. Get a decent cross to me and I'll get it in the back of the net." When I scored, even at training, I felt a release. Year 12 was too much, the pressure of an Overall Position and getting into uni. My parents suggested I could put a pause on my pursuit to play at the highest level to focus on school. Just for that season. Play a div lower, div one, at a team that was half the drive, halfway to The Gap, along the bike path. The new strip was green, white and red. Training was not compulsory or micromanaged and the players were mostly older. Some had husbands and children. To be accepted into sports science I needed an OP7 and had to take chemistry, biology and math B. I brought my chem textbook to games, but as if I'd have time to read it. The field was dark after six. Sometimes fog crept up from the nearby bush. One night a sighting of the shiny shape of a red-bellied black snake interrupted training. Snake decided to make the field its bed, sprawling across the eighteen-yard box like a defending wall. I stared at the snake in fascination, not used to seeing them in such a place, moving with caution. I would prefer to leave the snake where it was, but the coach was freaked. Coach called my dad over, and my dad got a stick that the snake, thick as a coke can, reached out and coiled itself on. He escorted the snake off the premises. The women hid their bodies here. The changing rooms were usually locked; only the men could use them—this club was not as giving to its women's teams—so we'd sit in a semicircle behind the dug-outs and slip undershirts over shoulders and under until they popped out. The women asked personal questions here with their eyes, ones that threatened to break me open. I kept my gaze on the grass while this ritual was happening. Sometimes I didn't take my undershirt off for the game. I left it on. I liked the way the sweat thickened to create an armor around my upper body. Like the snake, I did not want attention. I lived to be unseen. I would like to be kept where I lay. Don't look, don't look. Your gaze could get you in trouble. Don't think of seeing a flash of bra or torso or underarm. That waist is not for you.

Lesbian Mafia

I still wonder over how different our births and lives would be if we were not so rigidly trained into gendered forms of articulation.

Julietta Singh

When Alen Stajcic lost the Matildas managerial position in 2019, just five months before the 2019 FIFA Women's World Cup, he reportedly claimed a "lesbian mafia" was behind his sacking.

His contract was terminated in light of two confidential team surveys that revealed he, as coach of the Australian women's national football team, was partly responsible for an "unsatisfactory" team environment. Stajcic denied this, and it was then he reportedly referred to a group of players and staff who he believed were behind the decision as the "lesbian mafia." He would later deny using these words.

If there is a lesbian mafia, I've always wanted to join. Contact me through my website, please.

In all seriousness, organized football is as far from a lesbian mafia as you could get, and this has been proven on record by a panel of experts. An investigation by the Football Federation Australia (FFA) found Stajcic's claims were unsubstantiated. The independent panel was unable to uncover any evidence supporting the existence of a "lesbian mafia" and their report found that the removal was not personal.

I think it's always worth highlighting the use of terms like "mafia" and "Nazi" as a cheap rhetorical way to demonize something. For example, manufacturers of infant formula have referred to women who encourage the use of breastmilk as "breastfeeding Nazis."

Stajcic's comments were as familiar as they were hurtful. Whether he used that exact homophobic phrase or not, it was picked up by many of those in the Australian football community who disagreed with his sacking, and it was hungrily embraced by a sensationalist media. The damage had been done. This commentary opened the door for trolls, some who have been reported to police, to pile on hateful abuse of female footballers, queer people and women.

These are a couple of tweets at the time of this nonsensical "debate" that sum up the feelings of many.

Ben McKay
@benmackey

Wow is this FFA report bringing back bad memories reporting on the Matildas. I would just say sensationalising on the "lesbian mafia" is wrong & hurtful. It is an unnecessary othering of women and queer ppl in one of the few places they thrive in Australian sport. Don't buy in.

Nancy Hogshead-Makar, JD, Oly
@Hogshead3Au

Crazy theory that Australia's "lesbian mafia" was out to get the male coach fired. Riiiight, women are so powerful in @FIFAcom.
… Never mind the research that found rampant #AthleteAbuse, and a culture of silence under the male coach.

There's a rule I learned after decades of seeing this kind of thing unfold, and I'd like to share it with you. It's the "more than one" rule.

Put a group of more than one woman together and watch what they call them (bitches). Put a group of more than one man together and watch what they call them (nothing).

Put a group of more than one queer woman together and watch what they call them (dykes). Put a group of more than one straight person together and watch what they call them (nothing).

Put a group of more than one blackfella together and watch what they call them (blacks). Put a group of more than one whitefella together and watch what they call them (nothing).

In 1994, Australian cricketer Denise Annetts claimed her non-selection for the Australian team was because she was "not a lesbian." She held the highest batting average in Women's Test Cricket with 81.90 from her ten games and won the NSW Sportswoman of the Year in 1987. She lodged a complaint over her dismissal with the Anti-Discrimination Board. Her allegations of discrimination based on her heterosexuality and marital status resulted in the sudden ascendancy of women's cricket from media obscurity to the national limelight.

Annetts's complaint led nowhere. It is simply a footnote of history.

After being told all my teenage years that women's sport is rampant with queer women, I'm still trying to find them.

I'm sixteen years old, I have a crush on my much older teammate, Shon, but I don't really know I do.

We're passing the ball back and forth and getting to know each other.

Kick.

"Everyone thinks, just cos I play soccer, I'm a lesbian," Shon is saying in a bitter voice.

I freeze. Realize she's waiting for me to pass the ball back.

Kick.

"Yeah?" I can tell she's trying to gauge my response.

Kick.

"Yeah. I'm not a lesbian! We're not all lesbians! Why do lesbians have to ruin it for the rest of us?" To emphasize her point she takes an exaggerated lean back with her swing and says, "I make sure I don't play with lesbians."

Kick.

The ball comes roughly off my boot, and Shon has to shuffle sideways to retrieve it.

"Yeah, you're right," I chime in eventually, playing my part. "We're not all lesbians, why don't people get that? People say that about me too, coz I play. But I'm not gay."

As soon as those words leave my mouth, I feel a fresh pit form in my stomach ready to be filled with fears and doubts. Because I know that they are not entirely true. That I would, at any chance, accept Shon's hand on my waist. My thoughts do not go any further than this, a touch. I am buried in the sensation of internalized shame.

I soon work out Shon is not like me. She has a husband, and if she knew I was ... if she knew I liked her (in that way) ... well, I could never live with that. I could never live with that shame.

All day every day, I hear "gay" used in a negative context. So I say "I'm not gay" a lot that year. I say it over and over again, to myself, to others, as a rebuttal.

And I keep to myself mostly. I don't go out with my team for fear of somehow being exposed.

I say "I am not gay" more times than I will ever go on to say "I am gay."

I do say those words, "I am gay," next year, when I'm seventeen. I say them to my parents, and my brother, and my cousins, and my friends. And I feel like I've lost everything.

In Australia, it's been shown that sports participation rates of queer and straight players are pretty much on par with the general population, despite misconceptions of sport having more female queer players.

Monash University conducted the first quantitative research in Australia, the United Kingdom and Canada in 2020, which found nearly 90 percent of female athletes say most people assume they are lesbians if they play sports such as rugby, cricket, football or Australian Rules.

Outdated norms related to gender and sexuality affect us all. To avoid the label and the stigma that comes with it, even straight players outwardly perform straightness and normalized gender expressions.

I would get the shock of my life when I went out with my teammates outside football, even just to the club for trivia night or to the local pub. A lot of my butch teammates femmed up to the extreme and looked pained doing so, in high heels and dresses. I would hardly recognize them and would ask myself, what for? What are you trying to prove? Is this who you really are, or is this a result of the need to perform gender in a patriarchal and queerphobic environment?

In 2017, BBC News Africa reported on how stigma is particularly challenging for those from non-white backgrounds and those who live in non-Western countries. The Khayelitsha Cats is a rugby team established by Xoliswa Jubeju that is tackling anti-gay discrimination, sexual violence and HIV-positive stigma through sport and poetry. Khayelitsha is a partially informal township outside Cape Town, established in 1985 when large numbers were forcefully relocated there during the last years of Apartheid. Living conditions for the majority are poor, and it was called "one of the top five largest slums in the world" by Habitat for Humanity in 2020.

Jubeju explains that Khayelitsha is a violent place to be LGBTIQSB+. "We do have people who have been abused. They've been raped, assaulted, but they couldn't speak out because they are afraid that the people that have been abusing them will kill them."

Telling her own story, Jubeju said, "I had to be in a cage for so many years. And I had to sleep with a boy to prove to them I'm a girl."

The documentary shows the players sitting in a circle on the field after training. One player reads their poetry followed by appreciative applause from the group.

"I also decided to include some poetry sessions so that the people who are less sporty, they can jump into the poetry side of the club so that they can also heal without playing. It's a big part of the team," Jubeju explains.

I find Jubeju's leadership in the face of such adversity inspiring. I'm reminded of the damage and absolute wreckage colonialism and racism (in South Africa's case, inflicted by the Netherlands and Britain) have done to gender and sexuality in colonized countries, all while those in the colonies have made so much "progress" in promoting acceptance and outward love for LGBTIQSB+ individuals.

The criminalization of homosexuality was introduced to Africa by Western colonialists. It's much published that in Nigeria, a former British colony, the female national football team does not allow "lesbian players." Dilichukwu Onyedinma, head of the country's women's football league, said in 2013, "Any player that we find is associated with it will be disqualified. We will call the club chairmen to control their players, and such players will not be able to play for the national team."

I reflect on how almost three-quarters (67 percent) of the seventy countries where same-sex relationships are still currently outlawed are former British colonies. Most cases, the laws against consensual gay sex were put into place under British rule and were left there following independence. Homophobia in the Pacific and Caribbean is rife.

Musing on how toxic homophobia and transphobia can also affect heterosexual people, I think of white Canadian pop singer Shawn Mendes. I remember reading an article where Shawn explains how, at the age of fifteen, people labeling him as homosexual because of his mannerisms contributed to him feeling self-conscious, even though as he says there is nothing wrong with being queer.

> Everyone's been calling me gay since I was fifteen years old. I'm not gay and I'm like, "What does that mean?" I had these problems with the way my voice sounded. I'm

like, "How do I sit?" I'm always first to cross my legs and sit with a position of this feminine style and I really suffered with that shit. It kind of ended up becoming something I wanted to just be really open about and honest about. I think a lot of guys go through that and, even worse than that, there are just so many guys who are gay and in the closet and must be hearing shit like that and just being like, "I'm terrified to come out."

When expectations of gender and sexuality, which relate to racism and colonialism, become too much, we all suffer. Toxic performances of femininity and masculinity destroy the fabric of communities and relationships. There are so many ways to be. Why deny the world your authentic self? Why deny yourself the opportunity to grow?

Alex Blackwell was the first openly queer cricketer when she came out publicly in 2013. She says she "tried to listen with an open mind when an administrator told her there was a problem of predatory behavior in women's sport."

"Their concern is that poor behavior in women's sport is by the lesbians," the former Australia cricket captain told *The Guardian*.

I have felt profiled because I'm a lesbian, profiled as a predator. Lesbians in sport have been profiled as predators. That is very hurtful and I'm tired of that. It's really unfair to profile a group of people as good or bad based on a characteristic like sexuality or skin colour or religion … because perceptions of what goes on in team sports where there are lesbians doesn't match reality.

In the 2019 FIFA World Cup, five months after Stajcic's sacking, Sam Kerr captained Australia to a memorable 3–2 comeback win against Brazil.

"Suck on that!" Sam said emphatically to the camera in her post-match interview, a surprise departure from the normally practiced and mannered response expected of an Australian athlete. Many believe the comments were fueled by the homophobic and misogynistic abuse she had been receiving online as part of criticisms of the team's performances prior to the win against Brazil. Kerr had run out of patience with the fickle Australian sporting public. Prior to the tournament, the Matildas had been crowned Australia's favorite sporting team for some years running, but how many "fans" stood up to this online abuse?

Research released by Plan International in 2019 revealed that on Facebook more than a quarter (27 percent) of all comments directed towards sportswomen are either sexist, sexualizing, belittling of women's sport or otherwise negative in nature. It's a shocking statistic from an industry perspective but also from a societal one.

The analysis showed that sportswomen face three times as many negative comments as men (27 percent versus 9 percent) and that 23 percent of all negative comments directed towards elite female athletes are sexist (referring to traditional gender stereotypes or belittling women's sport, their athletic abilities or skills). These are the typical comments I see: "Nobody cares about women's football," "My eight-year-old son's team would beat them," "I would do number three and number five."

Although Plan's research did not go into sexuality, queerphobic comments directed towards women in sport are also very common. As high as 48 percent of queer women reported being personally targeted, with 84 percent of those having heard verbal slurs such as "faggot" or "dyke."

Homophobia is an issue for sport broadly, with Australian data suggesting that 80 percent of LGBTIQSB+ sportspeople have witnessed or experienced homophobia in sport. This includes 57 percent of gay men who report being personally targeted, while more gay men (41 percent) than lesbians (16 percent) said they had been bullied because of their sexuality. Meanwhile, 48 percent of LGBTIQSB+ sportspeople are afraid to come out because of the negativity it is perceived to attract, and so they hide their sexuality or gender identity.

I have been "out" as queer for sixteen years now, half my life, and the cliché "it gets better" is a proven truth for me. My family and friends have accepted and celebrate who I am and those who haven't are no longer in my close personal circle. However, it is so important to note that "coming out" is not a straight journey, so to speak. Mexican writer Asiel Adan Sanchez in their *Archer Magazine* article writes elegantly about this problematic promoted belief: "when so much of queer visibility is grounded in white history, white bodies and white gatekeepers, we have to question who benefits from coming out."

The choice to be publicly "out" as a queer person is not the only choice. Not "coming out" can be powerful too. Some of my friends and lovers are "closeted," for lack of a better term, for cultural, family or other reasons, or simply for protection of privacy, rejecting the Western ideal of a public declaration of (othered) identity and a typecast linear journey. Instead of "coming out" they "come in." What they do serves them. It is how they live their lives. Many reject labels altogether as they don't feel they're beneficial, rather restrictive.

Alisa Solomon wrote in her 1997 essay "Sneakers" that the rising popularity of women's soccer in the United States coincided with a new market for brands like Nike to sell shoes to. It was seen as important for the United States team and any other representatives to present as "wholesome, heroic and above all, heterosexual." Stories that these female athletes could tell at that time, according to Solomon, to market products and appeal to fans were: "a mother surviving cancer; a new baby; a modeling career. And never, ever, a girlfriend."

Some might wonder why swimmer Ian Thorpe and tennis player Sam Stosur "took so long" to disclose their sexual identity. There seems to be a sport in "outing" professional players who have not disclosed personal information. Have you ever walked in their shoes? Respect their choices. Don't go after individual players. Talk about the environment in general, how it might not be the kind of environment in which a player can feel comfortable to express their whole authentic self, and the double standard between straight and queer players and the pressure to disclose.

Sometimes I still think of Shon's words.

"Did you know there are lesbian teams?" Shon said. "Some teams have all lesbian players. I make sure I don't play with lesbians."

PART TWO

Bookmarks

The first time I remember seeing women's football hyped up, televised live and celebrated in a major way was during the 2007 Women's World Cup. Before that, there was a dearth of representation of women's football in the media, and limited opportunities to watch games. The 2007 Women's World Cup changed all of that, and I feasted my eyes on the games.

A key player who starred for Brazil was impossible to ignore. Marta Vieira da Silva, creative striker, twenty-one years old. She was electric, fearless. Comparisons to male Brazilian footballers—a bit of Ronaldo, a bit of Ronaldinho, all wrapped into one—fell short. She was her own phenomenon.

After beating Australia 3–2 in the quarters, Brazil went on to stun world number one United States 4–0 in the semi-finals. Marta scored two goals. Brazil lost eventually in the final to Germany 2–0, but Marta's individual performance was noted in the history books. She was the top goalscorer of the tournament, with a record seven goals.

The posters of Ruud van Nistelrooy, Dennis Bergkamp, Zinedine Zidane and Thierry Henry were ripped off the wall, Blu Tack and all, for this new kind of representation. The male players I had idolized in my youth couldn't compare to what I was seeing: a fierce and dynamic woman of color tearing teams apart. A symbol of female empowerment. The most exciting player of a generation. She is seen by many as the greatest women's football player of all time, and she would go on to inspire hordes of young female and non-binary people to lace up their boots. When she announced her engagement in 2021 to her Orlando Pride teammate, Toni Pressley, she became an inspiration for the Brazilian queer community and gave them strength in the fight against homophobia.

The opportunity for televised women's sport in Australia increased with the establishment of professional leagues. In 2008, the W-League began. Also in 2008, the ANZ Championship (now known as Suncorp Super Netball) started. In 2015, we saw the Women's Big Bash League kick off; in 2017, the AFL Women's; in 2018, the NRLW and the Super W (rugby union)—while the longest-running Australian women's sporting league, the Women's National Basketball League, has been going since 1981.

The establishment of the W-League, the professionalization of our game, the rise of international stars like Marta, and the increased attention and movement to gender equity—all those things that we had been wanting in the game—coincided with me needing to establish my identity outside football and family.

It's only now when I sit back and think about it, while writing this, I realize there are missing years in my life. I guess we all have them. From my high school graduation in 2007 to my uni graduation in 2010, there is a void of memory. I have to focus really hard to recall events and feelings from these times.

I think there was probably a resignation from me around that point that I didn't have the physical capacity to make it as a professional player. I wasn't delusional. I knew my determination and dedication could only get me so far. With the establishment of the W-League, a few of my ex-teammates were getting deals and it was exciting and heartwarming to watch them be part of this new chapter of women's football. Perhaps I was a little envious, a little forlorn, but I also had other things on my mind.

At the time, I was navigating "out" life, family, leaving my suburb and its associated memories far behind, reinventing myself, finding "me."

Some of this happened in Gadigal land in Sydney, where I timidly entered queer bars and pulsing live music venues. The thrills of sex and affection. Other times it was in the online world, where it seemed easier to connect with people than in real life.

Leaving school, leaving my suburb, leaving my bullies was a liberation. I felt like I could finally breathe. It was like I was starting again. But I still held so much fear.

While studying, I navigated many share houses across Brisbane, getting to know different angles of the city and different people. I didn't have a lot of money, but I dreamt a lot.

I was shy but made some good blackfella connections at uni, some of whom I'm still in touch with today. I remember the powerful experience of walking into the Oodgeroo Unit communal space in B block, as it once used to be, on February 13, 2008. The Wednesday of my first week at uni. I was ignorant as to what was going on. The TV was on. There was a hushed silence and a feeling of tension in the air. I was seventeen years old and had a haunted watchfulness that would lend itself well to being a writer. Parliament was shown in the background. Prime Minister Kevin Rudd was speaking. "To the mothers and the fathers, the brothers and the sisters, for the breaking up of families and communities, we say sorry. And for the indignity and degradation thus inflicted on a proud people and a proud culture, we say sorry."

Sobs, gasps, words of emotion from those sitting on the couches in front of me and standing beside me. There were mixed emotions in the room, especially when Opposition Leader Brendan Nelson spoke. The Aunties on TV and in the room turned their backs and tuh-tuhed at his insincere words and malicious undertones. I could see the long road they had endured to get to this point, and the disappointment they predicted they would feel. There was really a lot going on. People looked after each other that day. Cups of tea. Food. BBQ.

I felt a glimpse of understanding of the heavy weight of the history that had come before me. I could see what our older people had endured. And because of them, I was proud to sit there, as an

Aboriginal person, with other Aboriginal and Torres Strait Islander people, representing our people and our stories.

We went to Minjerribah for a welcome camp for new students. The staff cared for me, supporting me as a young blackfella worried about a lot of things. I felt so liberated to have left high school, away from the bullying. But I did have my guard up, waiting for it to follow me. At the welcome camp, I thought I'd be bullied like at camps in the past. I am glad to say it was the opposite. I was treated with kindness and encouragement.

*

In the outer north-western suburbs where I grew up, top of the agenda was sport. My currency was my football ability, which got me places in representative teams. Most of my time after school was spent going to training. Any spare time I had I spent practicing in the backyard. I spent a lot of time outdoors.

There was no real incentive to be engaged in the arts. I saw it as something that wasn't for me. Apart from attending NAIDOC at Musgrave Park, I would only enter Brisbane's art quarter, named in English after London's West End but with the Jagera name of Kurilpa (place of the water rat), at the age of sixteen, when Mum worked at the State Library of Queensland. It was there I saw coffee shops for the first time—outside of the Queensland chain café The Coffee Club, where my friends and I would go for hot chocolates after our church group on a Friday evening because it was the only place open at eight o'clock. In West End there were artisan bakeries too, beyond the Bakers Delight chain available in my suburb, and Greek, Italian, Lebanese, Indian and Vietnamese food. West End was only a thirty-minute drive, but it might as well have been another country compared to where I grew up. Here cafés were open to midnight, and there were bookshops and theatres. I did not know then the significance of Kurilpa/West End to mob. But I soon would.

Books and sports didn't seem to mix. I remember once being reprimanded by my coach for bringing a textbook to a game. I was sitting on the bench and knew I wouldn't come on. The message was clear. Be one thing in one moment. Be present.

I liked writing from an early age, thanks to Mum bringing us books back from the library. Due to her work, we grew up believing in libraries as places where our imaginations could thrive. When I read, I also imagined my own worlds. There were no Indigenous-authored books on the syllabus at school. None at university either. And, as far as I was aware of, neither Mum nor anyone in my family read Indigenous-authored books, so I have concluded that these works were deliberately made elusive to young Australian students. There are alarmingly few people who know who the Ngarrindjeri man on our fifty-dollar note is—David Unaipon—and if they do, very few know he is considered to be our first published Aboriginal writer. Some of his work was not attributed to him at first but to anthropologist William Ramsay Smith in 1930. It would be seventy years before his writing was repatriated and its author correctly acknowledged.

As a young Murri queer person growing up in Queensland, I felt a deep psychological shadow on my being. I did not see anyone who represented me on television, in movies or in books. I didn't understand the strange alienation I felt as one of very few Indigenous students at my school, even though I was part of such a strong culture and lineage to South East Queensland, my Country, my ancestral home.

All this is the backdrop to the transformative moment of reading *Swallow the Air* (2006) by Tara June Winch for the first time.

I was with Yasmin, a talented first-year student from Rocky, who I was tutoring in a computer room with no windows, before we had laptops. I was in my second year. Yas is now one of my most longstanding friends, but at the time we were just two First Nations people from Queensland studying creative writing. Through the university library, Yas and I were slowly discovering the rich canon of Aboriginal and Torres Strait Islander writing together. We were finding voices that spoke to us.

Yas had this book with her. I was immediately drawn to the colorful dust jacket. She let me have a look. We would both draw on *Swallow the Air* as inspiration for our own fiction. This young voice spoke to us more than any had previously.

Swallow the Air is broken up into twenty chapters, some of them slight, just a few pages long. It follows the character of May from the ages of ten to seventeen, starting with the death of her mother in the titular opening chapter, "Swallow the Air." The novel-in-stories flows from family members, using kinship as a guiding thread.

The book has won so many awards it is difficult to list them all, but it began by winning the 2004 Queensland Literary Awards' David Unaipon Award in manuscript form, with the original title *Dust on Waterglass*. Tara was in her early twenties at the time. The University of Queensland Press (UQP) editor Tara worked with, Sue Abbey, a white American-Australian, would become my mentor shortly after I graduated from university, founding the black&write! project at the State Library of Queensland. Over several years, Sue would give me the tools to become an editor of Indigenous-authored work.

Recently, while speaking about a very First Nations practice of writing relational novels-in-stories (see Jeanine Leane's *Purple Threads* [2011] and Gayle Kennedy's *Me, Antman and Fleabag* [2007] as further examples), I introduced a piece, "Cloud Busting" from *Swallow the Air*, to a new generation of university students at RMIT. The tutor told me it was hard to hold back tears when reading this work. I can't overstate how much emotion lives within these pages.

Swallow the Air is a breath of fresh air from an author who lists her influences as the *Charcoal Lane* album by Uncle Archie Roach and Uncle Tony Birch's body of work. Like these two Elders, Tara writes about fracture and repair with beautiful sensitivity. The child's voice is brought to life in Tara's characterization of May, who is willing to see the best in people.

When I touch the book's pages, I'm reminded of Yas, reading this book with her, and Yas's own lyrical and poignant prose, inspired by Tara's but undoubtedly her own. I remember a beautiful line in one of Yas's micro-fictions, poetically tracing the moon and saltwater Country. I hope my thought of her finds her writing and creating.

Another sister, Freja, is reading *Swallow the Air* currently for the first time. It sits on her bedside table.

I walk in to Kurilpa for a cuppa, following the river where thick, dense rainforest used to grow. I walk down Boundary Street, which Samuel Wagan Watson describes as "the line ... the limit/where the dark-skin were told—/DO NOT CROSS!" history tinged with violence but also pride, past Whynot Street, the title of an Oodgeroo Noonuccal poem against the removal of First Nations people, when there was a petition to get rid of them during the gentrification of the area, feeling the protest in the soil beyond the bitumen many generations strong.

I remember meeting Dr Sandra Phillips in the last month of my undergraduate degree. Sandra is a trained Murri book editor who had a few decades of experience by the time of our meeting. I would find out later she had also been mentored by Sue Abbey, while Sue was at UQP. These connections were starting to stick and my path was being made. She had just finished her PhD on the authoring, editing, publishing and everyday reading of Indigenous literature. It was surprising that we had had similar preoccupations over the previous three years but had never spoken over that time. That brief meeting with Sandra contributed to me feeling like I had a place in the reading and writing world.

Around 2009, I was watching W-League on the telly while studying, and I happened to look up when a young Sam Kerr was brought onto the pitch for Perth Glory. The commentators said she was only fifteen years old. Here was this laidback-looking kid, baggy purple kit swallowing her. She was something else. A bit different. Fast. Fearless. I immediately took notice. Her rise was extraordinary, of course. Barely a year out of playing her first professional match, she'd earned her first cap and scored her first goal for the Matildas. I don't know if I dared to think at that point: are we witnessing our own global star in action? Will she be what Marta has been for our game?

In those years, I was trying to forge an identity that would take me beyond football and family. But I would realize I always circle back to these things as my grounding.

EASTS

At twenty I was living with my first GF on the corner of Wel Rd and Vulture—two streets that make up the boundary blackfellas couldn't cross only forty or so years ago. My GF got closer to me than anyone else, but there were things I couldn't say as a Blak kweer living on the boundary. Sorry, honey, there're things I can't talk to you about. Me and my GF skateboarded to the flash deli but were too broke to buy anything, just looked. Watched Jolie films between assignments (*Hackers* a fave) in the single bed we shared. My partner got scared walking past the Gabba stadium at night. Not easy coding dyke with the cricket and footy crowd. Gabba a bora ring, but no one talked about that. No one mentioned stadiums have always been places of ceremony. Always was, always has been. I marched on Invasion Day and wearing my orange jersey. Ground at the mouth of Norman Creek. Once a fishing camp where nets and weirs caught hundreds of fish in tow rows within minutes. Mob would have crossed the river regularly to come fish here. Now the place was a big sports complex. Tennis on one side, rugby the other. Big private college behind. Still, water snaked through the fields. After a night of heavy rain, the club would close. The ground would reference its once rainforest, and I could imagine the dense foliage. Food and fiber grew here. That summer, during preseason, it started raining and it didn't stop. Training was suspended indefinitely. Me and my GF watched as the bread disappeared from the supermarket shelves. She left me when the flood warning came—fled to higher ground. I was there in the house alone as the water came closer, and the coppas all out and about evacuating people. I managed to stay. Water would not be tamed, filling the old ways. I didn't stay home and listen to the radio. I moved through the empty suburb to locate the damage inside and out. When the ground dried up, I joined the clean-up. The field was soggy in memory and touch. Salty. Sticks from the other side of the river had drifted over. Bream dotted the edges of the bank. When training resumed I didn't go back.

Flooding My Sentences

Aborigines from the Yugarabul language group knew of the cycle of drought and flooding in the Brisbane River or "mairwar" and accepted it as part of the life cycle. In 1890 the Upper Brisbane River Cooyar people told the legend of the flood on Magenjie or Big River. Although shared with settlers such as the McConnel family of Cressbrook in 1842, the newcomers gave this Aboriginal knowledge little credence. Augustus Charles Gregory, surveyor-general in 1893, dismissed Indigenous understandings of these matters as the unreliable "indistinct aboriginal traditions of a flood."

Margaret Cook

2011 represents a line for many of us in South East Queensland. There is a *before 2011* and an *after 2011*. The flood weighed deeply on our consciousness. It transformed the places we lived and grew up in. Many things we had never thought about, we thought about now.

At the time I lived close to Mairwar and watched it swell and extend its banks. Watched fridges float past. Cars. Boardwalks. Ferries. Looters hanging around South Bank. My home was not flooded, but my workplace was. My first day at work at black&write! was delayed more than a month. We lived in a strange sort of flood time. I remember listening to the radio, I remember watching Anna Bligh on TV, I remember the adrenaline first thing in the morning and the looking out of the window late at night, sleepless and wired. The lights going out. The shelves empty. The sound of rain when it doesn't feel like it will stop. The swirl of drain water. The smell. We all have flood stories. Of loss, of escape, of aftermath.

When our places flood, we also flood: our bodies, our memories, our sentences. The flood is like a swallowing. In the last month of 2010 and the first month of 2011, collective denial then collective fear then collective grief soaked us right through so that we were dripping, dripping, and we couldn't get dry. We tried sandbagging the limits and borders of our bodies, but we had not prepared ourselves for the deluge.

On a personal level, those floods were my wake-up call. I could not go back to complacency after that. I saw how racialized the issue was, how mob did not get a say. The colonizers had put a city on a floodplain. They had destroyed the rich wetlands, mangroves and other life to build up the city and extend the airport. I also saw how class intersected. Assistance came first to those in the wealthy streets, while the wreckage remained in the working-class suburbs for weeks.

My connection with Mairwar strengthened during that time. Water itself is blameless. It is sacred. But climate change is human-made, and floods are increasing, as are other weather events.

Living in the soaked place: mud, mold, mosquitoes. The pain of thinking how many animals and plants had been destroyed. How the size of the disaster could have been prevented if Elders and First Nations knowledge keepers had been listened to. I listened to Elders and my heart broke.

The past doesn't go away, it does not escape. It repeats if we do not learn the lesson. From 2011, I decided to dedicate myself to the fight and stand beside people who put their bodies on the line. I fight for Country in the ways I can. Fighting for climate justice is fighting neoliberalism and persuasive colonialisms, and it's also about giving Country and those who are Country custodians a voice. I write to resist the centuries-long suppression of climate truths.

I spent a lot of time as a youngster among mangroves, and my first major work was inspired by the mangrove, as a symbol of climate mitigation. For me, mangroves are like superheroes in their ability to provide protection, refuge, oxygen and food. Mangroves are strong enough to withstand storms and their timber is well versed to shield, to fight, to move over water. In my long story "Water," written in 2012, which appears in my first book, *Heat and Light* (2014), the mangrove comes back in the wake of yet another invasion, strikes back and takes its rightful place as a warrior protecting Country. This story was a way for me to absorb what I had learned about home into the creative force of fiction.

And yes, our sporting fields and facilities also flooded, sport was put on hold, and at first this seemed secondary to the other losses. Though when I read about Sterling McQuire and his Nerimbera Magpies Soccer Club, and other stories like his, I realized how deep an archive a sporting ground is.

In a profile written by Joe Gorman after the 2015 cyclone that devastated much of Rockhampton, Sterling talks about his connection to the place and how it extends beyond football. Sterling knows the ground intimately. He has lived in Rockhampton all his life and has become synonymous with the club, as a former player and the groundskeeper of Pilbeam Park. His heritage is Darumbal and South Sea Islander—his great-grandfather was taken from Vanuatu to Mackay. Sterling says:

> It's more than just a job for me. See I'm living on country, and living on country means you look after country. It's waste, and it's disposing of it properly. You know, keeping country clean. Same down here at Pilbeam Park— that might just be a little piece of ground but I'm looking after country. People say "why is he still down there," but we're custodians of the land. Nerimbera, it's a Darumbul name: I'm where I'm supposed to be.

With a cultural connection to the ground, Sterling is a custodian to sport on Country and a perpetual witness to the cost of climate change. "In 2012 we had a one-in-one-hundred-year event," he says. "We had 700 ml of water in twenty-four hours. It might happen every six or seven years before that we'd have a big flow-over, now it's happening all the time."

The extent of the 2015 cyclone damage to Pilbeam Park was devastating. The clubhouse was no longer standing, trees were flattened, there was a huge cost to rebuild.

Climate events put small clubs at risk of not recovering. And the memories are inundated too. The archives flooded. The history is bent out of shape and bruised and washed away unless there is opportunity to bring it back.

VIRGINIA

Used to cycle from Chermy for training and
games. Linked up to the bikeway, through three
kms of park, park that followed the water.
Always wanted to stop and watch the ducks
at that one bend in the creek, weave a basket
for my bike. Past the rugby fields, headphones
in ears. Moved through so much life, through
where villages once were. Now the bike path had
been made to go under the road and airport tunnel and past the Toombul shopping center, these
big invasions on the land. The days grew short, it
got dark quickly—I had three lights on my bike
and two on my helmet. The football grounds
were on a rise near the swamp. From where the
swamp started mosquitoes bit through clothing.
The old German camp was just at the back where
the hoop pine was—the first Christian mission
in Queensland. Nudgee Road at the edge of the
grounds. Water was everywhere, sugary water,
the fields slippery when raining, my ankles sink-
ing, water lifting up through my legs. Scratches
on my back from the mozzies. Shoulders sore
from riding. Shaking going down the hills on the
way home. Squeezing my eyes shut, thinking, if I

fall, I fall. Somehow the most peaceful moment of the day.

Queer club. Made friends with the couple that were into cycling. Two other couples in the team. Goalkeeper and right-wing. Center-back and center-forward. Felt comfortable with those girls, talking about girls. Goalkeeper dropped me home some nights, sometimes singing assertively to the same pop song, confessing she was in love with someone else. Two couples split up and two girls walked out on the club—the right-wing and the center-forward. I shook my head, offering a solution so it would not happen again—the team should introduce prenups on sign-on. You will not walk out on the club if you break up. I watched as the goalkeeper bought cheeses for a picnic with her new love at the open-all-night by-the-airport grocery store. I hadn't guessed the new love was on the team—the center-back. I started working it out. Seeing the tension. Stakes grew in fights over positioning and training schedules. The group broken—players stopped showing up. I couldn't score that year. Couldn't put it in. Had a lot of sex though. Maybe that was where my energy was going. Pushed up the collar of the baggy red strip to hide the bites.

Toads crept onto the field under the floodlights. One game I played with only half a team. I spun in circles to forget the score. I was prescribed orthotics for my bad feet. Calves got so tight I couldn't run. I started to drag my bike up the hills on the way home. I quit one game before the season was out and didn't think I would play again with the pain. No longer did I pass corroboree trees. I remained haunted by the place of ducks and water. The end of the chain of waterholes that started at North Star, my first club—while in the womb, while a baby, my dad bringing me back that ball. I spent weeks in bed with fatigue. My neighbor cared for me and got me out of the house and into the car. We drove past the field on Nudgee Rd and I saw the journey I used to make—saw my path as one of many—the place a crossroads of major treks. My neighbor took me all the way to Nudgee, where I met the sea. Aus flags displayed on every corner of the ocean front. The violence was so close.

Country Is Like the Body

On a night in 2014 by the fire at kuril dhagun (water rat's place) on Mairwar, Aunty Nancy Bamaga, a Torres Strait Islander woman from Saibai Island, spoke to a small, interested group about rising sea levels and the effects on Torres Strait Islander burial practices. She spoke with great weight and sadness about the tide coming to her island: the reality is that her people's homes and way of life are being compromised. It was an insight into the threat to our northern and low-lying places.

In 2008, the Australian Human Rights Commission's *Native Title Report* for New South Wales warned that the Torres Strait Islands were facing a "real possibility of a human rights crisis." Of more than two hundred Torres Strait Islands north of mainland Australia, seventeen are occupied. The Islanders that live in the Torres Strait make up about 20 percent of Australia's total Torres Strait Islander population, and live alongside the Traditional Owners of the inner island archipelago, the Kaurareg, who identify as Aboriginal. Torres Strait Islanders who live on these islands—and those who don't, like Nancy, but retain connections—are very concerned about biophysical change to their islands, feeling the effect on local flora and fauna and on the land and sea, which are all entwined with Islander culture and identity. Disappearing land means disappearing culture.

The language of loss

We need new ways of speaking about uncertain futures. The term "climate change" is often too vague and removed from the here and now of rising seas, changing temperatures and species devastation to sink in. Australians' habitats—our homes and our cultures—are at risk.

The changing climate disproportionately affects Indigenous people, and affects them differently. Because land and sea are inextricably linked with Indigenous cultural identities, a changing climate threatens ceremony, hunting practices, sacred sites, bush tucker and bush medicine, which in turn affects law, home, health, education, livelihood and purpose.

But there is a second sense in which Indigenous people are being removed from the language of climate change. Indigenous people feel a unique sense of responsibility to the land and to their children. Many communities have unique cultural resources and knowledge in managing climate, as well as experience in cooperatively managing climate with neighboring communities. And yet among those who recognize the need for urgent action to respond to a changing climate, there are few who look to Indigenous Knowledges for solutions.

Indigenous Australians have a lot to say. As Tony Birch blogs, "For Indigenous people, the impact of climate change is not a future event. It has occurred in the past, and it is occurring now."

The tide is coming

In 1948, severe flooding forced Nancy's grandfather to relocate from Saibai to the mainland, Bamaga, on the tip of Cape York. A tropical cyclone combined with high tides to create a storm tide. The sea swallowed houses on Saibai and Boigu and people had to be evacuated. The flooding caused erosion and a lack of freshwater for the community. Many, like Nancy's grandfather, never went back. Today the Bamaga community are descendants of these relocated Islanders. These were the islands' worst major floods in living memory—elderly Islanders pass on stories of the fearful event.

Each new flood, like the ones in 2005 (Mer) and in 2006 (Boigu and Saibai, Poruma, Iama, Masig and Warraber), brings back old fears. The waters are coming closer and closer. Every aspect of life is affected, from subsistence hunting to commercial fishing to sewage and infrastructure, churches and schools. An Elder well versed in the sea looks at the water and feels as if they don't know it anymore. It's scary, and so few are listening.

In 2012, Saibai was once again hit by high tides that swamped the cemetery, damaging sacred gravesites. Through Nancy's voice I got a glimpse of the extreme community distress that results from the degradation of graveyards and other significant sites like story places and midden deposits. She described sandbagging graves to save their beloved dead from the sea. These desperate efforts are not always successful. On other islands, such as Iama (Yam), homes are frequently taken hostage by the sea. If no conservation measures are implemented it could mean living there will no longer be safe.

Will Torres Strait Islanders again be forced away from their homes? It's already happening in the seas around us in the Pacific Marshall Islands and Kiribati. Interviewed by *The Guardian* in 2015, filmmaker Jack Niedenthal questioned what leaving might mean to island people: "If the land doesn't exist, what happens to these people for whom the land is the most integral thing?"

For many Torres Strait Islanders, moving off their islands is the "last resort." Cultural practices and traditional activities cannot occur (ideally) without the context of the islands where these people's ancestors were born. As Fred Gela, mayor of the Torres Strait Island Regional Council, says in the *Koori Mail*, "the land and sea in the Torres Strait is a critical part of our spiritual and physical identity." Islanders forced to move to mainland Australia, like the community that relocated to Bamaga, may create potential cultural conflicts.

A few months after Nancy Bamaga spoke in Brisbane, the residents on Saibai got some long-awaited news. To try to prevent a last-resort action and to assist in the survival of cultures unique to Queensland and the world, the federal and state governments were investing $26 million in seawall infrastructure for the six islands most at risk. The process of building and maintaining the seawalls is ongoing and is much needed by communities who have campaigned for years. Recent administrative delays have added to the frustration of communities who often feel their struggle to save their homes is going unnoticed. Despite efforts to raise awareness of their growing despair, they feel their voices are being enveloped by the tide.

The magpie geese

Like the Torres Strait Islands, northern Australia will soon be devastated by rising sea levels and warmer seas. This will mean a change of abundance or location of animals and plants and will affect co-dependent relationships with Aboriginal people. The Murrumburr people from Kakadu are noticing the effect of saltwater intrusion on the availability of traditional foods. Balanced Country is particularly important for sustaining populations of magpie geese in Kakadu.

Australia has many beautiful, distinct birds at risk of population decline, not all of whom can fit onto postcards. The magpie goose is one of these birds whose story goes mostly untold in mainstream Australia but who has a central place for many Aboriginal societies.

Magpie geese once were common in southern Australia before European settlement, abundant in swamps in places such as Melbourne and in coastal areas and inland river floodplains in places such as central-west New South Wales. In the early 1900s, clearing for agriculture and wetlands removal made these regions unvisitable for the birds. Today their range covers northern Australia from Broome to Brisbane, where I live. Bigargin is our Yugambeh word for the waterbird. Like the magpie, magpie geese are black and white. They are sturdy birds with long black necks and long orange legs and are referred to as a "living fossil"—the family diverging before the Cretaceous-Paleogene mass extinction event and preceding ducks, geese and swans.

The late wet season between February and April is a special time in the Top End wetlands, where up to 30,000 birds can gather. The birds develop family relationships of mostly two females and one male to raise their young.

The Top End identifies strongly with magpie geese and they are a big part of culture. As a totemic bird, they have their own paintings and ceremonies, and they are important bush tucker. Hunting magpie geese assists the transfer of skills and knowledge from one generation to the next and fulfils kinship obligations. Murrumburr people hunt magpie geese by various means: throwing well-timed sticks while the birds are in the air, or stalking and hand-catching underwater using hollow reeds as snorkels. The birds are usually roasted; the eggs are also eaten. Hunting trips play a great role in cultural cohesion and social interactions, and are part of looking after country. At the same time, Traditional Owners monitor environmental threats and practice traditional burning around floodplains. Seventy percent of the geese population in the Territory during the dry season live in habitats less than one meter above sea level. The northern coast is at risk of seas rising at four times the global average, partly because shallower seas are more prone to expansion through heat. As Stephen Garnett of Charles Darwin University explains, "As sea levels rise, the big spectacles will go. The wetlands of Kakadu will no longer be much of a tourist attraction. They will be invaded by sea salt. There's some evidence that it is already occurring."

The birds will also stop visiting as frequent cyclones change their habitat. It took three decades for the mangroves of Darwin to recover after Cyclone Tracy, as research conducted by Charles Darwin University has discovered. The findings show forests are dependent on an exact tide elevation, which means "even small rises in sea level will throw the balance into chaos, diminishing marine, plant, mammal and bird biodiversity."

The harvest of magpie geese has been estimated to contribute as much as $1.2 million a year to the Northern Territory economy, based on a market value of twenty dollars per bird and 60,000 birds.

Bush tucker is nutritious and does not have to be transported in. Loss of tourism is also a big concern for many Aboriginal communities, including the Murrumburr people.

Twenty percent of the bird population in northern Australia is at risk of dramatic decline in the next few decades, and the magpie geese are part of this. They have already lost their southern habitat—will they lose another? How will First Nations people cope with the loss of a totemic species so integral to their lives?

Many eagles protecting our country

First Nations Australians often look to our totemic animals for guidance in tough times. On my way to a white learning institution in inner-city Melbourne I noticed a statue dedicated to the eagle totem Bunjil towering over the street. I paid attention as Yugambeh people also see our Mibunn as looking over our country from the sky. Eagles—big, majestic birds, high-flying over land—have provided inspiration for nations across the country from coast to desert. Uncle Tony Birch explains the widespread message of Bunjil in Victoria on *Weather Stations*:

> The story simply stated, within Aboriginal culture, is that Bunjil the Eagle watches over all children from the sky and endeavours to keep them safe. This is not simply a "fairytale" or folklore (in a dismissive sense). The story of Bunjil has vital meaning in contemporary Australia for Aboriginal people. The story also acts as a guiding point for the sustenance of all peoples and the environment. The Bunjil story within Koori (Aboriginal) communities in Victoria comes with a high level of responsibility. It is incumbent upon adults and parents to care for our children. It is important that we provide them with education. That we nurture them both emotionally and

intellectually. In return we hope that when our children grow they will accept the responsibility of caring for each other and the environment.

When a child's learning is the land, disappearing land means knowledge can no longer be passed down. A child loses their education—the equivalent of libraries and textbooks turning to dust. Goori writer Melissa Lucashenko speaks often about how important identity is to the mental, physical and emotional health of all Indigenous Australians but especially the young. With interconnected relationships to land, identity is island, river, mangroves, forest and desert; identity is magpie geese, emu and spinifex.

It is fundamental that future Indigenous Australians can receive knowledge about how to live. This can only occur if we take the right steps to ensure our places are protected. "Language is fossil poetry," Ralph Waldo Emerson said, and indeed Aboriginal languages hold the most valuable and longest record of land and how to live on it. We must endeavor to retain language as if it is water.

A different kind of weather

Aboriginal knowledge and land management practices may have been able to prevent recent natural disasters, or at least reduce their impact. For example, Kaurna philosopher Uncle Lewis O'Brien is critical of the lack of a coordinated approach to contemporary flooding events:

> The Pitjantjatjara knew in 2008 the River Murray would flood in 2010. The Pitjantjatjara knowledge wouldn't have stopped the flooding, but it could have reduced the flood damage by way of more time being available to take precautions.

And if Indigenous environmental knowledge was more readily available [in 2011] they would have been forewarned and let the water go from the Wivenhoe Dam and this would have reduced the damage to the flooded areas of Queensland.

Indeed, to only look at 250-year-old weather records when Indigenous Australians have kept oral records of such events for thousands of years is short-sighted. Aboriginal and Torres Strait Islanders' ideas of weather, and the weather in most parts of Australia, don't fit into the neat, European model of four seasons. Take for example goanna season (in Arrernte country, after "winter," around September, when goannas come out). All First Nations have their own concepts and ways to talk about the weather.

In desert country, what are countrymen and women noticing? What uncertainty has crept into the homelands? Have soft eyes seen everything, or is this "a different kind of weather"? Like the Elder who gazes at the unrecognizable sea in the Torres Strait, reading testimonials of desert people dealing with fast-changing climate, the sad confusion they are facing can be easily imagined.

> *There are different types of fire now because of the different grasses, like buffel grass. The fires are hotter and fiercer and this affects what's happening up in the sky, it affects the weather. Now it's hard to know when to burn.*
>
> **Eastern Arrernte Elder**

> *In goanna season nothing was fat ... Bush tucker from trees is not coming in right seasons; not many bush bananas— not coming at the time we need them, after the wet. Wet was late bush tucker missed time to come out. Bush potato comes in winter-time. Last year we couldn't see the cracks ... Weather is changing, winter is shorter ... One month ago*

went over 100 kms to get kangaroo—nothing; and no goan-
nas. No bush tucker—bush orange, bush banana.

Trisha Frank, Mt Isa region

At some time last year the weather messed up the time we'd
go for bush tucker. Normally when rain came in Dec/Jan
we get Feb, Mar and April to go hunt goanna, bush tucker,
but this year we got one lot of rain, brought all that bush
tucker up and then next rain washed them off. We only had
first lot. But our old people say that the first lot are for the
birds and animals and the second lot are for us. But there
was nothing for us because the second lot of rain came [and
ruined them].

Jennifer Mahoney, Alpurrurulam

These are disturbing images of country changing too quickly. It now feels foreign to those who know it best.

Despite a history of marginalization, the powerful messages of Elders and Aboriginal people living on country are now being listened to by scientists, who see the benefit of adding these voices to facts. Elizabeth Kolbert's *The Sixth Extinction* (2014) describes the recent theory that we are in the sixth extinction event and aren't even noticing it. The book has a frog on the front cover, as frogs form an important part of the warning. But even forward-looking climate research like this is still behind, as Uncle Lewis describes: "I was influenced by my aunt, Aunty Vera, who used to say to me, 'Lewis, where've all the frogs gone?' She said that to me for forty years and I didn't do anything about it. Then I realized the university was starting to talk about frogs missing and I thought she was well ahead of her field, forty years ahead of her time."

Living connected to Country, there's no wonder Traditional Owners are steps ahead of science. Indigenous Knowledges are old knowledges. They are accumulated through years of trial and error.

They should be valued for what they are, a tool to meet the challenges of a changing climate.

Multi-nation thinking

Country is like the body. The body is like Country. You say your ankles are sore and stiff, but it originates in your hips and starts to affect your back and knees. Uncle Lewis talks of "a multi-nation" approach to climate, where Indigenous Nations worked together to care for the land and prevent disasters and waste. He points to the movement of wind and cloud from Western Australia to South Australia as just one way the country works like the body. First Nations groups engaged in "cooperative thinking." The movement of winds and clouds across Western Australia to South Australia is dependent on growing trees in certain places and lighting fires at certain times. "'When they cut trees down at Cummins [in Western Australia], the rainfall fell or was reduced [in South Australia].' So we got an indicator that's factual and we got to look at this."

Traditional knowledge is an underutilized resource in national climate change mitigation efforts. Not only is Indigenous knowledge rarely used for the prevention or lessening of natural disasters, the current legal system does not adequately recognize or protect Indigenous Australians' knowledge. There is only limited legal opportunity to protect Indigenous peoples' rights to maintain biodiversity practices.

The inability to adapt to climate-related changes with neighbors is also a problem for Torres Strait Islanders, as traveling between islands has been affected by sea levels. In the past, Islanders were linked economically and socially through a maritime trading network, just as they were linked with Papua New Guinea and Cape York Aboriginal communities.

Climate-related problems require holistic thinking. There are examples of Indigenous knowledge and science matching up to find solutions. In magpie geese country in the Top End, a collaboration between traditional knowledge and science has become a government-recognized model for "two tool box" approaches to climate change. Almost a decade ago, five Aboriginal land management groups from West Arnhem Land developed a plan to address the damaging effects of late dry-season wildfire. Up to a third of the Northern Territory was burned every year, and burning is the biggest contributor to greenhouse gases in the Territory. The West Arnhem Land Fire Abatement (WALFA) project began in 2006 and draws on thousands of years of local experience in expertly managing the tropical savannas. Strategic fire management practices protect the biodiversity of the land and reduce greenhouse gas emissions. The WALFA project has met its reduction target by 140 percent and the problems caused by the most fire-prone landscape on earth have been mitigated after being put back in the right hands. Similar strategies are being adopted in the Kimberley, Carpentaria and Cape York Peninsula. There are many initiatives taking place today that use this model.

Greater understanding and application of Aboriginal and Torres Strait Islander knowledges and practices will help with future challenges. The Ngadjuri people of South Australia were described as "weather prophets" by early settlers for instinctively moving before weather events like floods. We need our weather prophets now more than ever.

Warning

The United Nation Permanent Forum on Indigenous Issues is concerned about the huge challenges Indigenous people face and warns that these communities can't do it on their own. Indigenous people have the smallest ecological footprints in the world's communities and should not be asked to carry the heaviest burden of adjusting to climate change.

The Torres Strait and northern Australia face threats to unique ways of life that will mirror challenges faced by our central and southern Indigenous Australians. Climate change challenges Indigenous identities.

Recognizing the need for action to safeguard these identities is only the beginning. Indigenous culture needs to do more than just motivate a response to climate change; it needs to be a part of any response. Innovation and resilience have buoyed efforts in the past. They are needed now. When the government responds to climate change without seeking the input of its Indigenous people, the response perpetuates this country's colonial history.

As I listened to Aunty Nancy Bamaga that night in 2014 at kuril dhagun, I also felt the Brisbane River's presence, so close. So loud. This is a river I have spent my life near, but in truth I know so very little about its survival.

Listening is the first act of learning, and through learning we become not only aware but also appreciative of what is, and always has been, around us.

BAYSIDE

My dad always boasted he had been to every football ground in town, but he hadn't been to plenty, Bayside being one of them, and it was inevitable that we would get lost. He was hopeless with directions, saying it was because he was used to driving on the other side of the road, and I wasn't much better, even with last year's refidex spread out open on my lap. I blamed the dusk for obscuring the landscape, concealing the street names and the road signs. One eye on the time knowing I would get there way past the hour but knowing the coach wouldn't care and I would be in the starting eleven anyway. End of a service road. Smelled the sea beyond the mass of bush. I steadied the light on the roof of the car like holding a lantern. Tracing my thumb over where I was and where I ought to be. We needed to get back on Whites Road. I took a deep breath, trying to ignore the time, and worked out a way to get us out. Sense of relief when we saw the patchy fields, the car veering onto the gravel car park. It was twenty past, but my team wasn't in the changing rooms yet, instead sitting next to the fence watching the game before. I nodded to the coach. Some of the girls headed to the back. I bought a paper bag of mixed lollies from the box-shaped window of the canteen, then walked quickly past the closed referee's room and home team room. Away room was bare, grey walls, brown floor. Stretcher in the middle. Old wooden bench with the white paint stripped off. Foul smell, probably from one of the cubicles, two, adjacent to a filthy sink. Tape and heaves of mud and half-drunk bottle of Powerade on the floor. This was the game where I bled onto the ground. From a gash on my knee sustained in a collision that resulted in a goal I knew nothing about but claimed anyway. 1–0. The ref kept sending me to the sideline to patch up the wound, but the bandages wouldn't hold. The ref said I was at risk of a yellow card—for what?—so I ripped a piece of my teammate's green electrical tape and wrapped it around my leg three times. It held, and so did my team's narrow lead. When I got into the car, heater already running, my dad congratulated me on the goal, and I smiled. He put on the easy listening radio and quizzed me on who was singing the song. Creedence Clearwater Revival? There was even less light as we drove home, still not knowing where we were and why the trees whispered through the radio static.

Taking a Stand Against a Name

I am located therefore I am

Aunty Mary Graham

Throughout my life I have been confronted while driving through Queensland, passing signs of creeks and roads bearing names that sent shivers down my spine.

"Why is *this* called *this*?" I remember asking my parents, who shied away from my assumptions.

"I don't know," they would say, and the car would fill with uncomfortable silence for a few long minutes until we reached the next landmark. When I spotted a name with a questionable implication, the hair on the back of my neck would begin to bristle and my shoulders would grow stiff, as if I was caught in flight mode. During my childhood I grew to accept that these names and this feeling were just a part of life.

In 2011 I became personally acquainted with an Aunty who would forever change my life. Proppa cultural way, Aunty Linda McBride-Yuke introduced herself as the daughter of Uncle Lambert McBride, who was the best man at the wedding of my mother's parents, Cyril Currie and Betty Williams. Our kinship circles had been tightly interwoven for many generations, and she attended the same school as my mother and her siblings. They played together as children in the Blak working-class northside communities of Zillmere and Chermside. But this day marked the start of our close and formal relationship as colleagues, friends and kin.

116

We were at the State Library of Queensland for our first day as inaugural trainee editors of a pilot program called black&write!. As we walked the floors of the library during our induction, Aunty Linda was giving me a proppa rundown of who I was and who I belonged to, proppa which way, proppa link-up. I am not embarrassed to admit that when I first began my job at black&write! at the tender age of twenty there was a lot I did not know. Much of my life had been about avoiding attention and hiding myself from real as well as perceived threats.

Aunty Linda was kind with me and always forgiving. She never berated me for what I did not know, understanding the context in which my life was situated. Everything was said with humor. We laughed! Aunty Linda was steeped in politics from her pores to her bones. Her parents, Lambert and May, were active members of the Queensland Council for the Advancement of Aborigines and Torres Strait Islanders and campaigned to get rid of Queensland state protection acts, considered the most repressive in Australia.

Our work life was as literary as it was cultural. Slowly I began to open up to her, especially when she would give me lifts home from work. She was beautifully supportive of queer family members, and treated me and my partner with so much love and kindness. We worked together closely for five years. The whole time, Aunty was battling a respiratory illness that would eventually take her from us in 2019.

It was through Aunty Linda that I first heard about the Murri anti-racism activist Stephen Hagan, who was the editor of the *National Indigenous Times* between 2010 and 2013. Aunty Linda told me the story of Hagan's efforts to remove the word "nigger" from the grand-stand at the main sport stadium in Toowoomba. Toowoomba is located in the spine of the country's Whale Dreaming songline, also called the Great Dividing Range, and is the intersection of the traditional land of three separate groups: the Jagera, Giabal and Jarowair people. It's a place that has hosted age-old ceremonies, and is on the pathway to the important Bunya Mountains feast that connected all of us southern Queensland and northern New South Wales mobs.

It seems shocking today, in an international era of zero-tolerance for racially offensive names, that the journey to justice led by Hagan took nine long years (1999–2008) to resolve. In recent times a lot of change has been made. But to get where we are today, a lot of dogged determination was necessary.

The n word. My mother and her siblings grew up being called it. My grandparents grew up being called it. It is a word that is still hurled at First Nations people and settler people of color in Queensland every day. It is not a word that exists only in the past as much as I wish it did. I've never been called the n word to my face. I'm not sure if that counts me as lucky, but I'm pretty sure it's to do with my light-skin privilege rather than Australia getting any less racist. But that's not to say that skin color or appearance are the defining factors—people weaponize racial abuse against any First Nations people, just because they're First Nations.

I've had "the ABCs," as artist Gordon Bennett calls them (abo, boong, coon), and I've been called a monkey and an ape. The words have always made me feel indignant, like, "What gives you the right?" I've always felt the strength of my ancestors within me; through anger, through pride. If you accept a name, you accept a loss.

One day in 2020, I finally sit down to read Hagan's autobiography, *The N Word* (2005), cover to cover, at a place where Aunty Linda and I had a lot of memories together, the State Library. I read the book in one day in the Neil Roberts Research Lounge, taking a few breaks. It's late in the year, late for many things. It smells like summer outside, strong sunlight, thirsty trees. I spot a white woman chasing an ibis away from the library café, which is decorated with giant Christmas beetles. People are slowing down for the last few days of the year. Families are trying to get together, despite COVID-19 restrictions.

In *The N Word*, Hagan begins the story attending a rugby game with his family. A Cunnamulla boy, he had been living in Toowoomba for nine years with his wife, Rhonda, and two young children. Hagan's twin nephews were playing in the game.

When the broadcaster announced the first try has been scored at the "'Nigger' Brown end," Hagan and Rhonda immediately looked at each other and across at the wooden grandstand emblazoned with the sign "ES 'Nigger' Brown Stand." At every pointed mention of the sign by the broadcaster across the loudspeaker system, Hagan and Rhonda became increasingly distressed, and contemplated leaving with their small children. I know the feeling Hagan was alluding to. It's a nails-on-the-chalkboard kinda feeling, to say the least. Something inside you is dying. And you wonder why you are the only one feeling like something is wrong.

In 1962, the ES "Nigger" Brown Stand was named after local footballer Edwin Stanley Brown (1898–1972). Brown was a highly regarded rugby league player in the 1910s and 1920s, as well as a local businessman. He was a white Australian man and was given the nickname "Nigger" by his peers at a time when many Australians supported white-supremacist views. As Hagan explains,

> Edward Stanley Brown's birth certificate did not include the word, and irrespective of how he received the nickname, the word itself was racially offensive and definitely not a term of endearment. The nickname "Nigger" was bestowed—and later included on the sign—at a time before Indigenous Australians were even allowed to vote or be counted in the nation's censuses.

Hagan believed that it was the only sign in any public sports grandstand around the world to bear the word "nigger," and it must be disposed of. Thus began a series of lengthy and costly legal battles and widespread support, though with an equal spread of condemnation. Hagan was motivated by pride in his people and a wish for the younger generations: "I had a vision of my children playing on the oval with children of other races, free in the knowledge that they would not have to confront a relic of a racist past."

His first attempt in the High Court was dismissed, as Justice Gaudron rejected the submission that there was a link between the sign on the grandstand and racism. However, as Hagan's journey was to prove, there was a lot going on underneath the surface.

In my family, we were taught to be wary of Toowoomba. I was told it was a haunted place. I only went there on two occasions, both for football, to play South Toowoomba Hawks with my Gap team in the premier league. It's roughly two hours west from where I grew up. I remember how cold it was on a July evening. Those were the only times I would pack tracksuit pants in my kit bag.

In his book, Hagan describes Toowoomba in the late 1990s and early 2000s as a place where skinheads could terrorize First Nations youth with targeted bashings, and a non-Indigenous man supportive of First Nations rights could be called "a gin jockey."

As Hagan continued his campaign, he, his family and his supporters began receiving hate mail, including death threats claiming to be from the Ku Klux Klan. There were known clusters of the KKK in the Darling Downs region and the mail often had letterheads with KKK iconography.

Hagan's fight had stirred up the cloud of racism above Toowoomba. In the late 1990s, the region was under the spell of Pauline Hanson's One Nation Party, formed in 1997, which called for zero net immigration; an end to multiculturalism; a revival of Australia's Anglo-Celtic cultural tradition, which it said had been diminished; the abolition of native title and the Aboriginal and Torres Strait Islander Commission (ATSIC); an end to Aboriginal funding programs; opposition to Aboriginal reconciliation, which the party said would create two nations; and a review of the 1967 constitutional referendum, which gave the Commonwealth power to legislate for First Nations people. Hanson received 36 percent of the vote in the Lockyer electorate of Blair in the 1998 election (in Toowoomba North she got 24.1 percent and in Toowoomba South

23.7 percent). Overall, One Nation won eleven seats and received a state average of 23 percent of the vote, though the election was won by Labor's Peter Beattie.

The support for the "Nigger" Brown sign in the small city was a green light for violent white supremacists. In 1999, it was alleged a man walked up to the entry of the school that Hagan's nephews and many other First Nations students attended and handed his son a baseball bat, telling him to get rid of the "troublesome niggers." Hagan's sister, Pam, was stopped in the center of Toowoomba by two skinheads, one of them rolling up the sleeve of his shirt to reveal a swastika tattoo.

By 2000, Hagan's campaign had divided the city. Some First Nations leaders were initially against the name change, alluding to it as political correctness gone mad and saying that those who were offended were too sensitive. One former high-profile Aboriginal player said at the time, "I don't have a problem with it and when I read about it I found it quite laughable."

However, by late 2000 the tide was beginning to turn. A rally was held in the streets of Toowoomba. The publicity poster included the lines, "If a player called another player a 'Nigger' they could suffer disciplinary action including fines up to $10,000. The reconciliation process must begin with a commitment to racially inclusive public spaces. This means removing or modifying historic signs which cause offence."

Neville Bonner's niece Jennifer Bonner, whose two sons played for the Queensland schoolboys' football team, said at the rally "nigger is a filthy, evil word." She said the name did not have to be used for a public figure. "If his family want to use it that's their prerogative, but we are a proud race that have been degraded for too long … It affects us spiritually. It cuts into your heart," she said.

Hagan said, "We will get that word taken down from that grandstand so that the next generation of Aboriginal sportsmen don't have to run on to Athletic Oval and play under that sign 'Nigger.'"

Hagan lodged an appeal of decision in the Federal Court, but the appeal was dismissed. So, in July 2002, he and his team sent a submission to the United Nations Committee on the Elimination of Racial Discrimination in Geneva. In April 2003, they received the response they had been wanting. The committee recommended the removal of the offending term from the sign, stating that "the memory of a distinguished sportsperson may be honored in ways other than by maintaining and displaying a public sign considered to be racially offensive." The Queensland Anti-Discrimination Commission also called for the removal of the "Nigger" reference.

The UN endorsement made headlines all over the country. Russ Brown, son of Edward Stanley, joined Hagan in a photograph in front of the stand, which was published in *The Toowoomba Chronicle*.

Despite the decision and the support from the press, the Toowoomba mayor and Premier Beattie still refused to change the name. In 2004, the Australian government officially responded to the UN decision and said it did not propose to remove the "term in question" from the sign. Hagan had won the argument at the highest international level, but it hadn't resulted in meaningful change.

At the time of the book's publication, 2005, the sign had not been changed. Hagan concluded by saying, "nevertheless I will not give up on the promise I made to my family to have the 'n word' removed from the E.S. 'Nigger' Brown stand."

Hagan's fight for justice didn't end there. He campaigned for the change of the name of Coon Cheese, which was finally changed to Cheer in 2020 after the Black Lives Matter protests. And Carlton Football Club rejected his 2021 suggestion to commission a new club theme song. Hagan reasons the melody was originally based on "Lily of Laguna," a nineteenth-century song that contains highly offensive lyrics about Native Americans and Black people, which was performed numerous times in blackface.

Despite refusing to change the stand's name, in 2006 Premier Beattie, through his Natural Resources Minister Stephen Robertson, set the wheels in motion for changes to racially offensive place names following the lobbying of First Nations groups.

Rooted in hate and violence, the word "nigger" has historically been used in the names of products, colors and plants, and as a place name, in Queensland particularly. Elders want these names changed because they promote violence. It's different, say, to "Boundary Street" in West End, which references the historical barrier where our people were banned from entering Brisbane. Elders voted against changing this name because it carries history that should not be forgotten. It is not direct derogatory language.

In 1973, the late Birri Gubba and Mununjali activist Sam Watson was on a work trip in the Atherton Tablelands when he drove past a road sign bearing the name "Nigger Creek." He stopped the car and took the sign, one of two in the area. "I just got a couple of tools out of the boot and liberated the sign. I thought, this is a blot on the landscape."

It took forty-four years for the name of the creek to be wiped off the map, in 2017, following a submission by the Girringun Aboriginal Corporation on behalf of the Jiddabul people. The creeks have been renamed from Nigger Creek and North Nigger Creek to Wondecla and North Wondecla creeks. A further ten place names across Queensland have been replaced. However, some still remain.

I'm still on guard during road trips. Names I saw as a child, such as Murdering Creek and Murdering Creek Road on the southern side of Lake Weyba near Noosa, on Gubbi Gubbi Country, blatantly point to sites where the local people were massacred. In this example, it's offensive how little is widely known (or how much is covered up) about the massacre and loss of life—even the date (circa 1860)—though it is captured in the place's name. Hiding in plain sight. When I'm in places where ghosts scream of violence, I have learned to center myself through the wisdom of my Elders.

In 2008, Hagan finally got his wish, as the stand was demolished to make way for a new stadium. Toowoomba Sports Ground Inc. agreed not to use the term in the future.

Towards the end of Hagan's book, I'm startled and delighted to see a mention of beautiful Aunty. Hagan writes about being "moved to tears" after he read a letter to the editor Aunty Linda wrote to the *Koori Mail* in 2003, where she told of resigning her membership of the ALP due to Premier Beattie's lack of leadership over the issue. Aunty Linda knew words hurt, and she wasn't afraid to take a stand.

I text a photo I've taken of the mention to our mutual friend Sue. We've been texting a lot about Aunty lately, due to her ancestral homelands K'gari being on fire for six weeks because of four white visitors who started an illegal campfire. "Look who makes a mention," I say in my text. "Our star." Sue repeats my star emoji. "She's everywhere," she replies. Like stardust she spreads. I miss her, especially realizing that next month will mark another year that she has not been here physically. But always in spirit. The rains have dampened the fire, and the island is beginning to renew itself.

Today Toowoomba sits in the wake of the devasting 2011 inland flood. Floodwaters swirled angrily into the Central Business District after 160 millimeters of rain fell in thirty-six hours on top of a month's record rainfall, turning the normally calm West and East creeks into a frothing, angry river that killed two people on top of the Great Dividing Range. Toowoomba is also one of Australia's new regional multicultural cities, having accepted thousands of refugees from 2003 onwards from Chad, South Sudan and Afghanistan, as well as Yazidi refugees from Syria. This led Toowoomba to be declared a "Refugee Welcome Zone" in 2013. The name change of the grandstand was a significant and symbolic step in providing a harmonious environment for all those who now live on Giabal and Jarowair Country.

In 2019, my mum took offence at a name on a representative jersey I was wearing. I was playing in the National Indigenous Football Championships, and our team sported the name "Jinda Magic." The

124

name was taken from the word for woman in the Bundjalung and Gumbangirr Nation, and was chosen by our team captain, who is Gumbangirr. I've heard similar words, "jidda" and "tidda," used as terms of endearment for female relatives, and the word is similar all down the east coast.

My mum said the name of our team connotated the word "gin," which had been used a lot in her time as a derogatory word for Aboriginal women. Mum tells me that "gin" was used in many of the records of state surveillance against our people (as Aunty Linda used to say all the time, we are "the most documented people on earth"). The use of "gin" in these documents denied the women their names and humanity. They couldn't even be bothered naming the women they were documenting.

The other day I was with Mum and Aunty Sonnie at the pub at West End, the one we always go to, next to Open House, and Aunty Sonnie was telling us about her research, about having to endure seeing that three-letter word spelled out over and over again, a word used to imply Aboriginal women were inferior. "Don't even like the drink," Aunty Sonnie said, spying the bar menu. "Gross as."

I'm reminded that, for Aboriginal women of the generation above me, even reclaiming the word "jinda" can cause a heavy toll. Reclaiming language does not always bring us together. Sometimes reclaiming is not the best for everyone. I am determined that those who have held the burden in the past will not have to in the future. I will take a stand.

Personal Score

Like romance, competition has many faces, some of them ugly. In addition to showing me my grace and graciousness, the mirror of sports had reflected back to me my jealousy, pettiness and arrogance.

Mariah Burton Nelson

"Queer time" is a term for those specific models of temporality that emerge within postmodernism once one leaves the temporal frames of bourgeois reproduction and family, longevity, risk/safety, and inheritance.

Jack Halberstam

Temporal drag is a productive obstacle to progress, a usefully distorting pull backward, and a necessary pressure on the present tense.

Elizabeth Freeman

Season

By Queertime, at twenty-five, I grew restless and could not see what was in front of me. I felt rootless and lived alone; my friends were not family. Through this depression, I bought a new duck-feather pillow and ten-kilogram weights, and did what I had done since I was young: structured my life through football.

I lived through games: played and watched. Off-season, preseason and on-season. There was the meal at the pub while watching the game, always the wedges, always the Stone & Wood.

The A-League season came to a head fast. Soon my team, Brisbane Roar, were playing Western Sydney Wanderers in a knock-out semi. I had been feeling nervous all day.

The viewing was with other dykes at the pub on Melbourne Street, just up a bit from Musgrave Park. The most dykes ever seen in Brisbane. The two girls in front of me I only saw at games, a young Gold Coast couple, kissing and dancing at every chance of celebration.

Up 3–0 within twenty minutes and it was looking good. I even allowed myself to smile and laugh with the others. I was to punish myself for it, this ease, as another twenty minutes gone and the scores were level. I had another Stone & Wood as the game went to extra time. Western Sydney got the goal they needed to put them in the lead. How did we go from 3–0 up to losing 5–4? I leaned in to the girls in front of me. I saw it in them too, the defeatism. Nothing now to believe in. None of it would be there for me the following week. I felt my heart ache as I watched the couple leave before me, no longer holding hands. They did not play the game as I did, only watched. I still had my own football; the year had something for me yet.

New club

It was four minutes on the ferry, my new club. And another couple of minutes' walk down Oxford Street, past the bars and cafés to Memorial Park. I resigned myself to playing here because it was four minutes on the ferry.

I still got nervous joining a new club, meeting the girls, learning the unspoken rules. It was still challenging, no matter how many times I did it, or how old I was.

I scanned the girls for signs of familiarity. Creatives? Older women? Lesbians or bisexuals? This had become a ritual of self-preservation. Was it safe? The pack would strangle those not in with the crowd. Each time I took my gear off in the changing room I would be aware of this. Each time I smelled the start of a wounding joke I would run faster and leave the words in the wind.

The girls put on their boots. It started here—appearance. Coded in how they dressed. How short were the shorts? How high was the hair? So much straightness and so much time. A season of this.

Passing drills, technique-based exercises. Volleying, heading, bringing it down on the knee. These things came back to me after a while; it was a rhythm. Feet right and it volleyed off the foot into the hands of the receiver. Of course, the throw helped as well, as I told the girl I was paired with. "Perfect," I said to Kath, also new to the club, in colorful shorts.

When we entered a passing game, I saw Kath was a fit player with a good work rate and positive distribution. I knew before Kath told me that she was a box-to-box midfielder. It was comforting to know there was a decent player in the squad, but it also brought on feelings of jealousy.

In the break, I sat by myself on the wet grass. Kath called me back to the group; coach called a possession game.

I was picked to be on a team with fewer players and fought to get the ball a bit too aggressively. I rushed at Kath and accidentally stood on her toe.

"Sorry," already running to where Kath had put the ball, boxed Kath's teammate in.

When I looked back Kath was frowning, clutching her toe. Then she was grabbing my shirt, pushing her shoulder into mine as I was muscled off the ball. "Well done, Kath," the coach yelled out and I fumed.

I was scared to get to know the field. Shy of it. The entrances and exits. The grass. All seemed uncertain.

The group took another drink break, silent and out of breath. Some of the girls took the opportunity to sit down and stretch. I looked at Kath's sculpted calves. Her hands. Short fingernails, thick fingers, shiny skin. We were both covered in sweat. I was tired in the legs but wanted to show more in the next round of play.

When we got back to the game it was set up with two small goals. I was primed for this situation, scoring four straight up. Kath only got one late in the game. I didn't know why I had created this personal score between the two of us.

As the team jogged doggedly across the field in a pack as a last physical commitment, I tried not to notice those calves of Kath's again. She said she went to the gym with her boyfriend. I wished I had come more prepared for this; my body was hurting.

Change room

Walking into a half-circle of seated straight girls in the changing room, I held my breath. I felt a repulsion for these expressions of femininity I could not endorse. Kath with fake tan and mascara to play in and straightened hair, whitened teeth.

The girls did not take their shirts off in front of each other, hiding their stomachs and breasts as if they didn't have them. One by one they went to the closed toilet cubicle to change. When all the numbers had been taken and worn, the coach entered. He held up a whiteboard and began to put names to dots.

I looked at Kath across the room. We had been fighting for the same number and the same position. Luckily, the team required two central midfielders, so we could play side by side. We did need to learn how to pass the ball to each other. The coach and the other girls had noticed the bruising we gave each other in the training games. The coach put Kath's and my names together on the whiteboard. This felt unstable, easily altered.

The pregame warm-up went like this: running in lines, lifting knees, opening and shutting the gate, shuffling sideways. Passing in lines, passing straight and running straight, passing diagonally and running straight and passing straight and running diagonally.

I felt the need to beat Kath here but also to keep reserves for the game.

Goal

We only had one official for the match. Typical women's game. We paid the same but got nothing for it. When the ball went close to the sidelines the teams had to rely on the ref's approximation and our own honesty.

Kath and I killed it in the midfield. One assist and one goal each. We could have been playing for fun, but neither of us knew what that meant.

My goal: running deep from midfield, turning a player to get into the eighteen-yard box, hitting it with the laces across my body. Top right corner, goalkeeper no chance.

Kath's goal: a quick one-two with the winger, a sprint to get in front, dummying the keeper and slotting it in from close range.

Neither was better, but I couldn't help the comparisons. Not a team sport with Kath on the team, always there, always fierce, always pushing me.

We finished the game with a solid 4–0 victory and everyone was happy. Pats on the back for the performance. We ran out our tired legs, skipped the last few meters, stretched out hamstrings and groins.

The one official had gone, so the coach asked for a few to stay back to help pack up the equipment. There were two needed to take each goal back. I put myself on Kath's goal. We lifted it together. I was exhausted but determined to keep up my end.

"Go to mine." Kath said it quickly. I followed her to her car.

Kath's house was behind the club, as if staking territory. Radio and lights on inside. Midway through a nervous thought-sentence, Kath's lips, wet. We pulled off our sweaty clothes and left them in a heap in the corner of the bathroom. I found myself thinking I hadn't been with a woman whose chest was smaller than my own; Kath hadn't needed to wear a proper sports bra. I saw her with her back to me in the shower, the red lines the socks had made on her calves. The few pieces of grass in the cave of her back. My own thighs protested as I bent down to soap Kath's legs, feeling the muscles there, wondering if she was also feeling the pressure of the running, the movement.

Winning streak

The superstitions you keep when you're winning and doing well. An eight-hour sleep. No coffee that day. Noodle salad three hours before the game. Left boot on first. Laces tied twice. Before taking to the field I joined the circle, the team putting our hands together to chant the team song.

Kath and I continued to level our performance against each other. Every game counted.

Have you had penetration after football? Four fingers inside Kath, her sweat in my face.

I was bleeding, hated bleeding when I had to play. Kath had run much better, while I had felt heavy at times during the game. The pad had filled up. Kath had been quick to take it off of me as if she'd known I had been wearing it.

Sometimes during training games she would bump knees with me, stick a leg on my leg, or press against my backside, knowing the way I liked to come, teasing me about it. If all that was needed was this friction, then she might have been saying she could make me come standing on the football pitch, fighting for the ball.

I was less interested in the ball than I was in beating Kath, getting in front, holding strong. I felt better when I muscled Kath off the ball without cheating, without my elbows up.

We had been playing our positions our whole lives. Kath centered straight and I centered queer. We were not about to give it up.

Form

There was a potential problem. A disruption to the rhythm. I had a cousin's wedding to go to in Cairns. I missed training twice. While away I tried to make up fitness by running on the beach. The night I got home I hit the weights, pressing them closer and closer to my head.

I arrived at the game ready to go in my head, not so much in my body. I sat in the changing room and watched the coach name positions. My name was on the bench. Kath was starting with another teammate, Jill.

I stood by the bench, not used to this role. I did lunges and squats while watching the action, keeping myself close to the sideline to let the coach know I was ready at any time to make my way into the game.

Like usual, Kath had a lot of ball. When she tore down that left-hand side and the bench was vocal, my own cries of encouragement got caught in my throat.

I was watching Kath having an intense on-field battle with her opponent, a sturdy player. Kath kept trying to round her, but more often she got tangled.

Then Jill played another long ball; Kath ran on. Somehow she got there before the defender, smashed into the keeper. The ball dripped out of their collide, all held our breath, all thought it was going in the goal. I noticed I was the only one on the bench who was silent in that long moment. The ball hit the post.

The game continued, but something was different. The coach realized Kath hadn't got up.

Play was stopped and the coach rushed on the field to see how she was. Seconds dragged on, players in groups, me on the sideline wondering if it meant it was my time to come on.

Seeing Kath in pain, I felt safe. Must be something in my blood to feel this way.

When I took to the park, it wasn't the same. My goals were not as crucial. I missed the pleasure.

"You right?" I had said to Kath.

Her face constricted with anger, her voice a growl. "My knee's not right at all."

I had touched Kath's tears as she lay confined by pain. Perhaps that pain had been willed by me.

Conquer

Kath's injury was worse than the coach and our teammates had thought at the time. Her boyfriend rushed her to emergency late that night. The results of the MRI came: she had done her ACL. She wouldn't be back that season. ACL injuries are common in our sport, but it hadn't seemed possible with Kath. I had spent weeks hunting her weaknesses and hadn't got close to it.

I went to the next training session slightly stunned. I no longer had the desperation to catch up on the fitness I'd lost.

As I might have guessed, there was no off-field curiosity between us. I no longer had a desire to visit Kath's house without the football. I did scroll through photo updates of Kath's knee, swollen and strange-looking.

I ventured back to the pub, but all the screens showed rugby league and AFL and I had no narratives to place on these sports. It was out of season; there were no queers at the pub. I had no other hobbies.

I tried to create another rivalry, but Jill wouldn't take me up. Jill fell when I pushed. Jill yelled when I kicked. Jill told the others I was rough, and dirty. I sat by myself and looked at what I had destroyed. The pitch held the rhythms and the dents of my desire.

Somewhere along the line, I had stopped recognizing land as history. I longed to feel the stories of the old cross-river time, feel the land's occupation.

I started reading at home instead of lifting weights. I got heavy on the history of the place. As part of this, I took to walking along the river late at night. It was softer at that time. The bay breeze pushed through the river's heart. Though the small marsupials had been hunted out, I had once seen dolphins and hoped to again.

I was on track to finish the season as my team's best player, and my team's highest scorer, and these things would have meant something when Kath was around.

I only had the river, the wet smell of the ground, the Queertime breaths, the lust.

Birds and Football (Three portraits)

Kookaburra

At Memorial Park in Bulimba, the home field for the Southside Eagles, a kookaburra is a non-human spectator to the matches. He is what you could call a mascot. Except my feelings about that word are complicated. Where did the idea of mascots come about? I think about the issue of First Nations names and images being used by sports teams as mascots on Turtle Island, and the push to change mascots that carry violent and racist history. In Indigenous culture we have totems, animals that follow us and are significant to us, that look out for us. The kookaburra is my mate Greg's totem. Gugunyalu. He says Gugunyalu's looking out for us.

The early bird catches the worm. This particular kookaburra likes the night lights. Likes hanging out by the club at preseason—he swoops down for the bugs. They are territorial birds—when he sings he is saying, "This is my field."

Greg always notices the kookaburra during the game. Spectators notice it—they watch for it, better placed to see the movement. I always see the bird when I walk to the field from the ferry stop—it's almost as if it has picked me. Halfway down the street it tags along to the field. Sits in a tree or on a pole.

My parents like kookaburras. Dad spotted them from the house we grew up in and got me to come over every time, watch the birds make a racket. Dad was, and still is, fascinated by Australian birds. I'm newly fascinated seeing this strange, thick brick hurling itself through the air. They are unusual birds. I want to showcase them to the world. Where does the word "kookaburra" come from, I wonder? My research leads me to the Wiradjuri loan word "guu-guubarra," onomatopoeic of its call.

There are actually four types of kookaburra in Australia. The rufous-bellied kookaburra (lowland New Guinea, Saibai Island and Australia), the spangled kookaburra (Aru Islands, southern New Guinea and Australia), the blue-winged kookaburra (northern Australia, southern New Guinea) and the laughing kookaburra, which is the kind we are used to, living all over the east coast of Australia and introduced to places like Tasmania to eat snakes. The other species of kookaburras are quite different-looking.

When I was younger I wondered if kookaburras were really laughing. The term "laughing" was applied to the birds by settler-invaders, as a description of the noise this tree kingfisher makes. In the nineteenth century this species was commonly called "the laughing jackass." Is this an Aboriginal interpretation too? Could be a warning. The kookaburra and the lyrebird have a sing-off. Kookaburra starts laughing at the contest, and the lyrebird copies, thinking it's a song. Then the kookaburra laughs even more.

The kookaburra watches for the bugs to come out of the ground, comes closer when the game is starting, comes to sit on the goal's crossbar. Cheeky animals, they are. It is good for the team morale to have this bird. Give us a win. During the off-season he's not there. It's a symbiotic relationship.

Curlew

The eastern species of these wading birds spend March to August in Australia and then travel to Siberia, where they mate. We don't notice their absence, the population of 25,000 in the Moreton Bay area that suddenly leave. Our residents. Half of their lives are a secret to us. Like the curlews who change their plumage, I think I could spend half of my life white and grey in Australia, the other half brilliant bronze, red and gold in Rome. I receive a pending residency offer to live there for six months. To be someone else somewhere else. Life is easy with one pair of jeans, one below-zero jacket, one thick sweater, one light one, and a few undershirts and undergarments. I don't know why I haven't always lived like this.

These birds, mournful and secretive, on my school oval, raising their young. Most of this country's inhabitants are foreigners. Away from home, there's less of a political edge and more calm. No Australia Day celebrations. I could gain the plumage needed to live overseas, store fat, be well fed, have my rest and medicine. But home is home. And I am getting tired taking the flyways around the world. Country is calling me. I struggle to explain to my grant officer why I might need to turn down the opportunity.

How do the birds know the path? Their highways spread invisibly across the sky. Airplanes use machines. Migrating shorebirds might use stars, land patterns, gene memory, the sun or the moon, or earth's magnetic field. Scientists don't know. They suspect a combination. If the curlews lose their stopovers, we lose them.

Moreton Bay is an important habitat in the East Asian-Australasian Flyway, which is one of eight flyways in the world. The East Asian-Australasian Shorebird Reserve Network is an international chain of wetlands recognized for their importance to shorebirds. If I do return to South East Queensland, I want to see the V stretch across the sky on my way to training.

Normally I listen to *ABC Grandstand*, but maybe I'll stop now German research shows that magnetic radio waves on AM frequencies disturb and confuse migrating birds, disrupting their magnetic compasses, which could be in their beaks, iron-rich, fused with magnetite. I wonder where my compass is, whether it is in my mouth. This year I have swallowed love. I have swallowed hate.

Seagull

Birds get hurt playing football. It's a given. In Melbourne, hundreds of seagulls flock to AAMI Park and the MCG after hanging out in the city during the day. Attempts to chase away or deter the gulls by using an eagle have been unsuccessful. To go to the stadium is an interesting experience—all these fluffy things. During the 2016 FFA Cup final between Melbourne City and Sydney FC, a seagull got injured—dazed and confused, concussed. Sydney FC goalkeeper Danny Vukovic, usually an intimidating figure, stopped play to attend to the bird in his eighteen-yard box. The gull looked safe in those big gloves. Carried carefully to the sidelines. This is not uncommon at this stadium. The birds seem to take over the game, not caring about the play around them. Or maybe they understand, like the kookaburra. Maybe they are playing too.

While in Europe, Dad and I buy tickets for an Eredivisie match at Sparta Rotterdam stadium where the famous seagull incident occurred in 1970. Dad wants to see a player he used to coach, Kenny Dougall. He's my brother's age and I remember watching him play when he was younger at Samford.

We trail through Rotterdam. It's cold. Almost freezing. The game is not on till later, so we walk around. I note the architecture—it looks different to other cities in the Netherlands. Dad says it was destroyed in the war and then rebuilt.

Sparta Rotterdam stadium is one of the most iconic stadiums in the world. Built in 1916 as Stadion Spangen, named after the neighborhood of Spangen, it was based on a plan by the architects JH de Roos and WF Overeynder. It was the first club-owned stadium in the country. The name "Het Kasteel" ("the castle") comes from the small pavilion with two towers on the southern stand of the stadium, which was inspired by a castle that was on-site centuries earlier. We sit on this side. We get there early and appreciate the stadium before it fills up. The game is sold out (a usual occurrence for the 11,000-capacity stadium). The castle building, which is currently located along the length of the pitch, was originally positioned behind one of the goals before the pitch got moved to a ninety-degree angle between 1998 and 1999. It is the only remaining part of the old stadium, which has been renovated and extended extensively over the years.

The famous seagull incident occurred in a game with the local rivals Feyenoord, who occupy the big stadium across town. Feyenoord goalkeeper Eddy Treijtel launched a high goal kick that took down a passing seagull. Treijtel refused to keep the stuffed bird when offered it by a taxidermist, and the bird is on display at the museum at Feyenoord's De Kuip stadium and not in Sparta's museum, a sore spot for supporters.

Dad talks to some of the groundsmen before the game and tries to get into the north stand, which includes the corporate boxes and entrance to the players' tunnel. I'm not hopeful; I tell Dad we can't expect to see Kenny. We don't have the right ticket for that area. Our seats are in the east stand behind the goals and we sit among the passionate supporters. By now it's below zero and I'm feeling the cold. Wish I'd brought a blanket.

Sparta lose, Kenny doesn't get on and we don't see him afterwards, but I still have a good time. Not sure about Dad though. He spends the taxi trip from Eindhoven train station (it's 2:00 am, I'm falling asleep in the back, I may as well not be there) talking to the driver about his old playing days. This guy might know who my dad was, before he left.

Australia Is Open
(To hold! Receive! Take!)

Late January 2017, just before Invasion Day, I'm in Vigan, the Philippines, for a literary engagement. It is disorientating being away during the Australian Open. The evocative whack of the ball from end to end of the court was the sound of my summer as a young-fella, watching games with my parents in the school holidays, belly on the couch.

I played tennis during primary school. I have found you can always return to sport. It is constant. In more recent years I watched five-setters on the exercise bike in the gym in my former apartment building by Mairwar (I also read Maggie Nelson's *Bluets* [2009] on the treadmill) while setting my fitness goals for the year.

I feel like my body is a shell. Like I've become nothing more than a lover, and things have to change. Being here, having deep conversations on the balcony of the hotel with the other writers in breaks between workshops, has brought these realizations to the surface. Perhaps it's necessary to be fueled by something more, something else. To find some other sort of passion.

*

In late 2016, I left my apartment by Mairwar, moved briefly to Gadigal land, but things didn't work out with me and my girlfriend no matter how hard we tried. So I left quickly just before Christmas, crashed with friends, then flew overseas to my father's family, which guaranteed two Christmas Days, one on the plane, one in Mierlo. In the Netherlands there were fireworks, oliebollen and icy streets. Family warm and welcoming. By the time I got over my shyness and attempted the most basic Dutch, it had been four weeks. I flew to Melbourne, spent one night there, then flew here, the Philippines, joining a gathering of writers from the Asia-Pacific region. Past experiences were rising to the surface, darkness threatening to overcome. I had been seeking answers for why I was feeling this way.

Tonight, on the headspace chat, "Pip" told me I was experiencing "waves of grief." They aren't going to move on easily, Pip said. I have to learn how to give myself "permission to feel." I know I don't want to feel those things just within reach, deep dark despair and bristling anger. No, I'd do anything not to feel them. I also had to lie about my age to get onto the headspace chat. I'm six months too old now. And really, I thought I had figured things out when I was twenty-three, at the time of the release of my first book. But now, at twenty-six, it feels like everything has collapsed.

*

Nail marks on the foam block in my hands as I sat on the yoga mat inside the second-level yoga studio in Brisbane, before I left. And it all felt hard, the stillness, the listening. I would've done anything not to listen. I was no longer able to listen to music or read, for fear of triggering lines and images. Aunty Mel had given me a meditation book, which I could only read in the right mood. I kept telling myself throughout the class that I would feel better soon and at some point my anxiety and depression would lift.

In the beginning, it went so slow and was so hard. And then at one point I stopped thinking so much. Thia, the instructor, said we had reached the "heart's gap" position. All of Thia's words seemed body real. It was all flowing inside of me, that was true. My body began to speak. I went into a lying position, the small of the back against the block, and I felt everything drop. I suddenly got sleepy. And then all there was to do was the five-minute meditation at the end, closing my eyes, letting go. But I was still thinking about my pain. Tears were rolling down my face; I was grateful that Thia told us to put our hands on our temples. I covered up the tears, and kept my hands there even when Thia told us to move our hands to our scalps. I couldn't do that anyway. That was a place I couldn't touch, as it reminded me of my ex-girlfriend, who used to massage my head when I couldn't sleep, a comfort I missed.

Something I had started wondering about was what type of exercise worked for what issue. For example, were some sports better for anxiety, or PTSD, or depression? I tried as many as I could before I went overseas. Swimming produced high moods and less tension, but only on days one and three. Yoga was great all-round; I was less anxious and less confused after class. Lifting seemed to only improve my fatigue. But any exercise regimen had to be long and consistent to see significant change, and I dropped off after about a month. I told Aunty Mel I reckoned I could stay in bed all day if I wanted. Yoga is meant to improve breathing and internal focus. Running is meant to release endorphins, reduce food cravings, improve memory, lower stress levels and protect against depression. Strength training improves mood and self-esteem, regulates sleep and reduces stress. Tai chi helps concentration, physical balance, muscle relaxation and breathing. On walking on Country, I read how my reduced anxiety while around trees and plants can be explained scientifically (if I need it to be): the chemicals plants emit to slow the process of their decay can slow our minds down as well.

Walking feels cultural to me. Sandra Phillips writes it is "inherent to the experience of being Aboriginal." In the Philippines, I think about the ancestral walks I'd like to do when I get home. The Billy Drumley Walk honors our Yugambeh ancestor who used walking to bring his clan together under the threat of being torn apart. The long walk, more than fifty kilometers, stretches from Beaudesert, his home, to Southport, where his sister Jenny lived. He walked this route right up until he passed away in his nineties. Many of his descendants have walked it in his honor. Walking brings ancestral memory to the surface, as we embody those who have walked before us, an intelligent network of songlines that are thousands of years old.

The detours my ancestors had to make; even now, we change our routes to avoid harassment. Sandra cites "the suspicion with which we are received when we exercise our right to walk into some places." I sometimes don't even realize I avoid certain routes; it is subconscious. One of the roads where I have received verbal abuse is the intersection of the main road near my parents' house, an old walking track, now a major thoroughfare for vehicles. I notice my sense of unsureness when I walk here. It puts me out of balance.

*

I accompanied my Tante M on a grief walk while I was in North Brabant in the Netherlands. We didn't speak but still communicated feelings as we walked. My other tantes told me she'd been doing these long, steady walks since Ome had died, every Friday, in the forest. The week before it had been canceled. It was snowing too much and the road was closed to Stiphout.

She showed me a photo I took in 2013. She'd brought it with her on our walk. Ome took us on a cycling trip of Zeeland. The photo is of Ome and Tante unloading the bikes from the car, smiling up at me, chill of the North Sea behind them, Tante's jacket lime green. I'd forgotten I'd taken it, forgotten I'd sent it after the funeral. But it conjured up the taste of herring, coffee from the thermos, the wind blowing through the dunes, and my uncle's voice.

I saw three blackbirds that day. My cousin later said it was a good sign. He said they almost hadn't recovered from a virus the previous summer. The sky was beautiful, setting sun. We walked past the football field Aarle-Rixtel. Tante M likes football, darts, skiing. She has an appetite for sport to match my own. Bits of ice on the ground. Tante M's walking stick tapped on the road.

Pitch-dark and cold, walking on a little road. A pathway—also dark. Trees. Moon. Bird noises. Snow on ground—patches you had to be careful of. Her breath I could hear towards the end of the journey.

"How was your walk?" the rest of the family asked when we arrived at the restaurant.

I didn't know how to answer. All I knew was that the walk was done and we had spoken. Walk to grieve. Rewire. Reset.

*

In the Philippines, I plan not to acknowledge the occasion of January 26 to anybody (it is much easier being overseas).

All day yesterday I listened to the A.B. Original album, especially to "January 26" and "2 Black 2 Strong," and got angry. It pumped me up so much I couldn't sleep.

I get the TV working. The tennis is on the BBC, in English.

I wonder how Serena and Venus feel about playing on "Australia Day." Do they know what it marks?

The Williams sisters weren't my favorite players when I was in primary school. When I was young, my favorite player was Kim Clijsters, a Dutch-speaking Belgian with a famous footballer father and a ballet-dancer mother. She had a mean backhand and was so nice and had those cute dimples. I cheered for "our Aussie Kim," who was engaged to "our Lleyton Hewitt." The splits she did to get a seemingly irretrievable ball back in play were amazing. She was a good role model and my parents approved. I still love her. She won a few majors. Thing is, she had a pair of Williams sisters in her way. As an eight-year-old, in 1999, I remember writing on a cut-out to be plastered on the wall of our classroom, "I love tennis, but I'm sick of the Williams sisters winning everything all the time."

Did White Australia make me write that? I felt so much internalized pain and dislike of my body and my brain. I knew I was different.

Through the racist lens of White Australia and White America, the Williams sisters, as Black women, are less likely to be seen as "typical" women. Black women's bodies (whether African or Indigenous Australian) are masculinized through the colonial gender project. Black, not women. You can hear it in the subtext of the language that is used by commentators and pundits. Tennis is a white person's sport. Others are monsters. Muscularity is unnatural, instead of reflecting strength and achievement.

Claudia Rankine has written about the racist treatment of the Williams sisters in the United States, highlighting a few of the numerous incidents on court and in the press. It happened and happens in Australia too.

My Black athlete love kickstarted with Cathy Freeman in 2000. Oh my god. That moment is forever. Those 400 meters at the Sydney Olympics represent a long stretch for us to be where we are. Meaning-making in front of the telly. I grew to love my own skin because it was the skin of my kin.

I was in Year 5 at the time. For a school assignment, I was given the choice of studying Dawn Fraser, Rod Laver, Betty Cuthbert or Don Bradman. I chose Wiradjuri seven-time grand-slam-winner Evonne Goolagong Cawley. Mum helped out. She loved Evonne when she was growing up, and I can guess why. From tennis, to basketball, to football, to rugby league, many of our Black athlete moments have been shared and treasured with family. Perhaps it is no surprise that my isolation here in Vigan is palpable. Throbbing like a sickness.

Venus Williams has the chance to be in her first grand slam final since 2009, to create a possible match-up with her sister Serena. Venus is tied twelfth with Goolagong Cawley on the all-time singles grand-slam-winners list.

I come in at:

Vandeweghe	7	1 (40)
V Williams	6	4 (40)

Williams finishes the game with an ace. Beautiful ace.

And then two aces to win the second set (and to bring the ace count to nine).

Vandeweghe	7	2
V Williams	6	6

I am nervous before the start of the third set. Maybe Venus is too; we glimpse rare displays of emotion under her calm and cool exterior.

Both players look drained. Watching them serve, I know how hard it is to get the ball into the court when your back hurts and your legs are heavy. At each changeover they walk back to their seats with their heads down.

Venus has tried everything, the breathing, the psychology. Lift those hips higher. And she is so close.

The crowd realizes she has two match points on Vandeweghe's serve. Venus puts a hand to her chest and looks back at her box. Vandeweghe aces the first serve. And gets the other back through a Venus error.

Venus is smart on the next point. Another match point. Vandeweghe tries a second pacey serve and hits Venus's return long. As the ball bounces out at Venus's feet she lifts her hands and sinks to her knees. She gets up and dances out the relief, her joy, what it means. She shakes her opponent's hand and then the umpire's. Dances again. I haven't seen this before. She does not contain herself. She leaves her racquet on the court. She dropped it when she won.

When interviewed, she says she wants to "keep her moment in the sun going." Of the upcoming final she says, "It is unbelievable to watch Serena play tennis ... It would be a dream to see her on the opposite side of the net on Saturday."

*

"Tennis" comes from the French "tenez," translated to "hold!" "receive!" or "take!"—an expression given to the receiver by the server when the ball is about to be played into court. The early form of the game, "jeu de paume" ("game of the palm"), was played without a racquet.

What's the chance Serena loses her semi? She is playing Lučić-Baroni, a thirty-four-year-old Croatian who hasn't been in the limelight since a 1999 final against Steffi Graf. I vaguely remember her. "She's going to have to paint every single line though," the commentator says.

Lučić-Baroni   1 (30)

S Williams   2 (30) and then aces to make it 40–30

Lučić-Baroni won the first game—a great start for her, but now I almost feel sorry for her. Serena "devours that second serve for a two-game lead," as the commentator puts it.

I like Serena's outfit—black-and-white print. It's one of my favorites for a while. That bright-rimmed W racquet. I stand up and play my shots with her, pretending I'm holding a racquet.

Lučić-Baroni   2   1

Williams   6   3

Lučić-Baroni kicks the ball in frustration after losing the game, 4–1.

Serena applies hand cream between games for grip. I'm meant to be downstairs for the writers' workshop. But now she's in the lead in the second set, 5–1—what a point, what a forceful, exhilarating rally! I run downstairs to the workshop. I am late. Everyone wants to know the score. I say I don't know for certain, but it looks like a Williams final. There are cheers all around the table.

The workshop time the next day is changed so we can see most of the final. It's 3–3 in the first set when we turn it on. We sit on Else's bed, six or seven of us at a time, with beers and Original Pringles in long tubes.

The emotion is muted between the sisters. How do they play each other? What is going on?

Venus does well when she gets Serena in her backhand pocket, but then Serena gets Venus on her backhand. Venus is admirable, but Serena serves much better in the first set to win it with one break, 6–4.

The second set starts in a similar way. The rallies are long, and the sisters make each other work for every point. At 3–3 deuce, Serena absorbs the pressure to return Venus's serve into the corner of the court. She makes a tiny fist and her eyes show only concentration as she waits for the next serve. Venus doesn't get her first one in. Serena wipes away sweat from her neck as she makes several steps inside the court to an intimidating return position. She hits an unstoppable winner again straight off the racquet to be in front with a break.

As the match reaches its pointy end, Venus continues to play well and provide some sparks in the rally, but Serena has set herself to cruise control. Her error count goes down and she applies pressure with consistent heavy balls to either side of Venus.

Serena is serving for the championship at 5–4. The first point of the game goes to Venus, who hits a sweet backhand winner for 0–15. Then Venus makes an unforced error for 15–15. In a long, tense twenty-four-shot rally, Venus finds the edge, forcing the error from Serena. 15–30.

"Venus Williams take a bow!" the commentator gushes.

Serena responds with steeliness and wins the next point to make it 30 all. When Venus hits a forehand in the net, triggering match point, Serena pumps her fist in the air and yells, "You fight! You fight!" The umpire shushes the excited crowd and it goes eerily quiet before the next serve. Serena plays a strong point to beat her older sister

| S Williams | 6 | 6 |
| V Williams | 4 | 4 |

and claim her twenty-third slam, surpassing Steffi Graf and making her one away from Margaret Court—"our Australian hero" who, in retirement, is in headlines often for the wrong reasons, described by Martina Navratilova as "an amazing tennis player, and a racist and a homophobe."

I have a feeling that I will get to see Serena's next slam win, the historic number twenty-four—at the same time as feeling like I can't see my life beyond tomorrow. Sport works that way. (Of course, later we were to find out that Serena was remarkably playing eight weeks pregnant with her daughter, Olympia. And, after falling short in the

2019 US Open final, and retiring in 2022, this would be her final grand slam title win.)

The sisters embrace, racquets still in hand.

Mum and Dad Viber me after the match because they were watching too.

And maybe it is today that I start living, even though I spend sleepless nights downloading useless anxiety and breathing apps, taking Valium to stop the spiraling, and playing chess against the computer. Thinking, Black is beauty and White people don't get it more often than not, and Indigenous people everywhere, here, have trauma and extreme challenges that make everyday life feel like an existential crisis.

And Venus and Serena, the best sporting siblings of all time, are still served so much anti-Black racism.

I give my social media sites a scroll. White Australians are now happy to love the Williams sisters. Prickles in my legs. Vague thoughts of maybe going back to playing tennis socially when I get back to Australia, wherever I end up. I have some research to do about this world and my body and my heart.

PART THREE

BRUNSWICK

I was on Wurundjeri land. Excited to feel a new pitch under my studs, new boots to go with the new place. The football field was near the bend where Aunty Di Kerr led the annual murnong harvest at the Merri Creek. Wurundjeri people past and present were on all sides of the creek. Shivering under a heavy puffer jacket, I watched a team drill from the fence. Hesitated to approach. A friendly voice called out, "I think I know you. Are you the writer?" "Yes! I am the writer. Can I join your team?"

Team EvN

For me, football is a strong antidote to a world that doesn't always make sense. I knew there was always a game I could watch. I knew I was playing on Sunday. And I can tell you, it used to not be fun trying to keep me from playing when I was injured.

In 2018, in my second year living in Naarm, and my second season with the Brunswick Zebras, it wasn't just football itself that kept me steady, it was the team. I've been reflecting on what it means to be in a team and to have a team, and I do think that everybody needs one.

The very first day that I moved to Naarm, I joined the Zebras. I had planned on checking out a few local clubs, but in the end I only went to one. It was March and the start of the season was rapidly approaching, and I didn't have the time to learn how to get there. Brunswick Zebras was a short bike ride away from where I was living in Parkville—maybe fifteen minutes if I was confident—but, at first, I would often miss the turn-off and get lost, and it would take me more like an hour.

Right from the start, I was drawn to the ground that we played on, which backs onto the Merri Creek. On a cold, misty night, it could be the most peaceful place in Brunswick.

When I first moved there, there were, straightaway, people I thought I could be friends with. I still see those people sometimes and I like them very much, but it's been the unexpected friendships that have shaped me and who I am in this city. None more unlikely than my football friend Corinne.

When I first met her, I didn't think we had anything in common. She was loud, mile-a-minute, Californian, always telling inappropriate jokes and slide-tackling opponents.

I was, in contrast, shy, unassuming and scared of contact on and off the field.

I can't remember when Corinne first started offering me lifts to and from training and games. I was a bit nervous sitting next to her for those fifteen minutes because I didn't think I had anything interesting to say. I knew Corinne was going a long way out of her way to drive me. I was not on her route; I was a bit more north. (And no, this story is not going where you think it is.) She would be home way quicker if she wasn't dropping me off. And the more I would insist I could grab the tram instead, the more she would offer. I also knew that lifts are a gift, particularly in Naarm's four seasons of winter.

It has been a slow-burn friendship. In the beginning, I would just listen to Corinne talk about strange office politics at her work and what her boyfriend had cooked for dinner, without contributing myself. But multiply fifteen minutes four times a week over a year, and, well, at a certain point our teammates noticed that we finished each other's sentences.

We teased each other like siblings, and she knew what I was thinking—it was pretty scary. Corinne's unexpected kindness was especially noticed when I had a bad week. We started to see each other outside of football sometimes. We went to the beach or grabbed a coffee, and texted the weird things that happened to us every day.

On the pitch, she was great to play with. She was a fantastic defender with an eye for attack and I knew she had my back. Relationships like this one helped to offset the loneliness that I felt there, pretty strongly actually. It took me a while to admit that I was feeling lonely because I hadn't ever really been lonely before, which was quite a luxury, I think. Back home, the place kept me safe and I had hundreds of relatives nearby that I could call on if I needed to. And my best friends lived five minutes away. So, of course, it would make sense that living in Naarm would feel different.

I know a bunch of people there now. I've got to know their personal geographies—how they, if they're not Kulin mob, got there, through family, relationships, work, study, and why they stay. I was always feeling like I had one foot out the door to go back home. And as I reflected and grew my understanding and appreciation of what it's like to be on Wurundjeri Kulin Country, what it's like to acknowledge and respect Elders past, present and future, I often did so with my football boots on the ground, studs digging into the turf, sometimes bringing mud back home that dried quickly into a layer on my skin until I washed it off.

The Zebras were recommended to me by a friend, as they are known for being this really friendly team that has a long social history. There's even a book about them, called *The Mighty Bras* (2010). My team was made up of total overachievers excelling in multiple disciplines, be it refugee advocacy or Indigenous health and wellbeing. Talking with Emily, who's Wiradjuri from Central New South Wales, on that first night of training was a major motivator to join the team. This was a team that I could feel welcome in.

"You don't need to drive me all the time," I said to Corinne for the thousandth time, as she sped down Lygon Street. "I can make my own way to training. It's okay." And Corinne told me, "When I first moved here from California and I didn't know anyone, someone did the same thing for me. And I will always remember it."

The Zebs hosted multiple social gatherings per week. It was a little bit much.

We resembled a composite family—Aboriginal, Brazilian, Vietnamese, Italian, Scottish—and everyone legit loved each other and didn't seem to need time apart. It hadn't been my experience in the past.

So, I have to give a little 2018 season wrap because we did pretty well that year. We started strongly, registering a few hard-fought wins before we had a tough match-up against the youthful Ringwood—fourth on the ladder—at 6:30 pm on a Friday night with a storm forecast. In Queensland, that game would have been called off. It's not because we're soft, it's just dangerous, you know?

I was thinking of my backup plans, looking at the radar and stuff. But in Victoria, games are not canceled and we were still required to go out there.

Corinne picked me up and we spent a terrifying half an hour on the freeway that was pretty much like an ocean. When we got there the mood was low. We were told that the referee said the game was going ahead. We were warming up in the dressing sheds, but we didn't really have room to move. It wasn't our best warm-up.

Yeah, I mean, we can blame the conditions, but really we weren't mentally prepared for that game and we lost 4–2. I had to come off early with a foot injury. Corinne and I were seething silently and head-to-toe drenched on the way home. I felt like crying, I was so disappointed to lose that match, but it revealed how much our team was taking this seriously. That went on to be our only loss of the season. We were just like, "We're not going to lose again."

We did have three draws, which meant that we finished second, but it really felt like we'd won. We were so proud of how we went that season. At the team break-up, our captain, Bridget, read out a 7000-word end-of-season speech in which each player of the team was named after an ingredient in a Boston bun. Maybe you had to be there ...

Also, I was really grateful to have friends come and watch the games, and I encouraged as many people to come as possible. I realized that I did need a team. This is not the story of how a total loner like myself became a social addict. I still do appreciate my space and time and a day or two a month where I don't see anyone, except maybe people at the laundromat.

I've been learning that building a friendship only needs two things: time and openness. They were things that I had been poor at giving until I moved to Naarm. And I needed to reach out, so I'm reaching, and my arms have never been longer.

What I Want When I Want You

1.

In my late teens I become hooked on queer longing in writing, fueled by Jeanette Winterson and Dorothy Porter. Their writing affirms my emerging identity and relationships.

The (White-authored) writing in Porter's *The Monkey's Mask* (1994) and Winterson's *Written on the Body* (1992) is charged with risk, both in the use of language and the revealing of relationships normally underrepresented on the page. Their work climbs a cliff of sexual tension, peaks in one or more poetic and emotive love scene(s), and ends in trauma.

In my twenties I read Garth Greenwell's *What Belongs to You* (2016), narrated by an American teacher in Sofia whose obsessive longing for Mitko, a hustler he meets in a public bathroom, is destructive. Described by reviewer Arifa Akbar as a novel about "gay shame," *What Belongs to You* further suggests the trope that queer endings translate to tragic ones; queerness is broken by death, disease, discrimination.

After a while I find comfort in First Nations, Asian and Black queer, female and genderqueer writing, whose undercurrent of longing is intersectional. Queer Blak longing is charged by culture and community. Coined by artist Destiny Deacon in the early 1990s, "Blak" is a self-defining term used by mob, particularly urban-identifying.

In *Anonymous Premonition* (2008), Bidjara poet Yvette Holt's visions of the place I grew up in, Jagera and Turrbal land, are tongue-kissed with nostalgia, moving from river to bay beach to West End streets—all the places I have tripped my heart over. I measure desire and longing for other things: land, family, country, past and future. I discover my interest in writing and reading futurism as another vehicle for longing. Desire, in its most charged form, is specific to place.

My friend Nhã Thuyên, who I befriended in Vigan and performed with in Naarm and Hanoi, mesmerizes me with the desperate quality of their writing. In *Words Breathe, Creatures of Elsewhere* (2015), translated from the Vietnamese by Kaitlin Rees, the language pushes and pulses; in "hours of the ocean," I swim after the sound of their voice.

2.

After spending the year in Naarm I go back to visit Country and am confronted with nostalgia and idealization. Sentimentality is exactly what James Baldwin warned me about. Look at that sky, I feel-think excitedly, look at those trees. And I wonder if my futuring around working and living on Country is based on a slippery desire of the self.

My skin is warmer.

I get excited about writing about Country again.

3.

My friend drives us between Mullum and Brisbane, sun streaming in the windows. I'm sitting in the front. I was fine until this eleven-minute Erykah Badu song about longing came on.

The song starts with a beat, slower at first, repeating. Panting.

I want to jump out of the car.

The song jabs, getting faster, repeating three words that make up the title. I. Want. You.

And suddenly I feel so very aroused and aware of who is arousing me, my crush, back in Naarm.

My lap is too hot. My hips are alive.

4.

At almost eleven minutes, the song structure itself mimics unbearable longing.

That night I fall down a YouTube rabbit hole, and so starts a moment of being really into Badu, especially this song. I look up the live version on *Chappelle's Show*, condensed to four minutes. Badu, her backup singers and band are incredible, and there is even more in the delivery of the song. It makes me sweat.

I try to read and do yoga to get rid of my obsessive thoughts about the crush, hoping it will run its course before the summer's over, but it won't loosen its grip on me. I am not finding the right space.

5.

Later in the summer I find myself making love delicately with my crush, pleased with her nipples, long against my touch. Still not finding the right space.

"I'm attracted to you," I admitted exactly three hours earlier on Taungurung Country by a lake that reflected both the light and the shadow of our figures. "I'm attracted to you too," she said. The first release. The naming of what was there.

After she leaves in a taxi, not staying the night, I spend the next twenty-four hours listening to love songs, noting their tricky relationship with time. The verse and chorus can exist in different temporal spaces, which makes sense, as feelings of love and desire often deal with the remembered past and the imagined future, which could hold both hope and pain equally. The result is perceiving how much pain will be caused in the future.

When we think of the object of our desire, rarely are we thinking about the present.

Badu is suggesting that longing, sexuality and how we choose to negotiate them are out of our control, perhaps even genetic. Perhaps it is the pain of the past that becomes a grate over our bodies. I think of my patterns. And hers.

When White women want me, they want my identity. Since before I can remember, I have been objectified and sexualized by White women who were intrigued by my queerness, my Blakness and my body. Blak sexuality and desires have been the subject of much White fetishization and demonization, placed in contrast to a repressive colonial religious culture. They want my identity differently; my identity becomes about them. They want to talk about me, for me. They want the community, the approval and the absolution of guilt. They want to absorb the idea of me, small and theoretical, instead of the real me, which expands beyond stereotypes and assumptions. My body holds athleticism, hair patterns, softness and hardness, strength and pride and pain. I can't conform to the idea of me. In these exchanges, I interrogate positionality, power and politics.

There are no neutral narratives, suggests American writer Hilton Als.

When Blak women want me, this also becomes about identity. My crush stares at me from the other side of the lake. I stare back.

6.

Weeks earlier, I had lunch at my friend's place and talked about being single. We agreed that the longing we felt for another person or persons could possibly be the same energy we directed towards our writing, noting that it was therefore impossible to work intensely on a writing project and manage a blossoming love affair at the same time.

Leslie Feinberg suggests the surrender is more dangerous than the struggle. Is this why I find it easy to name what I want but difficult to name what I need?

What comes first—sex or writing?

Will she be top, or will I be?

I close my eyes so she can't see what's in them.

This is the space to put my longing.

7.

Lately I've been thinking about stoneness. As in, I'm wondering how much of my life has been about resisting the label of stone as if it was too much of a butch cliché tick-box of the 1990s. A label that would restrict me. Stones will sink you, after all. That's what I thought.

I've been reconsidering its relevance. Is stoneness about the body, or the brain?

8.

Then there's a reading at a Fitzroy bar that I attend, as a punter.

The featured poet there calls me out. "Oh my god, is that EvN? I love the way they write about sex and desire!"

I'm embarrassed. Partly for the attention. And partly because I haven't been writing that kinda longing writing for a while. Maybe I've outgrown it. Because surely she's talking about my debut, *Heat and Light* (2014), a book I wrote when I was twenty-one years old? The pressure of being sexy. That's the old me. How does one live up to the horniness of being a twenty-one-year-old writer?

Never mind. We are always changing and evolving. Published text has a way of fixing the author, like cement, but only to the reader. Outside the pages, we live on.

9.

On stoneness again: my crush sends me an erotic story she's written and it is illuminating to me.

I don't mind my lips being bruised. We often joke about her being a pillow princess. She tells me she gets off by lying back and she doesn't want to do any work. Through reading her story, where the protagonist gazes studiously at her lover's face, noticing the subtle differences of expressions and muffled moans while they fuck her, I see that her pleasure is tightly bound to my pleasure in pleasing her. The gaze is queered. Meta. There are no separate roles, no giving, no receiving. It is blurred, pandirectional, mutual.

10.

I can't listen to the song anymore. I watch another queer show. One of the lovers is shot in the final scene.

Why are we disappointed with endings that don't belong to us?

11.

Desire is not a design flaw.

12.

"I want you" are dangerous words for a Blak queer to say, but I say them anyway. I say them with every inkling of the consequences these words can bring. I say them again and again and again.

Family Is a Stadium

Labor of love

All amateur association sport across the country is propped up by the unpaid and often thankless administrative and manual labor of a group that consists largely of women. It was women who washed our team's kit when I was small, who cut up our oranges, who drove us to the emergency room, who nursed our wounds. It was women who ensured that the club functioned day to day, that teams were administrated, that scores were sent in. It was women who measured us for our kits, women who made flyers advertising our games, women who cooked spaghetti to feed us at the clubhouse after the games and made sure we had beers and soft drinks and Gatorade and hot chocolates.

Every club I play for I make sure I am on a first-name basis with these women because so often they are taken advantage of. They are sometimes noticed only when things go wrong—when the canteen runs out, when the cheque bounces, when there is no team photographer arranged, when the lights go out.

If you speak to these women, you find out just how passionate they are about the game, as well as the community. They know the ins and outs of the sport just as well as the coaches do.

When you view sport as being just about the players, you miss a whole spectrum of community involvement. I've always seen it as one big family that keeps on extending. There are people of all genders who are passionate about the game and who maintain the structure necessary so we can play it. As players, we also have club duties to maintain, and it is necessary for us to put hours into the clubs we play at.

I could never do a solid count of all the hours both my parents spent when I was little driving me to games, cutting up oranges and nursing my injuries. They've provided physical and emotional support. They are passionate about the sport, but their main motivation has always been about helping me get the most out of it. I wouldn't have been able to play without the support of both of them.

It is estimated that every year about three million Australians volunteer in the sport and active recreation sector. This is about half of the overall six million Australians who volunteer every year, meaning sport and active recreation is the sector that benefits the most from volunteering. Particularly at the community level, many sports organizations would not function without volunteers. Volunteers fill important roles as coaches, officials, managers, administrators, and board and committee members.

Volunteers also make sure that major sporting events like the 2023 Women's World Cup and the 2032 Brisbane Olympics run smoothly, with thousands of positions to be filled.

Gender discrimination and a lack of visible role models mean that men are more likely to take on leadership volunteering roles, while women are more likely to volunteer in "support" and "behind the scenes" roles. According to the Australian Sports Commission, the types of roles sport volunteers fill include: general support (55 percent); fundraising (45 percent); scorer or timekeeper (37 percent); canteen/bar duties (35 percent); committee member or administrator (31 percent); coach, instructor or teacher (28 percent); and referee (22 percent). Reasons for volunteering are varied, and volunteering provides benefits to a person's mental, social and physical health. For many, it's a labor of love; love fuels community sport. It needs a full tank.

Perspective is a beautiful thing

Family is a presence. It allows you to be present with time. It's family time that allows our moments to be fuller and deeper. Family is not separate from work.

In early 2020, proud Ngarigo woman Ash Barty fell short of making the final of the Australian Open, losing to Sofia Kenin 6–7(6), 5–7. The media scrutiny of Ash was intense as she was highly favored to reach the final, which would have made her the first Australian woman to do so in more than forty years.

Despite the personal disappointment she was no doubt feeling, Ash walked into the packed press room—full of people there to grill her on her shocking loss—with a huge smile. It was the smile of a proud Aunty, as she was holding her sister's newborn, Olivia, in her arms.

"This is my newest niece. My sister just had her, eleven or twelve weeks ago," Ash said to the crowd of reporters. "This is what life's about. It's amazing. Perspective is a beautiful thing; life is a beautiful thing. She brought a smile to my face as soon as I came off the court. I got to give her a hug, and it's all good. It's all good."

When Olivia let out a cry during the press conference, Ash looked at her and said, "I hear ya, sister!" Ash generously answered the crowd's questions, knowing that at the conclusion of the conference she would get to spend precious time with Olivia and the rest of the family.

It's hard to know if Ash anticipated the inflated response to introducing Olivia to the tennis media and including her in her public life. The comments were wildly disproportionate. *The Tennis Podcast* commentator David Law said, "I don't think the baby should have been in there," while former player Mark Woodforde said she was "using a young child as a shield to deflect the tough questions that all tennis players face when they experience a difficult loss." Broadcaster Catherine Whitaker weighed in and said it was "not appropriate in the workplace," and that Ash was using her baby niece as "a human shield," while analyst Matt Roberts called Olivia "a deflection" and "a prop."

As a professional athlete with a hectic touring schedule, Ash rarely got the opportunity to see her family, who had traveled down to Melbourne to spend time with her. Involving her family in her career, in moments both positive and negative, seemed like a very natural thing to do. More so, it's a very Aboriginal thing to do. We see family as a natural part of any occasion. For me, it was an epic moment of pride in family and the groundedness of Ash Barty as a human being. She was showing her roots, her everyday, and it was special.

The comments against Ash's decision were harsh and disrespected her Big Aunty Energy. It was just another example of society having an opinion on how women juggle work and family life.

White culture props up the atomized individual separately from their family and community in ways that are damaging, particularly to women and particularly to Black women. This completely ignores kinship systems in sport and doesn't see people as holistic individuals. We as First Nations people often see our siblings' children and our cousins' children as our own. As much as there may not have been any intentional disruption to her actions, Ash bringing Olivia onto the big stage as a power pair for me was like a big F U to White expectations of female athletes. All sportspeople deserve the right to have their children with them at work.

Ash had two vocal supporters for her actions, in close friend Casey Dellacqua, who said on *Offsiders*, "It's very well documented that she's extremely close with her family. Is it really that big a deal that she takes her baby niece in? Did it really stop any journalist from asking her a question?" and sports presenter Jim Wilson, who said, "I thought it was a beautiful touch with her niece. Why are we trying to pick something out of someone who is such a great role model, carries herself so well and is someone we should celebrate?"

In 2022, Ash Barty did make the final of the Australian Open, and she won. It was a feverish summer, one we will never ever forget.

And less than three months later, on March 23, 2022, came this note from Ash on social media:

> Ash Barty the person has so many dreams that she wants to chase after that don't necessarily involve travelling the world, being away from my family, being away from home, which is where I've always wanted to be.
>
> I'll never, ever, ever stop loving tennis, it'll always be a massive part of my life. But now I think it's important that I get to enjoy the next phase of my life as Ash Barty the person, not Ash Barty the athlete.

It's my Australian publisher who texts me to tell me Ash Barty has announced she's retiring from tennis at age twenty-five. First, I'm floored. I think it's a prank. Then I am filled with a heavy grief. I am being serious when I say out loud: how am I going to go on? How am I going to live now?

Ash's successes on the court have given First Nations people so much hope and jubilation. Joy we didn't think possible. We are so grateful. The 2022 Australian Open win was particularly moving. With the added stressors of COVID-19, the environmental crisis and ongoing racism, to see Ash create memories with Aunty Evonne Goolagong Cawley and Aunty Catherine Freeman by her side was something I could not put into words. I was on a high for days. It numbed my pain.

Her decision to retire only two months after this achievement and six months after winning Wimbledon, sitting firmly at the top of the rankings and one of the most highly paid female tennis players, shocked the world. It can be read as incredibly intelligent and astute. Retiring on your own terms and on a high. Ash explicitly said she wants to spend more time with her family and at home and give herself as a person the well-roundedness she deserves. This was entirely in line with how she lived her life as an athlete. I have flashbacks of her sitting in the press room smiling with her niece on her lap.

Writing for *The Guardian*, Tumaini Carayol said,

> While Barty's decision to retire on Wednesday at the age of just twenty-five, as the number one player in the world and during such a beautiful moment in her career, is a shock on the surface, the manner of her departure fits perfectly with the way she has conducted her career. ... She has worked hard, with ambition and drive, but her priorities have remained her family, personal happiness and mental wellbeing.

"I think the Australian summer was for everyone else but not for her," Ash's coach Craig Tyzzer said, revealing that Ash first told him she wanted to retire after her first grand slam win, the 2019 French Open.

We love and support our Ash no matter what. Today, I am even more aware of the sacrifices she has made to give us moments we will cherish forever. Perspective is a beautiful thing.

Playing with bub

Reading a 1978 *New York Times* article, I'm struck by the parallels between Ash and her mentor Evonne Goolagong Cawley, who spoke about having her baby with her on tour.

In the article there's a quote from Wendy Turnbull, an Australian player who toured with Evonne, who said, "life on the circuit is a lonely existence, especially for someone way up on top, like Evonne. Tennis players have the highest phone bills of any athletes in the world. Everyone has somewhere to keep them sane."

During her first season with baby Kelly, Evonne employed a full-time nanny and planned a limited schedule geared towards the major championships. She said it was "really a trial at the beginning to see if tennis and motherhood would mix." She won four consecutive tournaments, including the Australian Open.

In the article, she talks about being distracted if she heard a baby crying in the crowd, thinking it might be Kelly, and having to know where her baby was seated.

After the first season on tour, worried that Kelly might become "overtennised," Evonne turned down an offer that would have made her the second-highest paid woman in tennis, behind Chris Evert, knocking back close to a million dollars (more than $3 million in today's money). Instead, Evonne wanted Kelly to spend time with her grandparents, and she took two months off. This perspective reminds me so much of Ash.

I have known many folk who have had children while playing. Some planned the arrival of bub in the off-season to limit the time out. Returning to play was easier for some than others. It's a very personal choice and a personal experience. In team sports, teammates become like family members to children that grow up around them.

Queensland Firebirds netballer Kim Ravaillion said the main reason for coming back after her pregnancy was to play in front of her "little human."

Serena Williams, who famously won the Australian Open while eight weeks pregnant, said she plays for Olympia, to make her proud.

For many sportspeople, pregnancy is a part of life. Athletes benefit from sports participation and exercise while pregnant. Yet a pregnant professional athlete is still a site of scrutiny rather than being seen as commonplace.

Seven-time Olympic medalist Dana Vollmer swam the fifty-meter freestyle at a national meet while six months pregnant with her second child and had an overwhelming response on social media from women telling her about their athletic achievements while pregnant. She said, "it's amazing how strong pregnant women are and what we're able to do."

In 2019, the Women's Tennis Association (WTA) introduced a special seeding rule for players returning from maternity leave, protecting their rankings. These steps are important for athletes who may have once had to choose between being parents and continuing their careers. However, it has been criticized by tennis player Tatjana Maria, who says the WTA could do more to support pregnant players, as the seeding rule is the same as the long-term injury rule that all players can access: "In tennis, pregnant women are not referred to as pregnant, we are more or less among the injured players. In the case of a pregnancy, the same rules currently apply as for long-injured players." Being pregnant is not an injury, nor is it a disability.

Training and competing at a high level can have consequences for fertility. Doubles player Gigi Fernández struggled with infertility after delaying childbearing to focus on her career. "As athletes, you're so focused on performance and you train very intensely. I would skip periods." Fernández became pregnant with the help of IVF and suggests younger female athletes freeze their eggs.

Social attitudes are changing, with more athletes returning after pregnancy, and supportive sports doctors and supportive environments have improved their experiences.

There has been limited research on elite sportspeople returning to competition post-pregnancy. Athletes have highlighted challenges such as travel and breastfeeding, and generally rely more on shared knowledge between other parents rather than research, which is limited, hard to find and inconsistent. The Australian Institute of Sport's Mum-Alete Project, the first of its kind in Australia, aims to help attract and retain women in the high-performance system and to influence change to better support and improve longevity of female athletes, by identifying the impacts that pregnancy and post-pregnancy have on their decision to remain in sport.

In colonial-patriarchal terms, the family and the sportsperson were historically separated to achieve high performance. Men went away on golfing or fishing trips with other men to blow off steam about family life. Women were kept away from the team environment so as not to distract the team. But this separation between the sportsperson and their family is being broken down—largely because of the personal and political lives of female players.

Bush footy painting

When I looked at Josie Kunoth Petyarre's colorful, lively bush footy paintings for the first time, I was struck by how powerfully she captures sport as family and community, shown as a stadium. Matches have a family focus; they are about relatives and kinship networks. Her paintings often have the footy ground in a circle in the middle and the community around it, without a hierarchical sensibility of one being more important than the other.

Josie is based on her traditional lands at the remote outstation of Pungalindum in the Utopia region, and her artwork is inspired by bush footy, a big part of life in Central Australia. Her language group is Anmatyerr, and she comes from a highly respected artistic family. Her husband, Dinni Kunoth Kemarre, is also an artist.

Josie's first sport-inspired artwork was a series of sixteen sculptured football players (one for each team in the AFL) that she made with Dinni. Josie and Dinni sourced the materials for these sculptures on long drives looking for soft-wooded bean trees. The sculptures were part of an exhibition called *Centre Bounce* at the Australian Football Hall of Fame in Melbourne in 2007. The artists attended the exhibition opening. Visiting the city (and the MCG) for the first time spurred a new body of work. Josie captured the experiences of Melbourne football through an Anmatyerr spatiality, urban and remote sites placed in a system of exchange. Scenes of professional and community football were put side by side. The same story. For this work, both Josie and her husband were finalists in the Basil Sellers Art Prize 2008, a biennial prize for work that contributes to critical reflection on all forms of sport and sporting culture in Australia.

The painting shows how close the community are. The circle is the focal point, the oval representing not only a football ground but also a close-knit community. "Although it acts as pivot to this action, the football match itself is not exclusively preferenced, and in some works is completely overwhelmed by the scale of events going on around it," Henry F Skerritt writes.

That's what sport is to me—everyone doing things for each other. It exposes the personality on and off the pitch. Sport is a carnival, and family is a stadium that houses our lives and our dreams and our togetherness.

I love the way Josie's paintings crush the false opposition of sport and art, showing the disciplines aren't separate, despite the Western world not understanding the mind/body link. With Josie's painting, where sport begins and painting begins is not relevant—they are together.

Sporting interventions

... white people are happy to say that rugby league has done a lot for Aboriginal people even though Aboriginal people have done a lot for rugby league.

Jeanine Leane, "Whitefellas"

In Jeanine Leane's poem "Whitefellas," the sport is rugby league, but implicit in its reading is that you could substitute another sport in its place. Sport is often weaponized by political agents as apolitical and benign. Yet sport is both a social power we can use as mob and a weapon that can be used against us.

Dyirbal gumbilbara (rocky place) bama researcher and anthropologist Lee Sheppard's research explores how White-run NGOs use sport to engage and lure purportedly "at-risk" youngsters back into the education system.

Lee tells me Sport for Development (SfD) programs originated in Britain in the mid nineteenth century, targeting those perceived as needing a "hand up"—in this early case, working-class English men, women and their children. Sport was used then, as now, to develop character, a sense of fair play, teamwork, work discipline and other socially approved characteristics within these target populations. This model has been applied in the same one-size-fits-all approach on a "this or nothing" basis in Australia for well over twenty years.

"I call them 'interventions' because these SfD programs specifically target our student youngsters and Torres Strait Islander students," Lee says. "They are top-down, paternalistic, laced with deficit-based rhetoric, and incorporate Western Ways of Knowing, Being, and Doing. Their aims and agendas align with the government's CTG [Closing the Gap] policy and aims—i.e. employment, education and health. While their real plan is to achieve the government's and their own neoliberal aims."

At the time of the interview, Lee is yarning with communities on the eastern seaboard that have non-Indigenous-run sporting intervention providers the Clontarf Foundation (for First Nations boys) and Star Foundation (for First Nations girls) programs. These NGOs use different sports (rugby league, AFL, basketball, netball etc.) to lure supposedly at-risk youngsters into education and employment.

But as Lee tells me, the way these programs are led is "tick-box," not targeting the real at-risk young people but those who are already engaged with school. They do not ask parents, what are your specific needs? What are the wants and needs of your child?

Lee pauses there. She's a proud mother and grandmother. "Their Ways of Doing do not acknowledge our agency, and their dealings with our mob disempower and suppress our self-determination and are quite assimilationist as well. I do not like SfD interventions. It reminds me of how sport was used as either a 'carrot or stick' on missions with our old peoples. Not much has changed in their present incarnation. If they are to stick around, I would hope that mob in communities acquire, have ownership of, and run their own programs."

Sport as kinship

In direct contrast to SfD programs, Lee, with Dr Steven Rynne and Associate Professor Jon Willis, has written about how, when in First Nations hands, sports can be used as a self-determination tool to "offset the impacts of colonization, racism, structural violence and structural inequalities" and to celebrate survival in a culturally appropriate way.

First Nations sporting carnivals hold great significance for First Nations people. These carnivals represent "all-Aboriginal spaces," "places of belonging that are both spiritually and culturally significant to Traditional Owners and those in attendance."

The Koori Knockout is held on unceded Aboriginal land and plays a part in a modern-day corroboree. It is "reminiscent of a four-day traditional ceremonial dance and celebration, but also enables new social and cultural practices to emerge."

The first Koori Knockout was organized in 1971 by rugby players who were disillusioned with the New South Wales rugby system. Frustrated about scouts consistently overlooking talented Indigenous players because of racism, and players from the regions being ignored, and bolstered by Redfern as a hub for inner-city activism, the organizing committee were connected through kinship.

Today, more than 35,000 First Nations people participate in the event. It is one of the biggest First Nations gatherings in Australia. The event supports men's, women's, girls' and boys' competitions. Winning teams of the Koori Knockout go on to compete against the winners of the Queensland Murri Carnival in an interstate Koori vs Murri match.

Sheppard, Rynne and Willis write that the Koori Knockout is an example of "giving primacy to social, spiritual, and aesthetic values associated with heritage. This is different from the extractive industry's cultural offsets who give primacy to mainstream (Western) archaeological practices that continue to create disadvantage in Aboriginal Australia."

The carnival is also used to offset environmental losses, as well as those losses associated with the historical suppression of culture, by providing opportunities to re-engage with Country. Playing on Country is directly linked to the wellbeing of Country and mob, in that mob look after Country, Country looks after mob, and the celebration of sport on Country brings both together in ways similar to pre-European invasion.

First Nations sporting carnivals and organized teams are the opposite of sportswashing programs that don't benefit First Nations people and that have a direct link to the violence of colonization. Mining the land for talent—taking children away from their communities—is like mining the land for its resources, and for what?

At the hundred-year celebration of women's football at the Gabba in 2021, Lee McGowan and Fiona Crawford introduced me to Leonie Young (née Yow-Yeh), who was part of footballing history in the northern suburbs. She gave an emotional Welcome to Country and dedication to her mum, Iris, who had recently passed away, at the commencement of the event. Iris was the heart and soul behind Tiwiwarrin, the first all-Aboriginal women's football team.

When, one year later, I speak with Leonie on the phone, her kind voice comes through like an Aunty's embrace as she tells me about those good memories. Leonie grew up near me, fifteen minutes away in Keperra, where the family house remains.

McGowan and Crawford's research credits Leonie as one of Australia's first Indigenous female players. She first took to the pitch as a young teen in 1976. "Soccer back then was the love of my life. I played for the love of the game, in paddocks with no shinpads. I used to come home with big welts on my shins and big gravel rashes."

During the 1980s, Leonie became the first Indigenous woman to represent Queensland in football. A speedster, she played on the wing, and once received a letter from the Queen after scoring nine goals in one game, a letter that Iris kept tucked away with all her other sporting memorabilia over the years.

Leonie said of her mother, "Since I was little she pushed me to prove to myself I can achieve anything. She was there cheering me on since I was thirteen."

Leonie's younger sister also took up the game, as well as her cousins who lived across South East Queensland. Iris had an idea.

"Mum decided we'd start our own Aboriginal team. She got us girls together and came up with the name 'Tiwiwarrin,' which means 'fast and speedy.'"

Leonie's dad, "Pop," drove a bus round Brisbane picking up players, who proudly sported the Aboriginal colors, black, yellow and red.

> Before Tiwiwarrin there was nothing going on in terms of Indigenous soccer in Queensland. In our first year as a team we played at Geebung and made it all the way to the grand final where we lost by one corner. That's how they separated teams back then. There was no extra time. We weren't upset about that. It proved we were a side to be looked at—we were in it for good. Then we played in the church league where we won nine out of ten finals, setting a record that still hasn't been beaten. In this league we were accepted as who we were, and how we played.

Iris determined the girls' playing style, where do-it-yourself individual skills and flair were cherished just as much as teamwork.

"Mum used to say before every match, 'skin 'em.'" (Referring to the fast and efficient way the Tiwiwarrin players dodged and weaved past the opposition with the ball, leaving them in the dust.) "We played to sing, dance and to laugh. Mum would put on the music after a match—it was always Queen's 'We Are the Champions.'"

Sundays were full with laughter. "Mum, Pop, Uncle, Aunties and the rest of the family would be on the sidelines. They are very happy memories."

Tiwiwarrin was together for the best part of twenty years, and still competes on special occasions. At one point, three generations sported the jersey: Leonie, her daughter and two granddaughters.

I asked Leonie what the difference was when playing with family compared to playing alongside non-Indigenous players.

"It was no different. When I played with other teams it was family anyway. Because the way Mum raised us, she accepted everyone into our family."

When Leonie was talking, I pictured joyful scenes of family on the field and the sidelines. I didn't know about the team when I was growing up as they were around in the 1980s and 1990s and I started playing in the early 2000s. But I know of them now as an important part of history. My heart is warm thinking about the spirit of family and community flowing through the sporting fields of my childhood.

Our Descendants Are Watching

In 1824, organized theft of land and cultural genocide of First Nations people begins in what is now known as South East Queensland—the land of the Yagera, Turrbal, Jinibara, Yugambeh, Bundjalung, Wakka Wakka, Gubbi Gubbi, Noonuccal, Joondaburri, Ningy Ningy and Ugarapul nations.

In June 1859, Queen Victoria of England authorizes the separation of northern lands from New South Wales, establishing the new colony of Queensland.

In February 2019, I move back to live with my parents in my childhood home on Turrbal Country. I come back after two busy years in Naarm/Birrarung-ga (so-called Melbourne). My mum and dad have been living in Mparntwe (so-called Alice Springs) for the last six years and have just started their retirement.

At first, being back is strange for all of us, but we slowly settle in. My parents give me the room underneath the house, where I have a view of the bush out the back. The sun wakes me every morning. My writing table is outside.

My parents and I observe changes. More geira (sulphur-crested cockatoos) fly over the house, their sharp squawks impossible to ignore. I don't remember many of them when I was last living here, a decade ago. Neither does my dad. But we remember other birds, smaller birds, that we no longer see. We see fewer insects in the backyard.

I have conversations with my blackfella friends of a similar age, millennial babes through and through. We've been told that people, animals, plants and the rest of the living world must "keep pace with climate change," "keep evolving," keep adapting to the changing world. We speculate about the frightening changes we will observe in our lifetime. Should we have children? Would it be responsible of us? Could humankind become extinct in our or their lifetime? Should we live in a state of panic or try to enjoy the last days of the world as we know it? Which option would be the most respectful to our ancestors? What will a post-human world mean in an Aboriginal sense?

As a coping strategy, we dissociate from climate crisis through music. I fill all the gaps in my life with music. I obsessively scout artists to build playlists. The general theme is dance to decolonization through alternative jazz, soul, electronica and hip-hop. I fall in step with Baker Boy from north-east Arnhem Land, who raps in Yolngu and English. I add Miiesha, Laura Mvula and Nakhane. I imagine playing these songs on the last night on earth, inviting all my black-fella friends, dancing till the sun comes up.

I grieve the colonization of my people and fear that the efforts we have taken to recover and revive our culture will be too late, as human-created environmental change increasingly affects our land and waterways. As I learn more from my Elders and peers, as Yugambeh rolls its way onto my tongue, I think, is the little I'm doing enough? Maybe that's just shame and guilt talking, two emotions so easily pushed onto a colonized people's psyche.

It takes a while before I can contemplate the real question I want to ask. How can we heal and recover from the past while at the same time preparing for a dangerous future? Can one lead to another?

It does help, talking to my friends, realizing that I am having normal emotional responses to the circumstances we live in, that everyone else also feels torn up, anxious, exhausted and unprepared. My energy is scattered between the two disciplines of healing and preparing.

The intergenerational conversations I have with my parents are slightly different. In the living room where we have our dinner, the TV flicks over one commercial channel to another—segments on fish dying in the Murray-Darling Basin, 40 percent of insect species threatened, ocean acidification, habitat loss, floods, droughts, blizzards. I explain dugai terms like "Anthropocene," all the while knowing that Western science has never added value to Indigenous peoples' lives. We are creating our own language around this, my parents and I, embodied through our bush walks. We walk at the back of the house, and sometimes we fill a few water flasks, pack extra-strong mints and go for a drive, walk the familiar spots we used to when my brother and I were young. I am happy to be home. I am happy to be where my ancestors come from, belonging to this place, responsible for this place, in dialogue with this place.

When the settler-invaders came to the east coast they not only committed crimes of rape, murder, torture and brutality to Country and people, they also became narrative terrorists, a branch of terrorism that still runs strong today. The settler-invaders attempted to destroy all evidence of technology, occupation and culture—that mob were here, are here, that they built, lived and loved here. They did their best to rub an eraser over the land and claim it as their own. Stolen remains and cultural objects were taken to museums all over the world or kept in private collections. Farmers concealed or destroyed items found on their farms. Evidence like tools, huts, fishing nets, compasses and burial sites were destroyed or made their way to the storage rooms of museums.

After the landmark Mabo decision in 1992, farmers again hunted their properties for evidence of occupation.

In 2017, a Victorian farmer was fined $20,000 for intentionally harming Aboriginal artifacts. In the same year, more than 130 Tasmanian Aboriginal stone tools were seized in Sydney as part of an investigation into illegal online sales of cultural material. In 2018, the Clarence Valley Council in northern New South Wales was fined $300,000 for destroying an Aboriginal scar tree in Grafton. It held cultural significance for the local Gumbangirr and Bundjalung people and was registered on the Aboriginal Sites Register in 1995, making it an offence to harm or desecrate the tree. The loss cannot be quantified.

What non-Indigenous people kept and recorded served their narrative purpose. Whitefellas became the "experts" on our lives, our anatomy and our land, and everything that lived on it. At the time of writing, they are not ready to give up that title. But Aboriginal people know the settlers can never destroy everything; traces, connections, sovereignty remains, and all will be returned in time.

During the nineteenth century, archaeology developed out of antiquarianism in Europe and spread across the world. Archaeology is used by authoritarian bodies to shape certain visions of the past. Tensions between First Nations peoples and archaeologists arise for several reasons, including the fact that archaeologists tend to position objects as belonging to a faraway past, while First Nations peoples believe that disturbing these things has consequences for the present.

It has only been in recent years that museums have started opening their doors to community for items to be viewed, being transparent with what they own, and sometimes repatriating remains in collaboration with community, the result of many years of resistance and advocacy. The ceremony of returning artifacts might be one step towards healing for a community.

Australia's narrative terrorism manifests in legislation that does not recognize contemporary Aboriginal culture, conveniently failing to believe both in an ancient-modern continuum, and that Aboriginal experience is as diverse as the population. Instead, stereotypes prevail. We don't belong in museums.

Eualeyai/Gamillaroi writer and lawyer Larissa Behrendt's book *Finding Eliza* (2016) exposes mythmaking in colonial storytelling. Eliza Fraser fraudulently claimed to have been captured by the local Aboriginal group, the Butchulla/Badtjala people. Her narrative terrorism led to the massacre and dispossession of a whole community. Today, the island, whose traditional name is K'gari, is known as Fraser Island after Eliza Fraser, though Traditional Owners are campaigning for naming rights. They are still fighting today against the colonial story that has done such damage.

Djugun woman Georgia Mokak writes in her article about Behrendt's book:

> The Eliza Fraser stories are the perfect example of how stories have been used by Europeans for their own purposes or for institutional purposes, and how they create the ongoing stereotypes of Indigenous people in Australia and across the world. Any truths surrounding Eliza's relations with the Badtjala peoples were very hastily sacrificed for the traditions of the dramatic tale.

For mob growing up in suburbs like mine, the erasure of our existence—whether at school or the supermarket—is compounding. Extending beyond the imposed built environment, there's a deeper disregard for Country. It took me a while to figure out that a lot of my neighbors, teachers and classmates live their lives simply "forgetting" they are on Aboriginal land. I witness this psychosis, which exists alongside the green-and-gold haze of Southern Cross tattoos and Australian flags.

"Paris syndrome" is the name used to describe the condition that affects some people when they visit Paris for the first time. In reality, Paris is nothing like the glamorous city that the media shows. Tourists suffering Paris syndrome can feel shell-shocked by the clash of fantasy and reality, and sometimes they become so sick they need to be hospitalized.

Call it "Australia syndrome," the relationship that non-Indigenous people have with the land. The culture shock of being on Aboriginal land, the clash of fantasy and reality. Where are we?

For millennial babes, the internet is a flawless distraction. Being oppressed people without land rights but with high-speed internet is strange. One of the first things colonizers do is ban language and culture and block the channels for obtaining knowledge. Knowledge is power. But there are question marks about whether the internet really holds knowledge. Whether it really does connect us with each other. We can draw on many examples of it helping us organize our resistance. But we haven't called each other in so long. Remember what our Elders achieved talking on the phone, twirling that cord with one hand—and what they achieved before the phone.

Responses to the global climate crisis on the internet seem enticing but often leave me feeling hollow. I think about the strangeness of a meditation selfie. Decolonization is a hashtag.

After watching a documentary with Mum on Netflix about two white men who claim to be saving the world by spreading the word of minimalism, living more with less, I spend hours looking at #Blackminimalism, a movement of mainly British and American women from the African diaspora. I find myself on websites shopping for sports bras made from recycled plastic bottles and scouring pages for plant-based skin care. "This minimalism thing is actually encouraging you to buy," Mum points out. So much for being anti-consumerist and anti-capitalist.

I get sucked into one Instagram vortex after another, looking at the beautiful Black, Brown, Asian and White faces offering solutions to a crisis in consciousness. Are they doing it for the 'gram or doing it for the planet? It doesn't matter. I go vegan in February, plastic-free in March, and my parents roll their eyes, asking what will be next.

After countless hours opening tabs, I finally shut my laptop. I live each day knowing how precarious life is. I live in the past to comfort our ancestors who have experienced so much pain. I haunt-walk through my existence. It is my radical longing that I'm afraid of, so much that I push it aside. As a young queer Blak person, I want more.

When the Australian Museum asks me to be part of a project about love, loss and hope in the face of environmental crisis, I am inspired to create a photo series, *Pose, Your Future Descendants Are Watching*, as the answer to my self-imposed question: how can we recover from the past while at the same time preparing for a dangerous future? Can one lead to another?

I craft living objects and plant them in our backyard and on Country as evidence of our historic and current occupation. This act resists the colonial narrative. I make a soft basket with a clutch handle of tea-tree sticks joined together with dyed and natural twine, a digging stick standing to my shoulders and a coolamon, which I position on Country. These are items that not only heal a past but also prepare for a future. They are used to source food and water, to dig, to carry, made from materials that exist in balance with Country, without separation.

My parents generously drop what they're doing to help me make these pieces. Mum misses the Oscars and Dad delays mowing the lawn. They observe my survival. Their labor is one of love and support. As I watch them flow into work without hesitation or complaint I reflect on the Lebanese poet Khalil Gibran's quote, "work is love made visible." My childhood home comes alive with the sounds of carving, weaving and painting. The television is relegated for the moment, the computer sitting idle. When I pick at the scabs on my knees, my blood smells like the bush.

We find the right tools in our present environment and at our disposal: sometimes it's a rock, sometimes it's a knife from the kitchen. Black American author Audre Lorde said, "The master's tools will never dismantle the master's house." It is more essential than ever that we move beyond the colonizer's logic and reach outside the toolbox. Micah White, co-founder of Occupy Wall Street, said, "Let's reclaim our stolen tools." We can free our minds with the right tools. We can repurpose them and build something better, a better house—a safe house. When I walk through the bush with refreshed eyes (a refresh that doesn't involve a scrolling finger), I feel a sense of creative control. While planning and gathering materials for these objects and crafting them with my parents, my eyes change, my mind shifts. I feel calmer, my anxiety levels lower. No matter what has been done here, no matter what continues to happen, I will never stop thinking of this place as home.

I make my first toothbrush out of macaranga. My teeth and the plant acquaint in my mouth and my gums bleed into the wood. When we are not recognized, we are not well. We are cultural materiality.

Mum chooses blue as the central color of the living objects. We paint the digging stick a bright blue. This represents the past and the future, survival, diversity and visibility. The three of us were wearing that same shade on the day we crafted it. The coolamon carries painted macadamia nuts and gum nuts in electric blue and white, as well as gum leaves. The basket is made of blue felt. When Mum chose a color that made the objects stand out rather than blend into the natural environment, I knew I had to take these objects with me, instead of leaving them behind to be found as I had planned.

When I ask Mum what the living artifacts we have crafted mean to her, she talks about the artificial environment and machine-made things in our current era. She points to the digging stick, the coolamon and the basket. She says of non-Indigenous people, "They have no idea what it is and that it is still important, it's still used today."

Storying Care

I find opportunities to tell my story through my line of work. Us artistic mob share our stories through poetry, art, music, theatre and dance; through this, we celebrate who we are and honor those who have come before us.

One space (there are many) where we consistently struggle to feel heard or tell our story is the health system. A space traditionally for healing, "health" in Australia today reflects the colonial-patriarchal society brought to Aboriginal land by the whitefellas: classist, sexist, racist, violent, sterile, impersonal. Here, "health" does not equal healing in Aboriginal way.

we tell our stories
often we leave the doctor's room or
medical center
not understood
not listened to

The many mob doing incredible work in health tell us the system is broken despite pockets of positivity and possibility. As my Country-woman Dr Chelsea Watego writes, "While building an Indigenous health workforce is vital to improving health outcomes for our mob, we cannot talk about the health workforce without talking about power and how it operates in the colony."

I am an able-bodied queer Mununjali blackfella living in the city. Here, I refer to the words of blackfellas working in this space while also reflecting on experiences yarning with mob who live in the big three east-coast cities. Despite the privilege of living where there is choice and access, I have always felt invisible barriers to accessing medical services.

Health professionals have preconceived ideas about our care and our narrative. They come with a whole bunch of assumptions about our identity. These are framed in the questions they ask and the answers they assume, and will inform the direction they take our care in, controlling the story of our physical and mental health. In these spaces, we are the object. We are taken through colonial processes and may not even be asked what our opinion is. Voices die here. We've seen our relatives brutalized by the system, denied their humanity, denied their health justice. We hope for better for the living generations, but we have already seen despair in their eyes.

Colleen Lavelle, a Wakka Wakka mother of four with an inoperable brain tumor, writes on Black media site *IndigenousX*:

> Death by racism should be a category on death certificates, because the racism in hospitals is hindering the recovery of many Aboriginal and Torres Strait Islander people. Spend some time as a patient in a hospital and you soon find out that the medical profession is full of bigots and people who might not consider themselves racist, but have preconceived ideas on race and hold outdated beliefs in racial stereotypes.

Across all institutions, our mob are discriminated against and receive unjust treatment. "Death by racism": since 2008, half of the Indigenous women and girls who have died in custody did not receive appropriate medical care. "Death by racism": since 2008, a third of Indigenous men and boys who have died in custody did not receive appropriate medical care. One death is too many.

Colleen also blogs as "proudblacksista," sharing tips on how to survive the financial pressure of medical bills, as well as offering a platform for others with cancer to share their stories.

Named after Pitjantjatjara woman Dr Lowitja O'donoghue, who has devoted her working life to improving the health and welfare of her people, the Lowitja Institute in Melbourne is a national health-research institute run by Aboriginal and Torres Strait Islanders. In the Lowitja Institute's *Deficit Discourse and Indigenous Health: How narrative framings of Aboriginal and Torres Strait Islander people are reproduced in policy*, authors William Fogarty, Hannah Bulloch, Siobhan McDonnell and Michael Davis from the Australian National University discuss how the Closing the Gap policy framework uses victim-blaming and deficit discourse, a disempowering practice that represents people in terms of deficiencies and failures. Indigenous people are required to—statistically speaking—assimilate into a Western worldview. These neo-colonial measures for success create a "fictional Aboriginal or Torres Strait Islander person" who is "removed from kinship or social settings." The fictional average Aboriginal or Torres Strait Islander person cannot reflect the diversity of our people nor the different wellbeing values we have for ourselves and our families and communities.

For as long as I can remember I've experienced depression, anxiety and suicidality, and lived with the pain of seeing loved ones go through the same. I have been a patient of mainstream, queer and Aboriginal medical services, each with its own positives and negatives. I'm all too aware of a general lack of cultural competence and responsiveness in mainstream care. I believe in trauma-informed care with a holistic view of who we are as peoples. When seeking help in the mainstream system, I have been turned away by doctors. They didn't want to hear my story. Some doctors blame the patient for their distress, and play into the stigma of mental illness when patients ask for a mental health care plan: "You don't want this on your record" etc.

This country is a hotbed for ignorance. Harmful views are held not only by white health professionals but also by non-Indigenous people of color. Completely perplexed about our diverse identities, they force us to deal with their bewilderment and confusion. When asked persistent questions like, "I have other patients who say they are Aboriginal but don't look it, can you explain to me why?" I feel on unsteady ground.

When asked about our medical histories, we have to ask ourselves: how do we translate our histories and genealogies for/to you? How will you transcribe our histories and genealogies, and how will you use this in your narrative? Health records are primarily in text—they can't hold our full, true story.

I have had overly helpful doctors too. When I told one doctor I was Aboriginal, she said, excitedly, "We can do all of these tests." Although I appreciated a thorough analysis, the over-ordering and over-frequency of tests made me feel like an object—like a specimen. I wasn't sure if they were the right tests for me, either—they didn't fit me as an individual and what was going on for me. They felt like tests for the sake of tests. Invasive—an object having tests performed on them for data.

Data is used to build, and claim, story. Recently, the term "data sovereignty" has been used to describe mob's sovereign right to their own data: all data should be subject to the laws and governance structures within the Indigenous Nation where it is collected. This data should be accessible to the community. Unfortunately, we are a long way from that.

Currently, as Trawlwoolway scholar Maggie Walter and Māori scholar Tahu Kukutai say in "Recognition and Indigenizing Official Statistics: Reflections from Aotearoa New Zealand and Australia," non-Indigenous majorities produce and control this statistical data, and the results reflect the "limited and/or erroneous understanding of who we are" rather than our own perspectives.

The Lowitja Insitute's *An Evaluation Framework to Improve Aboriginal and Torres Strait Islander Health* stresses that:

> Ideally, Aboriginal and Torres Strait Islander communi-
> ties should host repositories for their own data. However,
> considerable capacity building would be required to

make this possible. In the interim, hosting data with a third-party organization should be considered. Any such arrangement would have to respect data sovereignty, as well as security.

In Aotearoa, a Māori data-sovereignty network called Te Mana Raraunga created a charter: the first ideal recognized data as "living tāonga," living treasured things. With data sovereignty, we can own our stories and free our spirits from the narrative constraints that have been placed on us and our ancestors.

In November 2018, Gamilaroi man Luke Pearson wrote a piece for the site he founded, *IndigenousX*, that brought together the concerns of many about an Australian Bureau of Statistics-governed health survey. His title posed the question: "Is the National Indigenous Health Survey Ethical?" Participants for the survey were randomly identified through a doorknock and told to invite the Australian Bureau of Statistic representative in to perform hearing tests and take height, weight and waist measurements. The survey's motto, promoted by high-profile Indigenous ambassadors, was "Everyone's story matters." The survey ran till March 2019, with results released in late 2019, and promised to create a national picture of Aboriginal and Torres Strait Islander health. The data is already being used by government to make decisions on the future of health policy. The catch? Consent. Participants were told that failure to comply in the research could result in fines of $210 per day. For blackfellas who grew up under extremely oppressive conditions, this was just another insult to freedom and dehumanizing practice.

nervously, my doctor looked up
from her screen of questions
and asked if I was part of the Stolen Generation.
when I said no
she didn't really know what to say.

Comparative to mainstream health services, Aboriginal spaces provide a lot of scope for the patient to tell their story. The National Aboriginal Community Controlled Health Organization (NACCHO) defines "Aboriginal health" as

> not just the physical well-being of an individual but ... the social, emotional and cultural well-being of the whole Community in which each individual is able to achieve their full potential as a human being thereby bringing about the total well-being of their Community. It is a whole of life view and includes the cyclical concept of life-death-life.

everyone looks more Indigenous in footy jerseys
most of the medical professionals are whitefella ones

the waiting rooms are storied places
mob from all over
the ability to access
different services under the one roof
black faces at reception
and free travel

women's privacy compromised
underfunded, overcrowded
we wait
we wait
we become waiting lists

In between appointments, I stepped out of the medical center to the regional art gallery next door. I was surprised to find, after speaking to the staff, that they had no Indigenous art on display or programs involving Indigenous artists and community.

I had gone from a building that told Aboriginal stories to one that did not, and it was disorientating. Mum and I butted in on the free art class taking place at the back of the gallery, and I drew out the aches of the appointments and processes and administration. As I described my experiences, Mum talked to me about autonomy. She talked about my grandmother, about "that generation that were taught to believe in rules, and the doctors, the authorities knew best. That didn't speak up. That were made to be silent. Don't be like that," she said. "You have to speak up."

The link between storytelling and health can never be allowed to be under-emphasized. What should we expect when we go to a place to get well? Full understanding. Responsible listening. Enhancing of our strengths. Drawing on culture and creativity and our family's values. And we should never feel alone. Never.

Queer health services—often white by design—sit awkwardly next to heteronormative Aboriginal health services. There is the potential between these two to have the magical, culturally informed, queer AF care that we don't have yet in this country.

Dameyon Bonson, a queer Mangarayi and Torres Strait Islander man based in the Kimberley, writes, "Indigenous people are not homogenous. But if you looked at our health plans, one would assume we all in fact are, or at the very least we are all straight, heterosexual, and that us Indigenous LGBQTI mob simply do not exist." Dameyon is the founder of Black Rainbow Living Well and has expertise in Indigenous suicide prevention and strategizing male health engagement.

Dameyon says Aboriginal and Torres Strait Islander health "lacks the discussion and framework for cultural competence, cultural appropriateness or cultural responsiveness specific [to] Indigenous LGBQTI needs." This exclusion causes anxiety and depression in our LGBQTI mob, and adds to the challenges and complexities we face in our lives.

we live our lives in
patience, hoping we can
wait out all of it.
what happens when
our name is called?

A First Nations Canadian friend brought my attention to an essay by queer Cree writer Billy-Ray Belcourt called "The Body Remembers When the World Broke Open." The first lines of this essay gave me shivers. "I am trying to figure out how to be in this world without wanting it, and perhaps this is what it is to be Indigenous. To be Indigenous is also to be hurt on the way out, if the 'way out' is crowded by the past's razor sharp edges."

For me, living with hurt is difficult and requires daily resourceful-ness. Long-term planning doesn't feel possible.

For mob seeking immediate support when experiencing sui-cidal thoughts, there are limited culturally safe options. There is no Indigenous suicide-prevention line or web chat—like the youth-specific (headspace), queer-specific (QLife) etc. counterparts—even though mob are most at risk.

Quandamooka woman Leilani Darwin, the winner of the LiFE Award for Excellence in Aboriginal and Torres Strait Islander Suicide Prevention, writes at *HuffPost* that "compared to non-Indigenous Australians, Aboriginal and Torres Strait Islander youth aged fifteen to twenty-four are four times more likely to take their own lives, and those aged twenty-five to thirty-four have almost three times the risk of suicide."

Trauma creates trauma. High rates of Aboriginal and Torres Strait Islander suicide and even higher Aboriginal and Torres Strait Islander lesbian, gay, bisexual, trans, intersex, queer, brotherboy and sistergirl suicide rates are our current reality.

Leilani founded Dulili Voices, a consultancy that focuses on incorporating the lived experience of community members into ser-vice delivery in a culturally competent manner. She says the reality behind most of the policies and frameworks that impact Indigenous people's lives is "do it and consult with communities later."

When people's health narratives are not heard, it can have a devastating effect. They blame themselves for their pain. They hurt deep inside. They live a life half lived. Poor health gets in the way of other things they may want to achieve. The focus is on surviving, not thriving. They die young. Whole families and communities suffer.

Arts and wellbeing are entwined, and the wider arts industry should take a holistic view of Indigenous storytelling. We are people living with the past-present-future inside of us. Our bodies remember. They remember colonial violence and silence, but they also remember the ways in which we lived lives with purpose, compassion and balance. They remember swimming in well-kept waterways, they remember emu oil on skin, they remember yam and bay bug and bunya nut, they remember language, dances, music, song.

When we tell our stories, we are baulking stereotypes and saying, "I am not your fictional Aboriginal or Torres Strait Islander person—I am real." When we tell our health narratives, we are healing ourselves and each other.

France 2019

I am in Europe during the 2019 Women's World Cup. I'm having an exciting and stimulating time teaching a poetry class in residency at the University of Bremen. Mum and I duck off for a weekend to catch a Matildas match in Valenciennes. It's been a dream of mine to see a Women's World Cup in person since I first watched the tournament on telly in 2007.

The World Cup is only just beginning, though its presence is everywhere. The level of advertising is something I've never seen before. I'm in the chemist in a small town in the Netherlands and there're cut-outs of Lieke Martens and Vivianne Miedema in front of a toothpaste display. I'm in the subway in Lille and Amandine Henry's smile is on the vending machine. I'm on the train and young women crowd around mobile screens watching their heroes. There's a TV hardware ad that keeps popping up in which a girl breaks a wall with her skills. The hole in the wall is the perfect metaphor for how the Women's World Cup broke through so many barriers.

In Australia, Matildas captain Sam Kerr is sport's most marketable face. Her sponsorship with Nike sets her total earnings at more than a million dollars. A few years ago, this kind of representation for a female athlete would be unheard of. These athletes are finally being celebrated and remunerated for their football ability. Everyone knows the tournament is on. It feels like the women's game has finally arrived.

Mum and I get to our hotel in Lille the afternoon before the Matildas match. Ash Barty is playing in the French Open final. We ask the hotel staff to put it on in the breakfast room. It is just us, screaming joyfully at the TV. This win feels like a good luck charm for the next day.

Mum and I have a brief look around town (bookstores, lunch) before heading to the stadium by train. We recognize many other gold-and-green jerseys, including someone in the infamous 1993 "spew kit," which is said to have inspired this year's Matildas kit, with its graffiti-like arrangement of color. Mum paints one of my cheeks green, the other gold.

Looking at the snapshot of countryside out the window beside me, I think about the origins of the national sporting colors associated with Australia since the late 1800s. The Australian government describes the colors as having "strong environmental connections." "Gold conjures images of Australia's beaches, mineral wealth, grain harvests and the fleece of Australian wool. Green evokes the forests, eucalyptus trees and pastures of the Australian landscape." I wonder how these colors influence how we think of ourselves.

Mum talks with everyone we come across. We make friends with an Italian couple painting their small child's face blue. We walk to the stadium together with the rest of the 15,000-strong crowd. An estimated 600,000 people are watching at home. The atmosphere is building and so are my nerves.

I underestimated Italy. I thought the Matildas would beat them easily. We go up 1–0 with a Sam Kerr goal (penalty, keeper save, Kerr with the rebound), but I start to get nervous when Italy gets one back through Barbara Bonansea. The Italian fans are upstanding and louder than the Australian support. Bonansea gets the winner in the dying minutes. It is only a group match, but it's not the start we'd hoped for. Still, we are glad to have gone to the game. We loved just being there.

I arrive back in time to teach my class on Monday. When I get the chance, I watch matches in the pub opposite my accommodation, which displays every flag of the tournament outside. They are showing every match live, so I don't only watch the Matildas, who win their other two group games, I try to catch every match I can.

Cori—who is in my class and picked us up from the airport when we first arrived—lends me a copy of *Freshwater* (2018) by Akwaeke Emezi with a warning to go carefully while reading it. Even so, I am destroyed by the book. I am not a careful reader. I sob into my hotel pillow.

The Matildas lose to Denmark in their knock-out match. Kerr has a good tournament, finishing equal second-top goalscorer. But it's not the result I wanted. The final is between the United States and the Netherlands. Naturally, I go for the Dutch, whose star duo, Martens and Miedema, are slinky and lethal in front of goals. Cori is American and they and their German wife are rooting for the United States, who are so jam-packed with stars they could play their second team.

United States co-captain Megan Rapinoe's heat map on the field is just too hot. Her fire curls in and out of the left wing, her smart quick runs proving unbeatable. She wins the tournament for the United States, as well as being individually recognized with the Golden Ball and Golden Boot. Off the field she's all grace and glory, taking a public stance against racism, homophobia, transphobia and misogyny.

"I feel like this team is in the midst of changing the world around us as we live, and it's just an incredible feeling," Rapinoe said after the team's 2–0 victory.

All twenty-eight members of the United States women's national team filed a discrimination lawsuit against US Soccer before the Women's World Cup—relating to equal pay and working conditions. The lawsuit stated: "Despite the fact that these female and male players are called upon to perform the same job responsibilities on their teams and participate in international competitions for their single common employer … the female players have been consistently paid less money than their male counterparts."

The Matildas, Australia's most successful football team ever, have also campaigned tirelessly for equal rights. In 2015, they received a pay increase that would not have been achieved without strike action.

The top Matildas annual salary increased from a measly $21,000 to $41,000.

Total prize money awarded to teams participating in the 2019 World Cup is just 7.5 percent that of the men's in 2018—though the World Cup ensured the employment of many women as referees, commentators and journalists, and FIFA has committed to long-term reform. Record sponsorship, attendance and global rating make women's football an important economic site to watch.

The conditions for women in countries like Australia and the United States pale in comparison to some of the other teams in the same tournament, however. There is a huge gap between the rich and poor countries. One example is Jamaica's Reggae Girlz, the first national football team from the Caribbean to qualify for the Women's World Cup. Without the support of Cedella Marley, with help from the foundation named after her musician father, there would be no team, with the players and coaching staff receiving no payment for their work. Marley spearheaded an international fundraising effort several years ago and things kicked off from there. Jamaica do not progress from their group but do score a goal against Australia in a 1–4 loss.

Current African champions Nigeria organize a sit-in at their hotel following their last-sixteen loss to Germany. They are asking the Nigeria Football Federation to pay outstanding fees, some of which date back to 2016. This is their third public demonstration of this kind. After hours of deliberation, shorter than 2004's three-day sit-in, the Football Federation agrees to pay the fees.

To take on the European residency, I was away from my club— where I was playing first-team football—for almost six weeks (five matches) in the middle of the season. I tried to keep fitness up while I was away, doing weight-bearing exercises in my hotel room and jogging around the block, but I knew nothing would replace football fitness and it would take a few weeks on my return to regain touch.

At the time, I knew Australia and New Zealand were bidding for the 2023 Women's World Cup, but we hadn't received confirmation yet (this would come in June 2020). I wondered what our cities would look like transformed into spaces that held love and pride for the women's game. I started to dream of what that could look like.

CABOOLTURE

The artificial turf prickled the backs of my legs as the teams sat in a circle that symbolized the coming together of clans at this First Nations football tournament. My culture and love for football were so close, so entwined, but the forests were on fire nearby so the smoking ceremony under an already smoking sky felt like something to endure. I closed my eyes and tried to repel the fear, the fear of not being able to handle the stifling conditions throughout the day. Heat is a mental thing, not just a physical thing. The Gubbi Gubbi songpeople were singing their way onto the pitch while the fires were burning north near Noosa where forests were out of control. I told myself to play with and for my people, to put my foot on the soil, to do my best, to hustle, even though I was playing the unfamiliar number-six position, to fight and to hold the team together.

Tomorrow I would wake up sick as anything, my lungs full with the wrong kind of fire. At least I knew I gave everything on the pitch, and with three draws, including with the eventual winner, Newcastle, my team didn't win a match, but we didn't lose one either. I remembered vaguely my half-time pump-up speech in the last match like one you'd see in a movie, some of my tiddas looking at me with eyes rolling, everyone heat-delirious. "We just have to score one goal, just one goal, and we can make the finals. We can do this, I believe we can. Let's give it our all and not leave anything in the tank. Let's do it for each other!" The last half of football went by so slowly. I tried on several occasions to make a run into the box from deep in midfield, but my legs moved too slowly. The ref blew the final whistle and I collapsed onto the ground.

Virus in a Scorched Land

We started 2020 struggling to breathe.

As a 240-day inferno of fires burned across five states, dust storms and severe smoke hazed the cities, affecting 80 percent of Australia's 25 million people. Masks were sold out in every store. Australia is known for our clean air, but the bushfire smoke haze caused a widespread health emergency and we were told to close our windows and shut our doors to stay safe. Still smoke was getting into the buildings. For months, the population breathed in air pollution up to twenty-six times the minimum level considered hazardous to human health. Many could not breathe.

The year started quietly, in near silence. It was a time of surviving and mourning. Over 18 million hectares burned, two years' worth of CO_2 was released into the atmosphere, thirty-three people lost their lives, over a billion native animals and plants died, and 5900 buildings were destroyed, including over 2800 homes.

"The sky was red, black ash fell like snow, and smoke choked the whole east coast—even New Zealand felt the effects of our fires. All while the government keeps selling our water and land," Bee Cruse said of the inferno. Bee's Monaro-Yuin Nation was one of the worst-hit communities. Yuin man Warren Foster, from Wallaga Lake, said, "We need our country to be healthy so we can be healthy. We need the animals. If that is all lost, our spirits die when they die. This might be a wake-up call for them now to listen to us Indigenous people on how we do our cultural burning."

On March 19, I sat on a Yuin beach holding blackened wood that the tide had swept in. It was my first time on Yuin Country and I was taking a moment to tell the spirits who I was. I expressed my sorrow for the devastated Country taking steps to heal itself after the bushfires. I had not been to this place before the fires. I spoke to Yuin Country as a Murri from South East Queensland who could not comprehend what was no longer here, what had been lost. My closest exposure to the previous summer's fires was a blowover of smoke in November 2019, from fires in the Sunshine Coast, before fires had started burning in the southern states.

In Queensland, there were 8000 bushfire incidents between September 2019 and January 2020, and more than 7.7 million hectares burned. After a day playing fixtures at the National Indigenous Football Championships on Gubbi Gubbi Country north of Meaanjin in almost forty-degree, hot, thick, blustery conditions, I'd gotten home and not wanted to move. The next day I realized I had become sick from inhaling smoke from bushfires burning over one hundred kilometers away. Advice not to exercise in such conditions, especially for asthmatics like myself, would come later, as fires swept the nation. My fatigue, body aches and sore throat healed in a matter of days, but the fires would take months to burn out; at one stage we thought the country would never stop burning. (I would visit the burned place of those 2019 fires two years later. I sat on the Country and listened to Traditional Owners tell the story of tree ancestors, local vegetation and where non-Indigenous land management had gone wrong.)

From the safety of my lounge room, in front of the television, I watched the many, many fires in a state of anguish. Ten percent of children affected by the New South Wales and Victoria fires were Indigenous, despite First Nations people in those states only being 2.3 percent of the total population. Authors Bhiamie Williamson, Francis Markham and Jessica Weir explain how First Nations people live with "perpetual grief," and how grieving after fires is vastly different for mob than it is for non-Indigenous communities.

On Yuin Country, I told the ancestors I would tread carefully. I explained I was there by invitation from my friend. Laila had planned a week away many months earlier, when we had talked about being "burnt out" by our city lifestyles. How silly that phrase felt now. I further explained our intentions on Yuin Country to the Yuin spirits: "to love." Laila and I spent our days phone-free, bushwalking and ocean swimming. Nights were for scrolling COVID-19 news, but we obsessed less than we did in the city. The disease seemed far away from us and the quiet spot we had found, even though we knew restrictions were about to take effect. Laila helped me finish a poem in which I speculated what might happen in the next few months.

The infection rate doubled while we were away, and I knew I had to get home. We rushed the three hours to Sydney airport, which was a mess. There was protective gear strewn all over the floor and hardly any people. I told Laila not to wait around; I didn't want to expose her to the virus. I waved, not sure when I would see her again, and boarded what felt like the last flight back to Brissie.

I worried many people would forget climate change as a new major event went "live" around the world. Because, of course, it was hard to worry about so many things at the same time.

The government had not paid attention to the warnings about the fires. Reports came of fire chiefs being effectively gagged from mentioning the impact of climate change on bushfire risks. They said that they self-censored out of fear of losing their jobs.

The combination of drought, fuel and wrong vegetation had created a ticking time bomb. Indigenous fire management, based on a deep understanding of the land, plants, animals and weather systems, is an ancient technology and could have been used to prevent the fires. Through interpreting signs in the landscape and talking to the spirits, First Nations practitioners burn the country slowly, so animals can escape. They burn coolly, so the fire only reaches the vegetation it needs to, cleaning up country, providing food security, supporting waterways. Cultural burning is in sync with the seasons and breeding times of animals. Indigenous people have been crying out for more autonomy over the land they know well.

Many First Nations people took COVID-19 to be a sign from the ancestors. The meme "kinda feeling like the earth just sent us all to our rooms to think about we've done" became popular on Blak social media. My Aunty sent it to me after we dropped off some supplies. I think it had particular importance for blackfellas cos we need a reason for everything, to know that the ancestors had a lesson for us. One billion animals don't just die without retribution. This was a strong message that we were doing things all wrong and that a shelter-in-place could provide some time to think about what we could do next. Perhaps we could imagine and build a new world order that was democratic to all the people and put the environment first.

From the start of the outbreak, heightened prejudice, xenophobia and racism were documented around the world towards people of Chinese and East Asian descent. Incidents of anti-Asian racism in Australia increased and the Asian-Australian friends I checked in with had been the targets of racial abuse. Racist incidents occurred on public streets, in supermarkets and shopping centers, and on public transport. Incidents also occurred in schools, universities, workplaces and other spaces. A doctor friend told me a patient at the hospital refused to see her and any other staff of Asian heritage. I was appalled. It was convenient for white Australians to be mistrustful of people from China when, in fact, in the early days, more infections came to Australia via people arriving from Spain, Italy, Iran, the United States and the United Kingdom.

COVID-19 warnings were developed in many different languages, such as Arabic and Mandarin, and some Indigenous languages, to make sure the messaging was getting across to migrant and First Nations communities. Many created their own resources for their communities to be able to survive the crisis.

In 1918 and 1919, the Spanish Flu devastated First Nations people, hitting them harder than any other demographic in Australia. In the Cherbourg community, four hundred kilometers north of where I live, unmarked mass graves have only recently been discovered.

At the time, the government had full control of every aspect of Indigenous lives. We know autonomy remains key to our survival in times of crisis. We can't forget the past as it influences our present, and we are hungry for a hopeful future.

A week before I flew home from Yuin Country, Home Affairs Minister Peter Dutton became the first Australian minister to be diagnosed with COVID-19 after arriving in Brisbane from the United States. Prison abolition and First Nations rights activists Deb Kilroy and Boneta-Marie Mabo were on the same plane as Dutton and believe they were exposed on that flight, as they themselves tested positive after arriving in Australia. Boneta-Marie is the granddaughter of legendary Indigenous land rights campaigner Eddie Koiki Mabo, whose community comes from the Torres Strait Islands in the north of Australia.

Just after I returned from my trip south I planned to go to a fundraiser for First Nations women in prison. I met some friends in West End at a bar near the corner of Boundary Road and Vulture Street where the Aboriginal flag is permanently painted on the road. We were told that the fundraiser would not be going ahead next door because of Deb and Boneta-Marie being in quarantine. For many of us, these were the first people we knew who had contracted the disease. As we gathered around the bar catching up, we began to suspect this would be our last community gathering for a while.

One friend had had an interaction that morning with a man who entered her shop claiming to have the virus. She had closed the shop early; there had been no business. Another friend arrived in a shocked state, clutching her neck. She had just been involved in a car accident. Both she and the other driver had been rushing to the grocery store. The daily news was awash with stories of empty aisles at supermarkets as rice, pasta and canned foods disappeared from the shelves. Our country made international headlines with violent brawls over toilet paper. My friends and I were embarrassed. We knew that there was a lot more at stake and that there were other ways to clean our bottoms. Many of us had lived in generational poverty with little more than a tin of tuna to last the week. Some of us had traditional diets, surviving off the land. The pandemic woes of white Australians did not resonate with us.

Supermarkets began introducing special hours for shoppers over sixty and those with disabilities so they did not have to compete with the panic-buying stockpilers. State and federal governments imposed restrictions and urged Australians to stay at home. The National Farmers' Federation told consumers not to "panic" as there was "plenty of food to go around." Minister for Agriculture, Drought and Emergency Management David Littleproud declared that Australia has "the most secure food security in the world."

Not secure for some. This statement omitted the inflated price of food in remote Indigenous communities, and the lack of food sovereignty and/or access to clean drinking water. Aboriginal Australians and Torres Strait Islanders have poorer health outcomes and a lower life expectancy than the non-Indigenous Australian population, particularly those living in remote areas, and this, along with overcrowded housing, makes them one of the communities most vulnerable to the virus. Our Elders in the community are living libraries, as they hold knowledge vital for the next generation.

Communities shut down to visitors and border restrictions were introduced. My friends, two sisters who belonged to the community of Minjerribah, took a ferry to the island the next day so they could be with their parents.

A proposal to evacuate Elders from the remote Anangu Pitjantjatjara Yankunytjatjara communities in South Australia to Adelaide was not put into operation. The Northern Territory developed a remote health pandemic plan, with NT Health setting up a number of remote clinics. All non-essential travel to the seventy-six remote communities was banned, and in May health officials suggested that this should stay in place for the foreseeable future. The travel restrictions remained in place until February 2022.

On the banks of the Darling River in New South Wales, a group of Barkindji families set up a tent town to escape overcrowded accommodation. They believed they would be safer from the threat of the disease in tents along the river than in housing in town.

When the cruise ship *Ruby Princess* freely discharged 2700 passengers without quarantine in Sydney Harbour, some of my First Nations colleagues were quick to point out the irony of ships being allowed into the country carrying an infectious disease. This was especially trenchant in the year a tax-funded re-enactment of the 250th anniversary of the landing of Cook's *Endeavour* was due to occur.

The health gap in our nation was made apparent on March 29, when the prime minister urged Australians over seventy and Indigenous Australians over fifty to stay at home. My mother, sixty-seven, was stuck between feelings of caution and defiance. Why should she have more restrictions placed on her because of her race?

By that time, we were hardly leaving the house anyway. Mum, Dad and I have never felt luckier to have bushland behind us. We went on walks sometimes, but the birds also visited us in our back garden. Sulphur-crested cockatoos, kookaburras and crows. When I saw birds flying overhead I thought of flocking, a group moving in the same direction but keeping their distance. Physically distancing from each other but remaining unified. The sky was a lot clearer thanks to an easing of pollution. We saw more stars in the night sky. With gyms and playgrounds closed, we noticed more walkers in the national park. Just before nightfall we would see keen photographers trying to capture the elusive barking owls. Kangaroos were out in force in the mornings and the late afternoons, encroaching into urban areas. Green shoots appeared in the areas badly burned from the summer's bushfires.

The expensive air-filtration masks I'd bought my family to handle the smoke from the fires were transferable to this crisis. We wore them when we went to the supermarket or post office or had to use the train.

Mum got a puppy just before the COVID-19 pandemic started, after seeing an ad online with a photo attached (a squishy black-and-white blob) and falling in love. After we lost our beloved Max in 2013, I said if we ever got another dog I would name them Marta, a football name. Marta turned out to be an anxious border collie cross kelpie who needed a lot of love and attention. She likes to play football just as much as Max did, but her favorite game is frisbee.

I kept in touch with my friends and colleagues through online catch-ups. A particular favorite was a weekly roundtable for First Nations artists and arts workers hosted by the Australia Council for the Arts. We laughed and cried together; for many of us, this was the highlight of our week. We heard uplifting stories of our kinspeople embracing bush food, hunting, fishing, gardening and weaving. We talked about how we could come out of this crisis to a stronger place, in which we'd have data sovereignty and ownership over our land and cultural practices. We heard sad realities about our young people suiciding, COVID-19 creating a mental health pandemic hitting those who were most vulnerable. We brainstormed ways to help our young people make sense of this crisis. We urged ourselves to be cautious of disaster capitalism, whereby conservative governments would use the crisis's emotional and physical distraction to sneakily greenlight controversial coal mines and other threats to Country.

On Sunday, May 24, 2020, one of the world's oldest sacred sites was destroyed by mining blasts. The mining company, Rio Tinto, was granted legal permission to blast the over 46,000-year-old site belonging to the Puutu Kunti Kurrama and Pinikura Traditional Owners. The Traditional Owners were deeply troubled and saddened by the destruction of the rock shelters and they were frustrated by the inflexibility of the law. Viewed as out-of-date, inefficient and ineffective, Western Australia's *Aboriginal Heritage Act 1972* was replaced with the *Aboriginal Cultural Heritage Act 2021*, with a co-design process underway, a step towards ensuring Traditional Owners are at the heart of decision-making.

In October 2020, after 1772 submissions, the Royal Commission into National Natural Disaster Arrangements, otherwise known as the Bushfires Royal Commission, delivered its findings on the long-term effects of the bushfires on both the land and people's health. First Nations people told the commission that Aboriginal and Torres Strait Islander voices were routinely ignored in post-disaster commissions.

The Bushfires Royal Commission had a total of eighty recommendations in its report, including two recommendations (18.1 and 18.2) regarding Indigenous land and fire management. It stated:

> Australian state, territory and local governments should engage further with Traditional Owners to explore the relationship between Indigenous land and fire management and natural disaster resilience. ... Australian, state, territory and local governments should explore further opportunities to leverage Indigenous land and fire management insights, in the development, planning and execution of public land management activities.

The wording of these recommendations, "engage further" and "explore," doesn't feel strong enough in its intent to change the structure of land and fire management. Long-term secured funding is necessary to achieve First Nations people being able to manage Country now and into the future.

I have many thoughts when I think about the fires, the floods, global warming, species devastation and the ongoing displacement of people off their traditional lands. I think about the rare macadamia trees that were destroyed in the fires in Queensland. Macadamia trees are one of my community's totems, and their nuts are an important food source. I was devastated to learn of the loss of the trees.

Experts report the smoke that many Australians inhaled contained particles that can enter the bloodstream and affect every system in the body, causing many health issues. We don't know enough yet, like we don't know enough about COVID-19. Psychological stress was reported as being a lasting effect, and we are expecting that especially children will face post-traumatic stress for decades to come.

Climate change is the greatest health challenge we face, and most days I wake up feeling anxious and overwhelmed. I try to stay hopeful. I rely on the strength of my family and friends who tell me we have faced challenges in the past and we have overcome them. We belong to Country. Country doesn't belong to us. I speak to the ancestors. One of my Aunties comes to me in the form of the sulphur-crested cockatoo. Aunty KRG tells me to keep fighting and hold my head up high. And I will, to honor her.

Indigenous communities in Australia have been lauded as being highly successful in preventing the entry of COVID-19 during the peak of the pandemic and in the face of threatening national disasters. Many non-Indigenous communities want to "learn" how Indigenous and migrant communities practice resilience so they can apply it to their own communities. I am highly skeptical of the rhetoric. My mother and I talk about the term "resilience" as being very similar to "re-silence." A repetition of a harmful history.

"Re-" words in First Nations policy speak are dodgy. For example, reconciliation: (re—to repeat, continue) + (conciliation—to placate or pacify). Indigenous communities still remain highly vulnerable to potential future waves of this disease and potential future pandemics also caused by climate change. Many of our communities have substandard living conditions that should make all Australians ashamed. We should not have to continue being "resilient." We should not have to continue to fight for the health of our land, our waterways, our culture and our family. Why are we continually asked to change? It is the systems themselves that should change.

In March 2022, a week after experiencing 80 percent of our expected annual rain in three days, I am watching a climate scientist on TV explaining the recent devastating flooding event in Queensland and New South Wales as a climate-change-inflicted phenomenon that scientists are still trying to understand. All they do know is that it will happen more. She describes supercharged rivers in the sky, a phrase that makes my spine twitch, not because it's a fantastical image but because it is so real. This is part of First Nations cultural scope. We know there are atmospheric rivers in the sky. I have just worked on a children's book that included rivers in the sky. They are powerful. When they are supercharged, when they are part of a blocked weather system, they can cause devastation. We deeply understand the powers and extreme threat of nature—we have been warning about this for a long time.

There is talk of a rebuild and building futures. Before anything more is placed on Country, two ceremonies must occur: the lives that were lost, the homes that were destroyed and the objects that were laid waste must be remembered; and the inventory of Country, First Nations philosophy, must be brought to life.

What Survival Feels Like

Remember these poets who invited us to lean-in close/bear witness to their love/be part of what survival looks/feels/tastes like.
Natalie Harkin, "Refuse/Return/Remain"

Sitting inside this emergency room called Australia, through the sense of warmth and communion we've ceremoniously crafted in our writing, we find it's populated with people we love. So now, already, the walls of the room are looking more beautiful, and maybe someone's opened a window or two and there's a fresh breeze blowing through. We sit here together. The presences of women and others who have paved the way for us surround us. We got Aunty Oodgeroo and Lisa Bellear, and Aunty Kerry Reed-Gilbert—warrior women. This country's Indigenous poets and storytellers are all here with us. It is already feeling like we can tackle some of the most damaging and violent institutional aspects of this country with a bit more love.

*

Blak sovereign erotics
While walking through the streets of Sydney, after just finishing up a conference, Jeanine reminds me that our Aunty Kuracca KRG wrote erotica. Deadly! I'm glad to remember that. It makes me think of the awesome chats Aunt and I had about the craft of writing. She was inspired by my short stories, which made me real proud, and I was inspired by her fierce AF poetry. And we both loved writing erotica. It is always really powerful to celebrate Blak sexuality/ies and desire/s. The Blak sovereign erotic has the power to give the settler patriarchy the middle finger. Blak sovereign erotics have

always been an understated threat to empire/s. There is fluidity and freedom in our sexuality. I love writing powerfully about sex and love. A sovereign erotic takes back control of Blak sexuality and how we talk and write about it.

When I get home from the conference and put my suitcase down (the other thing Aunt told me to do was to get a Qantas lounge membership, but I never listened), I walk my street to reorientate myself with home. I see a single feather. Kuracca fly over the houses at the same time every day. The feather left behind is not all that you are but a reminder that we flock together. Kuracca keep flying, keep singing.

*

There is an effect in the intimacy we create in our words, as First Nations poets. I have to thank Natalie Harkin and many others who bring their readers with them in their fight for literary justice. In this way we are reminded that we do not spend any time alone, even though institutions try to divide and isolate us. Through our positionality, we can make the young blackfella feel safe and supported. Although our words go to a greater readership, it feels like we are speaking directly to the individual.

My most recent full collection of poems, *Throat*, went out into the (big, wide) world in May 2020 with a small group of readers specifically in mind. The writing of *Throat* was the crafting of a selective space where I could be intimate with a chosen few people, places and ideas. The book was written as if I was having intimate conversations around a dinner table. *Throat* is an unselfconscious work that exists inside of what it has built. As its beginnings were found in the intersections of people, I felt less inclined to build up a backstory or censor its language and ideas. The door had already been opened.

*

Aboriginal business
1.
It's not my business, I say to my sister,

215

But someone at work told me a few weeks ago:
"I have an aunt, we all have just found out she was adopted.
She always looked different, acted different too."
Uh-huh.
"We always knew. Very different, olive skin.
She looks Mediterranean. One of her parents must be something,
    maybe Lebanese."
Uh-huh.
What year was she born? What hospital?
Uh-huh.
It's none of my business.
It is your business, my sister says.

2.

Not Asian enough, my friend says in a group chat about her mixed-
    race son
she herself is Vietnamese but the words seem to jag at me
maybe because of the proximity to *not Aboriginal enough*
the years of juggling shame and alienation and not knowing
who was safe to talk to and whether my mother, brother or I could
    get chastised or even worse, attacked
for daring to say we were Yugambeh and proud.

                              *

Ways to be political
Bold and bright vs subtle and silent. There are ways to be political
that don't seem very political but understand there are inner and
outer lives and what we do in public and private are different things.
Ways to be political are ways to love each other and ourselves.

                              *

This country murders Aboriginal and Torres Strait Islander people
on a daily basis, as well as murdering animals, plants and other forms
of life on the continent. For us there is no difference between land,
sea, sky, earth and people. We all are related. Ecocidal and genocidal
practices combine to devastating effect, like what we saw with the

bushfires, which displaced communities for the third, fourth, fifth times. Until there is a clear sign that things are changing, Australia will remain an emergency room with an overwhelming number of casualties. This form of Australia is cataclysmic for everyone. Our mobs were hit by a brutal colonizing machine that continues to affect our autonomy and our way of living. Despite all this, we have survived.

*

[untitled]

Blaks at the back of the conference. Rating everyone's acknowledgements. And generally making everyone feel unsettled. Watching the Good White Person Olympics as they each stride to make their mark on reconciliation. They say they want to respectfully listen. How can you listen when you have fly lures in your ears? What you gonna do when you're in the water? What is between the crocodile's jaws?

*

Feelings (in the colony)

Shame. Guilt. Hopelessness. Worry.
Fear. Despair. Nervousness. Anticipation.
Loneliness. Boredom. Longing. Frustration. Grief.

*

Political

Forgive me, Nana
I'm a political animal
I'm a push back kinda Blak. I need to be noticed
I hope you will understand who I am today
My ability to speak, sometimes easily
Comes from your strength in keeping your children safe

*

We have a lot of "unfinished business." I have a lot of unfinished business. And that's a huge motivating force, perhaps why I continue to do what I do in the writing, editing, publishing and community spaces. Love is not labor if it is reciprocal. I write and work hard, and it is sometimes painful but also joyous. I enjoyed writing the intimacy in survival. My Creator Spirits and Ancestors are smiling down on us, I know it.

Ask me if I'd rather be in good health or writing, it would be the former every day of the week, and I struggle to reconcile myself with the fact that a lot of my most truthful writing comes from periods of deep impenetrable darkness, depression and loss.

*

Would I?
The answer's yes. I would make love to myself. 100 percent. If you asked me that question a few years ago there might have been some hesitation and some questioning about the practicalities, maybe. But I'm in a position where, if the offer presented itself, I would be keen. I'd be DTF, no questions asked. I'm not on any of the apps but if I was I would def slide into my own DMs.
What do you do to turn yourself on?
Walks, being outside, stars, being in water, floating, poetry, textual pleasure
What do I want from my relationship with myself? How do I relearn to be intimate with myself?
When I'm by myself, I declare myself my own lover. I get the scented candles out
The mood lighting just right
I whisper all the things I am proud of myself for.

*

Along with the drawings and photos, my darling mum kept my first poem, which I wrote when I was eleven years old. School was a violently oppressive place for me. It attacked my personhood, and I hid inside myself. Then I discovered books and found somewhere else to be. They facilitated my imagination. It took me some time to learn how to write. My parents patiently helped me trace out the alphabet. "Y" I found most challenging of all. There are some letters I have still not mastered.

My Year 1 teacher gave me extra support outside of class, I think after conversations with my parents. We sat together one lunch break.

She asked me to write a response to Sally Morgan's *My Place* (1987), my own little book about "my place," "my family," "my belonging." This feeling of creation stayed with me. I felt a sense of pride. I told my mum when I got home I wanted to be a children's book author.

So, from an early age I wanted to be a writer, to express myself in this way. Throughout the depression and isolation in my schooling years, writing was my savior. I would keep the back pages of my schoolbooks free for my scribblings. It made me feel safe.

My life significantly improved in the years after I left high school. No longer was I daily in places that tolerated my bullying and torment. I had space. I got to explore outside my suburb. I visited Sydney and immersed myself in the queer visibility there. Soon I had friends. People I could be myself with.

*

[untitled]
can i kiss you or am i way off the mark?
can i bury my nose into your neck and breathe in your tattoo and
    necklace
do you think we could have something
in common
do you think we could have something
warm and fun and free
despite these dark spirits
circling us like sharks
despite depression and colonization
you know, those things that don't leave us
do you think we could?

*

The ancestors of this lyric
When arriving I have to tell you the Europeans did not consider the
ancestors of this lyric   people
When arriving I have to tell you the Europeans did not consider the
ancestors of this lyric   as having a relationship to land

When arriving I have to tell you the Europeans did not consider the
ancestors of this lyric   as having culture
When arriving I have to tell you the Europeans did not consider the
ancestors of this lyric   as having science
When arriving I have to tell you the Europeans did not consider the
ancestors of this lyric   as having human rights
When arriving I have to tell you the Europeans did not consider the
ancestors of this lyric   as having the right to write poetry or tell
     stories of any kind
I need to tell you the ancestors of this lyric have made this page and
     are writing
back through us   every line, every word

*

[untitled]

Eh, murrigirl at UTS law school tutorial. You're cool, murrigirl. You
look like my sisters from Minjerribah. I can see the sea salt in your
big eyes, mouth twitching ... you're gonna say something? You know
you gotta talk, murrigirl. I know you got a lot to say. Don't let these
whitefellas hog the curriculum. We talking treaty and constitution.
I can tell how smart you are by how hard you're listening. Deadly,
I'm so glad you spoke up. Your voice is beautiful and luckily those
white ones were respectful enough to know what you were giving
them. I'm smiling at you until we get a chance to yarn ... Oh, true,
you're not Murri? Your mob's from the Pacific and you grew up
here? Really, you're not Murri? You got everyone claiming you. We're
so close to the ocean, girl. Pasifika and White but you don't know
if you can ... Mixed-race mob're no less valid, we're hot! Yours in
solidarity, Sis. Keep going.

*

University and the workplace were places where I found purpose
and communion with Blak women and women of color. I have relationships now decades-deep, and these continue to support me.

I trawled the university library and found the words of Lisa
and Oodgeroo. They nestled deep into my soul, like soul sisters. I

marveled at their strong voice and sharp focus that crystallized on the page.

I began to write with little fear. To be Blak is to always write with fear, but I was comforted by the intimacy of those who had inspired me. And to write on Country is the deepest privilege. I feel no shortage of energy from this land.

Where did *Throat* begin and how did I find the intimacy in survival poetics? Beginnings are always plural.

Throat began in October 1990 when I opened my eyes and lungs to Turrbal land. Though it may have begun much sooner.

Throat began when I did not let myself speak for many years but carried the burdens of many in my burning larynx.

Throat began when my darling friend Paula met me in Sydney's south, on Dharawal land, in 2017. I was undertaking a residency at Campbelltown Arts Centre, and as a community arts person from Western Sydney she had been asked if she wanted to meet me. Generously, she brought me a large stack of 1990s poetry books, anthologies and literary journals from women of color she thought I should read. These books transcended countries and borders, but I found an intimacy in their descriptions of what it meant to be queer and brown and born female in oppressive places and to deal with trauma and pain. Late that night, I flipped open the pages to a poem called "Serious Pepper" by Black British performance poet Patience Agbabi and came across the lines that would later become the epigraph for the book. *no one's found until they find themselves / hurting in the back of the throat.*

Throat began when I was living in Wurundjeri country and suffering a relationship breakdown that left me broken and unsure. I spent a few nights staying with my tidda who was a few blocks away. In another bed I woke up writing.

take me to the back of my throat

A month later I was spending the summer in Bundjalung Country, neighboring Country to my mob, visiting friends and family. "I think

I have a manuscript," I said out loud for the first time. "It's called 'Back of the Throat.'"

*

Mirror
This lover has this big wall-length mirror that sort of was a bit intimidating when I first entered the room. But now we're on the bed, and we've warmed up, and I open my eyes, and take a little peek behind me. I am looking back at the image of myself. I see a dark-haired beauty, me, on top of her, a tall, slender, long-limbed redhead. I see the beautiful formation of our bodies together. I see our shared pleasure. I see our shiny, taut skin. I see her fingers finding me. And I'm kind of surprised how much I find this image of myself, me, as sexy, us as sexy—that I just feel aroused and not the least bit awkward or self-conscious. I don't need to close my eyes. I feel really in the moment. I see us from the outside, I see us from the inside. I see the visual, the textual, the ephemeral. I come watching her fuck me in the mirror. My eyes flicker closed, open, closed. I feel her groan as I groan and I revel in the aftershocks, pressing against her fingers, her thigh, her lips, her chest. I look away from the mirror, though the mirror is still there.

*

I had not a manuscript but twenty poems that seemed to be moving together. I was writing about friendship, family and love. I was writing about powers I knew I had and powers I didn't know I had. Within the intimacy I constructed on the page, I was exploring the spiritual and the erotic. Audre Lorde writes in her essay "Uses of the Erotic" about how women can revolutionize the anti-erotic world through harnessing the power within themselves and bringing it outward, the erotic offering a "well of replenishing and provocative force."

take me to the back of my throat I'll stay

Throat began when I left Wurundjeri country and moved back home. In my bedroom at the bottom of our house, prone to leaks every time we had a big rain, I read Cree poet Billy-Ray Belcourt's

This Wound Is a World (2017), Sāmoan poet Selina Tusitala Marsh's *Fast Talking PI* (2009) and Filipina-Australian poet Eunice Andrada's *Flood Damages* (2018). Soon, the books were flood-stained too.

*

Aboriginal stereotypes

Aboriginal men and their shoes ♥ a brotha loves to show off new shoes—whether fresh-out-of-the-box sneaks, bush boots or take your pick!

Aunties and their goodbyes ♥ gonna be a long time on that curb as Aunty just won't let you go for a good hour!

Uncles and their jams ♥ every Unc can play a bit of guitar if given the chance.

Bookish Blaks ♥ can't walk past a second-hand bookshop tru god they're gonna be in there for an hour.

Blak on Blak couples and the way they talk ♥ these ones are likely to develop their own language within the first six months that is a mix of both of their mobs' lingo. No one can understand but just let em go all right?

*

Black Bitch

When I first see the trailer for the series I feel a prickly ache in my spine. The title feels yucky, triggering. I think maybe it will give them permission to call us that, more permission than they already have. Black women and people who are femme-presenting, we are either one of two things: meek or a bitch. How many times have I been called "shy," how many times have I been called "angry"? And nothing in between. Call me meek or a bitch, but I'd like to think I'm also twisty, kind, understanding, affectionate, funny, flirtatious and uncompromising.

I wonder why the *Black Bitch* title there in Toronto and *Total Control* here in Australia? *Total Control* doesn't seem to mean anything. I'm confused. I talk about this with Andrea and Jeanine, both older Aboriginal women. They don't mind the title *Black Bitch*, actually. Maybe it's a generational thing? They think it's a reclaiming. And I'm starting to see their point. Depending on who is saying it, it can be a racist and sexist insult or a deliberately provocative reclaimed term, J says. And A says she would wear it on a T-shirt. *Black Bitch*. I wouldn't wear it scrawled across my chest, but I think it's cool to think like that. It reminds me that language can always be taken back and used to our advantage.

*

I loved being back with my family, but being grounded in Queensland I missed my kin in other places, my sisters and tiddas. Those who chose a creative life. I wrote to them in my poems, about the things we had been through. I wrote of the racism, sexism and discrimination that haunted our lives, that was invisible to those who could not know what it was like to experience it. I wrote as if I was inviting them all over to eat with me, these people who loved me and who accepted me for who I was: sit down and let me make you a big AF pot of pasta, with a bit of river mint from my 2018 garden to season.

After finishing *Throat* I felt depleted of creative energy. I had written a life into this book as if to keep a record of my existence. I didn't feel like writing poetry again for a long time. Aunty KRG passed. To mourn her loss we came together, physically and through words. Gumerahla wanyi ngay.

The poems interspersed here are written in response to a coming back into the world again. They aim to be at their heart a gathering. An intimate gathering in a time of survival. Poetry by no means seeks to resolve anything or answer questions. In fact, it is more useful if it creates more questions. Critical questioning is an act of love. When our words meet the spaces that open up to the soul lyric, we are bashful and grateful. We shift focus to others. This could be what survival feels like, knowing there are others like us, that this will continue. And we are grateful to live in a world of poetry, of song, and language.

PART FOUR

2023

as imagined in 2020
In 2023 we will not
keep our reality to ourselves
there will be Blak people on television
narrating joy instead of survival, and I will rub my eyes
until the vision is seen and believed.
In 2023 Aotearoa and Australia will host the party of all parties
the whole world watching
a thirty-two-team competition will open doors, our neighbors
Papua New Guinea will qualify for the first time
Iran's national team will honor Sahar Khodayari in a blue strip.
In 2023 no fires will burn so wildly out of control
sacred business in the hands of First Nations practitioners.
In 2023 I will go to the supermarket
fill a shopping cart of food from Blak businesses
knowing my Unaipons sustain Country.
2023 brings me closer
to the question Cave asked
Is there racism in heaven?
I'm not sure yet
but I know I will rest when I'm dead
we will keep our face masks on hand
we will be taking all precautions not to
piss off our planet again
the virus is around, like all living things
but if we are talking about something

that deliberately and callously kills
yes, police and state violence will be suppressed
and what kills us (historically) will
make us stronger (figuratively).
In 2023 we will disbelieve a time
when women went to jail for unpaid fines
children were handcuffed
refugees were imprisoned indefinitely
oh, it will seem so long ago.
In 2023 our politicians will reflect what this country has always been a
place of deep spirituality and respect for every little thing
the state election will be contested by two First Nations candidates.
In 2023 I will turn thirty-three
recognize my face is more like an eagle's
older, and stronger
my eyes have never been so fixed.
In 2023 outside Meaanjin Stadium
kids will be backflipping like Sammy, forwardfacing the truth
Megan Rapinoe's allyship will no longer take center stage
our Matildas will have three First Nations players in the starting eleven
a dramatic penalty shootout will see Australia
make the final through a Lydia save and a Kyah conversion
the final will be played to eighty thousand fans
they will not allow tickets to bigots
crowds will descend on Cathy Freeman Park.
I will call my mother and say
even if we don't win the final tonight,
we have won.

Trans Sporting Utopias

My vision of utopia would be where I wouldn't have to choose [between queerness and cultural identity].

Willurai Kirkbright

In March 2021, from my home on Turrbal and Yagera Country, I spoke with Arlie Alizzi (he/him), Zakaria Shahruddin (he/him and they/them) and Louis Blake (he/him) to get an insight into their fitness and sporting hopes and desires. More than just finding out about how the landscape has affected other transfolk in sport, I was searching and trying to learn from other people's stories to make sense or to have validation of my own personal score with sport. There was not real representation of trans and gender-diverse voices in the media, so I searched for reality (from real people, lived experience) to help me with my own experience. We spoke about utopias (and dystopias) in direct and indirect terms. Talking about sports is a way of talking about life, and our conversations flowed into the personal and the relational.

Trans and/or gender-diverse (TGD) participation in sport is about inclusion. TGD people, particularly First Nations, are the most systematically marginalized people in society. This is a group that accounts for some of the highest mortality rates across the world.

A year earlier, I'd heard the story of a local trans girl who loved running but whose parents were told she was not allowed to run in a representative school competition. When the parents argued that their daughter's right to participate in the event was within the rules—her testosterone levels were still low, pre-puberty—it was suggested she could run but not get a placing. This is not acceptable. The parents protected their daughter from this information so as not to upset her. She's just a kid. How would a parent tell their daughter she is not allowed to run because the state sees her gender as invalid and her very being a threat?

Fewer than 20 percent of trans people play sport in Australia, and even fewer participate in team sport. Often LGBTIQSB+ children grow up feeling like they don't have a place in sport where they can be themselves without fear of judgement, harassment, abuse or violence. When TGD people are denied sport, they miss out on enduring friendships that often transcend divides. TGD people do not pose a threat to sport, but they are the survivors of vicious transphobic campaigns to exclude them from it.

If sport is "sex-segregated," heteronormative and explicitly trans-exclusionary, what kind of world is created, violently policed and upheld? These spaces are forceful dystopias; complete departures from the liberated lives our ancestors had.

These dystopic places are the places where I've been told:

"Line up according to your skin color."

"If you are a dyke you should find another team to play in."

"Girls can't play with boys."

"You can't play with the girls either because you look too much like a boy."

I have been subjected to degrading questioning about my gender during games. I have heard homophobic and transphobic slurs addressed to opposing players from my own teammates and have stood in frozen silence. I've witnessed anti-Blak, anti-Black and anti-Asian racism. In these dystopian places, First Nations cultures and peoples are continuously erased and violated. I grew up in these places.

Sovereign genders

Let's not forget we live and play sport on First Nations land. Let's not forget the impact of colonialism on gender identities. Colonial gender binaries hold up the Western patriarchy. TGD identities—including sistergirls and brotherboys, pan-First Nations terms that describe some TGD people in Aboriginal and/or Torres Strait Islander communities—don't fit into the rigid colonial understandings of gender.

These identities have always been part of our cultures. Brotherboys are Aboriginal and Torres Strait Islander people who are assigned female at birth but live their lives through the boy spirit. Likewise, sistergirls are assigned male at birth but live their lives through the girl spirit. These terms encompass both gender identity and cultural identity as well as roles in community and society. In the Tiwi Islands, sistergirls are traditionally called yimpininni. Identity is respected regardless of how sistergirls might look, as it's the spirit on the inside that counts.

In other parts of Australia, some of the First Nations language around gender identity has been lost due to genocide. Some of this language is being revitalized.

Elsewhere in the Asia-Pacific, Jaiyah Saelua, the first transgender player and fa'afafine (an umbrella term in Sāmoa for someone who identifies as a gay man, a trans woman or non-binary but with female characteristics) to play in a FIFA-sanctioned game, explains how sport and Indigenous gender identities co-exist in Sāmoa. "It's very common, actually, for fa'afafine to play sports," Jaiyah says in an interview with *The Guardian*. "Sāmoan society has no limits on what fa'afafine can pursue in life."

The first sport

Arlie and Zakaria, or Zaky, have been friends since 2015, when they met at a party. Arlie is Yugambeh (Kombumerri) from the Gold Coast area. He grew up in Ocean Grove and Queenscliff in Victoria on Wathaurong Country. Zaky grew up in Malaysia. Arlie and Zaky tell me that talking sport with each other is a way to take a break from their identity politics; sport is something they have in common apart from being trans.

> AA: The first sport was basketball. I was eight. I played in a team that was, in theory, mixed. But I was the only girl on the team. I played tennis. It was pretty fun. When I played tennis in town, I played on a boys' team because there was no girls' tennis in town.
>
> In Ocean Grove at the time, girls played netball, and boys played footy or cricket in the summertime. It was [a] very gendered binary. I remembered seeing one boy playing netball once. When I played netball I was goal defense [GD] and goal keeper for five or six years and I loved it. I got really excited by being good at playing defense. I got a real power trip from interrupting other people's scoring. I had a bit of a role for myself there.

> ZS: I was also a netball GD so I had the same brawl! And I did really like defending my people. I come from a sporting family. My dad played football for his state growing up. It's hard to assign class in Malaysia, because it's a youngish country, but my dad would consider his family lower working class. There were not a lot of opportunities to get Western-standard education in the village: playing soccer was a way for him to get out of the village. He got scouted at an away game and then moved to [Kuala Lumpur].

My dad met my mum while he was playing soccer. Just imagine his long, curly hair; he had a Vespa and he was playing soccer for the state. My mum was like, I think you need to go to school. He got into university because of soccer.

There were no girls' soccer teams when I was growing up so I went into all sorts of other sports. In primary school, I did a lot of shot-put and long jump, which I was very good at. I got in the state finals for badminton, which I was very proud of. Before high school, I was always in three different team sports at the same time. I really like team sports. I had ADHD so I wasn't very good at chatting with people, but in team sport [I had] a structured goal. In high school, my family told me to stop doing sports and focus on my education. There was an understanding in my family that sport was good to build the person you are but not something you should pursue. My dad always said, "I was never going to play internationally, I just wanted to get out of the village."

We loved sport. There was six of us kids so we could play a lot of sports in teams of three. You can play a real game with six. Dad played with us. We had a ping-pong table. We had a badminton divider. We had a soccer goal; Dad would always be the goalkeeper. I don't know if this happens [in Australia], but in Malaysia we'd put the Adidas slides on our hands: that's how you would [play] goalkeeper. Everyone wants to be goalkeeper for some reason in my house so we'd have to find a slide and put it on one hand and whoever put it on their hand first was goalkeeper. But because my dad was the person who decided when we played, he would have already had his hand in. Sport is still a big part of the family: we watch badminton almost every night.

AA: I was a Collingwood fan through my mum's side of the family—they grew up in the Altona/Williamstown area and would go to Victoria Park on weekends. I got into Collingwood real intense and one person I remember keenly following as a kid was [Noongar player] Leon Davis. He was the star shooter, the small forward. I watched him a lot.

I remember the 1996 Olympics in Atlanta. That was one of my earliest sport-spectator memories. I was watching everything, but I especially liked watching track and field. I loved watching the runners.

ZS: In 1998, the Commonwealth Games were in Kuala Lumpur. I was part of the dancing troupe at the opening ceremony. That was a very proud moment.

Louis

When I first meet Louis Blake in 2019, he is about to start testosterone therapy. He knows he will soon have to quit playing elite futsal with his team, as they compete in the state women's league. He knows he has to tell his team he is quitting and why.

Louis grew up in Essendon in a sports-obsessed (especially AFL) family, with a sports journalist for a dad, a cousin who played over 300 games for the Sydney Swans and an aunty who was a champion runner. He played women's footy at high school but fell in love with another sport when he was fifteen.

"Prior to Australia being in the [2006] World Cup, I thought soccer was boring—they play the whole game and don't even score. Following Australia play in the World Cup—I realized less scoring can make it more exciting. [I've been] hooked since then."

Louis's AFL tackling and hand skills transferred well to goalkeeping, which became his natural position. He joined a futsal team, an indoor version of the game.

"I loved it even more because I'm a short guy and I play in goal. Sometimes in outdoors you see a goal sailing so high above your head and going in and you go, *ugh*, there's no way I could do anything about that. With indoor I can reach the top of the net. I was hooked with that. And you're more a part of the action."

In 2016 he joined the elite women's league at Futsal Oz and helped his team to a 2019 Australian championship.

"I was operating my whole life under the assumption that I'm a cisgender straight woman. Transmasc people aren't represented in sports whatsoever. To see trans men in sport you have to seek it out. I don't think I've ever seen anything about a trans man doing well. Mainstream society doesn't even know transmasculine people exist, let alone play sport, let alone be good at it."

Louis speaks about inclusion in AFL, the sport he grew up with. He tells me that the AFL Women's (AFLW) had a pride round, and the Western Bulldogs had a jumper with a number of pride flags printed on it.

"That was really powerful. But I still note there are no trans women in AFLW: Hannah Mouncey was blocked from playing. You put [a flag] on your jumper, but do you walk the walk?"

Mouncey, who represented Australia in men's handball before transitioning, was barred from entering the 2017 AFLW draft. The decision the panel made "took into account the stage of maturity of the AFLW competition, its current player cohort and Mouncey's individual circumstances." Mouncey's testosterone level in serum had been below the recommended 10 nmol/L for at least twelve months. The AFL later said it was "concerned about the disparity in body size and bulk that Mouncey may have over the existing AFLW cohort after only a year of semi-professional training" and that she may nominate for future AFLW drafts. The AFL came under fire over its handling of Mouncey's case and she withdrew her nomination for the draft the following year, citing poor treatment from the league.

"She still gets so much shit and abuse," says Louis. "She's become the poster girl for transphobic abuse, designed to discourage other transgender women. The message is: you're not welcome."

When I meet Louis Blake again in 2021, he is no longer playing women's futsal. "I had to walk away from the elite level and the elite club. My teammate was like, 'Why can't you just keep playing?' And I was like, 'Are you serious? Because I'm a man.'"

Not comfortable playing in a women's league and not sure if a men's league will accept his registration without questions, he plays in a mixed futsal team in a social league. He is anticipating another process that will affect his sport: gender-affirming top surgery, due a few weeks after we speak. "I think I'm still seen as a woman; I think it's because of my chest."

Mixed futsal league rules that require a minimum of two women on the field at a time enforce a gender binary and create discomfort for Louis.

"They should just say what they mean: you must have at least two people on the field who have been disenfranchised due to their upbringing and haven't been able to train in this sport since they were a little kid. The whole thing is not set up for me. I don't fit into this whatsoever. Well, I do—I'm just a man—but I don't think they see it that way. I think it will be interesting to see what happens when I come back after top surgery, whether that changes. Over time I'll be even more masculine. I'm in this weird in-between stage at the moment and partially that's why I didn't want to play and will be taking six months off to transition a little more. I've wanted to avoid the whole in-betweenness because sport is not set up for anyone who is in-between in any way."

After surgery, Louis will be unable to exercise for at least six weeks. He doesn't know how long he will be unable to play futsal, but he assumes as a goalkeeper it will be longer than an outfield player. In keeping, there's a lot of getting hit in the chest.

Louis is daydreaming about what playing sport might feel like after surgery. He can't wait to find out.

Power

There is an active movement to exclude trans girls from sports, community and opportunity. Articles in the press "ask" if cis girls will be safe if trans girls compete in girls' sport, failing to care about the safety of trans girls and trans women. To put the inclusion of TGD people in sport up for "debate" in this way can do real damage.

"It affects me," Louis says. "I'm like: they're talking about us again, the people who have no idea of what we go through or any of the science, even though they think they do. Do I want to read the comments on this, or do I want to have a good day?"

American former college basketballer Kye Allums has said, "Forty-one percent of people in the trans community have attempted suicide—I was one of them." Kye says later, "That was all because of someone who didn't take the time to listen to what I said—who didn't care, who didn't value me as a person and who just saw me as, 'Oh, you're just this story.'"

"Muscles aren't gendered," writes Siufung Law, a genderfluid athlete from Hong Kong. "My body is a genderless body. Masculinity is different to muscularity: having muscles doesn't make you masculine."

Intersex athletes, such as South African runner Caster Semenya, a cisgender woman who has naturally occurring higher testosterone levels, have been vilified in the media and told by their sport their bodies are wrong. Their bodies are not wrong. When Caster won her first world championship in 2009 at the age of eighteen, the headlines were about her body—"manly," "narrow hips"—rather than her achievement. *Time* magazine ran the headline "Could This Women's World Champ Be a Man?" on an article written by William Lee Adams. The treatment of intersex female athletes in the sports world shows how female athletes are put up to a racist, outdated and colonial judgement of what a woman should be.

Stopping sport and starting again

ZS: I stopped playing sport when I was fifteen. Stopped altogether. I had an injury while playing rugby, a slipped disc in my spine. My parents told me to stop playing at around the same time. Up until then I had been playing for my state in badminton and I had to stop. There was no real conversation about needing to heal; I just didn't play again. I think it was my parents slowly maneuvering me out of sports.

I definitely didn't miss sport at the time. I was quite busy being a teenager and having a lot of queer feelings. Around that time, I had my first relationship and it was all-consuming. Now though, I wish I had had the support to stay physical.

AA: I stopped sport when I left my hometown and I moved to the city. I didn't have any money or any social connections in the suburb I moved to. My mental health was terrible and I took up drinking and partying—that was also quite fun. Being physical wasn't a priority. I didn't come back to regular exercise until 2015.

That's the year me and Zaky met at a party. I was quite deep in addiction—I had been for about five to seven years. That night was one of the last nights I got drunk. I wish I could remember what we talked about.

I got into boxing in 2015 with a good friend. The boxing gym was a fairly positive social environment for me for a time. There was a lot of people of color there. There were a lot of strangers who had different lives to me. Heterosexual people in their thirties who had careers—who I never would usually come into contact with or have a conversation with. We would pair up and be given exercises to do. It was a way for me to safely come into contact with parts of the world and parts of the community that I had no confidence talking to. I was like, these people are so different to me, we probably don't agree on anything, though we would spend quite a lot of time suffering. I like combat as a sport. The idea of hurting each other but it's okay. You get punched in the face; it's fine. Nobody shames you for that. It happens to all of us. It's sort of like a safe place to be a little bit of a failure.

I took up powerlifting in late 2015. Both powerlifting and boxing gave me something to do while I was trying to quit drugs and alcohol. After a while, doing both at once became too demanding. I had to choose whether I liked being punched in the face more or lifting weights more and I chose powerlifting.

Powerlifting has become the most important thing for my overall health. It's saved my life. It helps me to stay focused. It's helped me build skills that I've been able to transfer into my work life and social life and it's given me a lot of tools for sobriety as well.

My first competition was in 2017. I spent some time in Vancouver. I didn't go to Canada to train, but I got to experience a more developed powerlifting culture in North America because they have a lot more of a community and it is a bigger sport. I competed again in 2018 and 2019.

During the lockdown, competitions weren't happening. I'm about to compete again so it's been eighteen months. Under lockdown, working out became a bit of a lifesaver. I clung to it to give me some routine and make me feel like life continues. But it was a bit hard because my training space moved from the gym to my home. The gym is this outside space that I feel like I've studied. Instead of the journey from my house to the gym letting me build a mental space in which to train, now that space is literally ten meters away; just open a door in the house and you're there. Having to build that space mentally for myself here is a different process. That affected my training a bit but once I got used to it, the transition back to the gym was hard again.

There's been a lot of self-esteem talk for me recently. I've been working through a lot of inadequacy, self-doubt, vulnerability and fear. Also, every time I approach a competition, in the lead-up, there's a point, three or four weeks out, where I consider quitting the sport and doing something else.

That point was last week. Last week I felt weak and bored and I wanted to try something else. I felt intimidated every time I went to the gym. This week feels a little bit better.

Arlie lifts

Arlie lifts in his garage in Footscray. He wears a loose muscle tee and short shorts and Cons. Tattoos adorn his muscled calves and his left shoulder. His long, curly hair and moustache give me 1970s vibes. He has that cheeky Kombumerri twinkle in his eye and a wry smile.

Arlie lifts in his garage on a schedule: four days on, three days off. The weights are set against the brick wall. On his off days he jogs along the Maribyrnong River. Running is a different discipline, another kind of body knowledge, which he's not sure has helped his lifting but which has helped his anxiety.

Arlie lifts the bar without weights first to warm up, squatting, pulling and thrusting his hips in a precise motion. He then starts to set up the weights on the bar, beginning with 20 kilograms of the 200-kilogram weights that were a combined birthday present from a group of close friends for his thirtieth birthday.

Arlie wears a weight belt around his waist. He practices taking deep, deliberate breaths before he attempts a heavier weight. He is trying to create a moment for himself, less than one minute of his focus directed towards a singular movement. It's a mental habit honed over a number of years. His aim is to perform carefully and well. In this moment, he wants to be confident and precise, to be in a sweet spot where his arousal level is just right: not too excited, not under-excited.

He sighs and shakes out his arms and legs before approaching the bar again. He claps the bar and wiggles his feet so his heels are facing inwards, almost touching, and his toes are facing out. His feet straighten up and his arms tremble. Larger weights are applied to the bar.

He closes his eyes and breathes in, preparing to deadlift 150 kilograms.

Arlie lifts the weight. Triumphant.

I want to live

In my teenage years, the butch-shaming and gender-policing laced with racism amped up in both my school and sporting environments. This came from adults too; sometimes teachers and parents were just as bad. Between the ages of twelve and seventeen it was relentless and I disassociated to get through it. They told me I was different, but at the time I did not have the words to explain myself, and I shouldn't have had to.

I have never felt like a girl or a woman. I feel masculine in some ways and feminine in others, as if there are two spirits living within me, harmoniously. As a person who is often paralyzed by the fear of disappointing others and making mistakes, at some point in my life

I told myself: it is very difficult, EvN, to be anonymous, and you're going to have to push through your fear. It is going to be difficult for you to do nothing.

When I came out as trans non-binary in my late twenties, I did so slowly and as if I was dipping a toe into hot water. I knew many of my family and friends had fixed ideas about my identity and I fluctuated between being patient and firm with them. I remember saying to Zaky in 2018, "People always get my pronouns wrong, so I don't care what pronouns people call me. It's not life or death."

Reflecting on this now, I realize I was in a place from which I couldn't see a way forward. I wasn't being honest with myself or with Zaky. I was not respecting myself. In the years since then, the more I listen to myself, the more being misgendered begins to gnaw at me.

Poet essa may ranapiri writes, "when you transition your memories become liquid." Recently I've been feeling increasingly uncomfortable in my sport, as if the gendered systems and articulations and exclusions can no longer be ignored. Negative experiences, such as transphobic abuse from spectators and microaggressions from coaches and teammates as well as the collisions between the personal and the political, give me a soul ache. I hear whispers in the dark on a quiet night. I am asking myself, *do I belong here?* For now, my desire to play has waned and been replaced with the desire to live.

Zaky walks

Zaky walks twice a day, before and after work. He walks five kilometers in the morning and five kilometers in the afternoon, sometimes more. He walks his rescue dog, Kichu, along the Merri Creek Trail, which is near his and his wife Caroline's house in Fawkner. Kichu, a fluffy, white Japanese spitz with heaps of personality, has helped Zaky solidify this routine. He has trouble prioritizing his own wellness, but Kichu makes it easy.

He often walks Kichu through Bababi Djinanang, the Wurundjeri name for "mother's foot," which forms part of a system of native grasslands along the Merri Creek named using Wurundjeri words for parts of the mother's body. The grass is very green and lush and the creek is bubbling from recent rain.

Today, Zaky is in the mood to climb a tree. Caroline holds Kichu's leash; Zaky scales the tree, gets really high. As a kid Zaky loved long jump; it made him feel like he was flying. Growing older, he remembers how agile he used to be. When he was younger, he would jump off and do a flip on the way down. Now he thinks he might die if he tried this. The fear. The uncertainty. He doesn't know how his body would respond.

Zaky slowly makes his way back down to earth.

In the last few years, no sport or fitness regimen has stuck with him. There's always been something. Work. Community. Family. There's the pain in his back. He has to be careful with it. There's the capitalism of fitness and sport that has often put him off. But walking feels like something that can't be commodified.

Zaky walks.

Walking makes Zaky feel like he is in control of his life again.

Futures

In 2019, Sport Australia partnered with the Australian Human Rights Commission to develop guidelines for the inclusion of TGD people in community sport across Australia. Sex Discrimination Commissioner Kate Jenkins said at the launch,

> Unfortunately transgender and gender-diverse people are sometimes excluded from sport or experience discrimination and sexual harassment when they do participate. While some reported positive experiences of inclusion,

others described how they had been excluded from the sports they loved because of their sex or gender identity.

These guidelines aim to help organizations create and promote an inclusive environment for TGD people. In theory, trans people's right to participate in sport is protected by human rights laws and anti-discrimination laws. Yet they are still excluded. Barriers still remain.

The pressing need for change, for things to get better, often leads to utopian-imagining discussions within marginalized communities. The German Marxist philosopher Ernst Bloch says the essential function of utopia is to critique what is present. And so I ask Louis, Arlie and Zaky to share their visions for a queer and trans sports utopia.

LB: It would just be where trans people are free to play as the gender that they want to. I don't know whether that means we abolish the gender segregation of sports. That in itself involves lifting women's sport, but this is, of course, a utopia. It would just be that women are encouraged to play sport at an early age in the same way men are. And there's absolutely no difference; the pay is the same.

People think women need protection from men; they are in their own category because they couldn't possibly compete with men. But in my experience they absolutely can. People only ever talk about the absolute top elite level, Olympic-and World Cup-level.

Assuming the barriers for women in sport were knocked down and they could compete on an equal level with men, I don't know if you'd have to have a testosterone-level category almost in the same way they have weight categories in boxing. Exercise is so much easier since I've taken testosterone: I recover faster, I see results quicker, I can go for longer.

In this utopia, it will be fine to be gay. In women's sport, there are a lot of gay players. It's much more normalized—but it's still not great: there's still homophobia. In men's sport there's absolutely nothing. I would love to see a world where you could have two boyfriends on the same team in the AFL—or on a World Cup team, maybe.

In this utopia I would have been able to see myself represented in the AFL. There would have been guys like me. Trans guys and queer guys like me. I wouldn't have had to live the first twenty-five years of my life with something presented to me as life and nothing outside of that: I would have seen myself. By seeing myself, I would have realized I was trans and queer much earlier and it would have been a normal thing.

Some people say, how can you be into sports as a leftist? Because it's so hyper-competitive, hyper-masculine, so brutal, all of those things. But I think that ignores what sport can be—and that's community. What I really love about sport is the story—I get that from my dad being a sports journo.

I don't feel like I could ever turn my back on sport, no matter what. Even if sport turns its back on me.

AA: For me, the gym is full of people running towards their own utopias. There's this famous statistic that people who go to the gym as a New Year's resolution tend to quit by Valentine's Day. They are so invested in a future body that they have in mind. But being so invested in the future means expecting and waiting and building towards something to such an extent that you miss what's going on in the present and prevent yourself from existing in that moment. As a trans person, you watch this happen around you, month after month, year after year at the gym; you see cis people in that kind of utopian pursuit all the time.

My former coach, Mary Gregory, is a trans competitor in masters powerlifting. She was allowed to compete in the women's division until she broke records. There are some interesting proposals being put forward by organizations like the International Association of Trans Bodybuilders and Powerlifters in the United States where they are suggesting that federations have an MX category and everything will be okay. They are trying to re-envision the gender categories in the sport and it's just rehashing the same things over and over again. Every time you create a gendered structure around the sport, it's going to affect the way that people see themselves and engage in the sport. They are trying to design a perfect system that works for everyone—that doesn't work because the whole idea of sports being fair in the first place isn't real. Most of the time trans people just want to get out there and exist in a sport and enjoy training. If you can't pause and exist in that moment, there's no point.

There's something really interesting happening in Melbourne now. There's a trans man, Sam, who's the second trans man to compete in powerlifting in Victoria; I am the first. He's a personal trainer. He's lovely. He's building his own gym for trans and gender-nonconforming people.

ZS: I would like to play sports with some people who are trans and some people who are not trans. I enjoy the company of people who are not trans. Those people are my community. I deserve to have a community that is not separate: spaces that are niche give me creepy vibes. The tools being used to create these separatist spaces are also the tools that have been used to oppress us. I have never felt more dysphoric than when I produced one of the shows with Myriad, our trans art collective, and someone asked, "Are you FtM or MtF [female-to-male or male-to-female]?" And that was at a trans space.

[EvN: This intrusive question is an example of a microaggression. Often people don't know what microaggressions are and commit them unintentionally—even "woke folk," as Zaky illustrates here.]

My utopia isn't a trans utopia. My utopia is a utopia where everyone gets to find pleasure and joy in moving their body, be aggressive and be strong and be together in that space despite their gender. Which in itself is a trans utopia. It's my utopia and I happen to be trans. This is what I hope for the future.

I've been thinking, if I have children, what would their lives be like when they are my age? What do I want to do in my community to ensure they have that? A part of me feels like if they have a safe world, where we are not so hot that we are burning, they can choose what they want for the future for themselves.

Louis, Arlie and Zaky's utopian visions make me hyper-aware of my own hope for the next generation of LGBTIQSB+ children who want to play sport. For these kids to grow up with "no limits" on their lives, in Jaiyah Saelua's words. For there to be no fear for these kids. Maybe this could even inspire me to connect with football again.

The young trans girl I mentioned who was told she couldn't run for her school at representative level? Her parents did get a response from the relevant sporting organization, backtracking on the suggestion she could run but not have her place recorded. She kept her spot in the race and she competed with the other girls. She ran her heart out. She ran her race in the category of the gender she identifies with.

As it should be.

I can't help but pause here with emotion, a whole lot of emotion. And as I finish writing this, I hear about the first out trans and non-binary athletes to compete at the Olympic Games—in Tokyo, 2021. This feels like wonderful news, but there should be nothing new about it. My utopia looks for a day when TGD people's inclusion in sport is not news and not up for debate, when no one has to fight to have a space and when we move on from reports of inclusion to reports of playing.

Playing—and living: I insist on doing both.

Challenging the Binary

The gender binary as an organizing principle for the institution of sport once excluded female athletes. Sport was often used to demonstrate male supremacy through physiological differences. As Bronwyn Adcock writes, "when sport arrived as an organized social phenomenon with the Industrial Revolution, women's bodies were judged as too unsuitable and inferior to take part."

When women began to be "allowed" to take part in sport, only certain sports were deemed suitable—for example, tennis, golf and croquet, though with different rules than for men. Women-only sports clubs were first created during the 1900s in Australia, with the establishment of the first bowls and rowing associations. Paternalistic medical authorities continued to be against women playing some sports, however, suggesting it would cause infertility.

Lines were drawn and enforced. Sometimes these were written, sometimes implied. For example, it was illegal for women to play football in Brazil from 1941 to 1979. In America in 1950, twelve-year-old Kathryn Johnston became the first girl to play Little League Baseball, as no one had thought to make an explicit rule to exclude girls or women. This was quickly redressed; a ban was in force until 1974.

Fiona Crawford and Lee McGowan write about "a tacit fear that the women's game would detract attention and income from the men's game" as a key obstacle to women's football in Australia. Football gained some traction in Australia after an initial match played in 1921 at the Gabba in Brisbane attracted 10,000 people. Momentum stalled altogether, however, following a ban on women's football by the English Football Association, where the women's game was also thriving, with the association committee ruling that "the game of football is quite unsuitable for females and ought not to be encouraged." As part of this ruling, clubs were asked to refuse the use of their grounds for women's matches. This stopped progression of the sport in Australia for about fifty years, until the 1970s, when local leagues were created in most states and the national league was formed.

Though women were allowed to play a larger selection of sport from the 1970s, the desired female athlete was white, straight and young, and the way she played sport had to be seen as desirable to the male gaze.

In 2022, an outdated AFL rule prohibiting girls over fourteen from mixed-gender competition came to light when a fourteen-year-old, Abby Weir, wanted to continue playing with her teammates at St Arnaud in regional Victoria. The club wanted her to continue playing, but the AFL rule prohibited her from doing so and she was left on the sidelines, running drinks for her old team. Abby applied to the AFL and was granted an exception, probably the first of its kind, after they considered the shortage of players in community sport and the travel required to play in a female-only competition.

Non-binary athletes further challenge the rigid concerns of gender in organized sport but in an exciting way. Playing sport while openly identifying as non-binary broadens the spectrum of how people can be when they play. It exposes the gender hypocrisies in forced gendered uniforms, gendered facilities and pay gaps. It demonstrates that we don't have to play "like" girls or boys, we can just play as ourselves. When I was growing up, I used to play in both boys' and girls' competitions. I found myself moving and shifting. This was a natural fielding position for me.

When non-binary people come out in sport and are like, "we are here," it ruptures the binaries that organized sport hinges on. It makes us all more human. When we remove gender as a condition of play, we become freer. Non-binary people in sport also break down barriers that are harmful for all of us. For some of us, mainstream gyms and sports settings are places of public hangings, while others feel comfortable in those spaces. Regardless, having non-binary participants in these mainstream spaces alongside a commitment by the organization, team or gym encourages inclusivity and acceptance.

Openly non-binary professional athletes include footballer Quinn, who won a gold medal with Canada at the 2020 Tokyo Olympics. A few months before the tournament, Quinn came out as non-binary and transgender, and adopted their prior surname as a mononym. They continued playing in women's competitions based on their sex assigned at birth. When the media used their birth name when they came out, they said on their Twitter account, "it's crucial to write about trans people using their name and pronouns." Their Olympic win marks the first-ever medal for an out transgender and non-binary person.

In Australia, Gold Coast Sun Tori Groves-Little and marquee Carlton player Darcy Vescio both came out as non-binary athletes in the AFLW in 2021. Darcy had a history of activism on trans issues, included wearing the transgender colors on their mouthguard at an AFLW pride game and ensuring they were also included in the design of the guernseys for AFLW pride games. Growing up, they had stopped playing competitive football at the age of fourteen, when they were no longer allowed to play with the boys' team, due to the rule mentioned earlier. Darcy didn't pick up the sport again until they moved to Melbourne from Wangaratta at the age of eighteen and joined the Darebin Falcons in the Victorian Women's Football League.

When Darcy came out as non-binary on social media, they included this message: "There's a lack of understanding, but there is a willingness to understand that, just as strongly as you feel like you are a man or a woman, that's how strongly I feel I am neither of those things." Non-binary football broadcaster Brihony Dawson was there to commentate on the moment being "absolutely huge."

Darcy was heavily involved in negotiations for a new collective bargaining agreement in 2020 that argued for fairer gender pay distribution and redistribution of wealth. They were part of a minority of AFLW players who held out for a better deal. This was improved even more in August 2022, when the AFL Players' Association agreed to a significant boost in salary. The minimum salary increased 94 percent, from $20,239 in 2021 to $39,184. The best-paid players—two per club—will receive $71,935, up from $37,155.

On coming out, both Darcy and Tori were received positively by teammates, who adopted gender-neutral language to make everyone feel included, going from "girls" to alternatives such as "athletes," "footballers," "everyone" and "folks."

Tori said, "In a way, I hate it, because it's like, 'Oh, we can't say this because of Tori, we can't do that because of Tori' … but I'm glad because I feel like that's the way society should be. We shouldn't have to use those gendered pronouns to single people out."

Tori said although they do not feel uncomfortable competing in a women's competition as a non-binary person, they understand others might feel differently. "I think the W in AFLW is something to feel proud about. [Australian rules football] is something that, obviously, women have fought very hard to be a part of, to play a male-dominated sport. So for me, it's actually something that I'm really proud of … The W means everything to me."

Tori brings up an important point. The W or M in the name of the league is individual to the person and can be seen as inclusive to those who don't identify as either. Through this lens, W or M does not undermine trans identity nor conform to the heteronormative colonial gender binary.

Other out non-binary elite athletes include: Timothy LeDuc, figure skating, who breaks the cisheteronormative mold of pairs skating; Layshia Clarendon, basketball; Laura Goodkind, Paralympic rowing; Robyn Lambird, wheelchair racing; Maria "Maz" Strong, Paralympic seated shot-put; and Alana Smith, skateboarding.

When non-binary sports writer Frankie de la Cretaz interviewed Layshia Clarendon and other non-binary athletes, they prefaced the interview, "It's generally considered bad form to focus on the particulars of trans people's bodies, but as a professional athlete, the decisions Clarendon—or any trans athlete—makes about their body are incredibly consequential," before including the list of questions Clarendon considered before they decided to take steps to have gender-affirming surgery and come out as non-binary:

> What will the recovery look like and how will it impact my 2021 season? The league and my team have a right to know a lot about my body because it affects my play, but is there anything personal that the league can't ask me about? I know I am going to publicly talk about my top surgery, but what if another player has top or bottom surgery and doesn't want to share that with their team or the public? If the league doesn't support me, can I be fired?

Clarendon's list is highly illuminating for those who have never thought about the complicated considerations a non-binary athlete, especially one who is thinking about masculinizing or feminizing surgery, must take into account.

When an athlete introduces themselves as non-binary there needs to be coordination between player, club, teammates and the league. Normalizing pronoun use for each player helps. Think ahead to all the scenarios where a player might be misgendered—social media, website, commentary, uniforms, match day, functions and presentations—and ensure commentators, coaches, teammates and officials are prepared and educated. There is ignorance. People have been honest and told me I'm the first non-binary person they've met. Peers can point out when people use gendered language on autopilot. As the numbers grow of those willing to let their teammates, fellow athletes, club and/or sporting body know they are gender diverse, a well-supported environment can make all the difference.

*

It's the A-League's inaugural pride fixture in 2022, the players are wearing rainbow numbers and socks, and Coopers Stadium on Kaurna land is awash with rainbow flags. I have mixed feelings. On one hand I am excited about the representation, which is long overdue, but I'm also stressed. Are pride rounds a form of rainbow washing? my friend asks. It's complicated, I answer.

At the same time, a harmful bill is being considered in parliament to exclude transgender people from single-sex sports and to discriminate, for the first time, against children under twelve. It is hard to hold these two things together. The celebration and the discrimination. When I see our current prime minister is supporting the bill, I don't want to read the article. I feel hopeless. The rights of LGBTIQSB+ students and teachers are being discussed in the name of so-called religious freedom, with detrimental effects on people's health and self-esteem. The Liberals' cynical election campaign attacking the rights of transgender people brings back memories of hurtful comments I've heard on the football field—the intrusive questioning of my gender when I reached a certain age and it was no longer cute to have me play in both groups. Gender-diverse young people I know are anxious and stressed.

In Josh Cavallo's promotional video for the pride games he says, "whether you're a boy or a girl, no matter what the color of your skin, everyone deserves to play football." He doesn't explicitly mention trans people or those who do not fit within a gender binary. Maybe I shouldn't be surprised. He's doing his best, I guess. He's trying to stay afloat, I can imagine, with all the homophobic abuse he's received since becoming the first cis male player to come out as gay while in the first division of a professional football league. There was an overwhelming amount of support for him from the football community. But we need intersectionality. We can't leave transgender, gender-diverse and gender-questioning children and adults out of pride rounds or forget that pride is rooted in protest. Josh's lack of inclusion for gender-diverse athletes may have been unintentional, but it still erases and excludes those who do not fit within the gender binary.

As I watch the rainbow flags being collected from the stands, I remember Amart All Sports giving away rainbow shoelaces about ten years ago. I was really excited and went out and ordered them. At the time, they represented for me my sport supporting LGBTIQSB+ people. I still have them. They are sitting in a pair of Tims I don't wear anymore and need to dust down and take to SWOP. Queer promotion that upholds the rigid gender binary and fails to recognize gender diversity can feel stiff and corporate.

Under a toxic gaze in the highly binary sports world, transwomen are having their right to compete debated while non-binary athletes are rarely discussed. Women's and men's competitions aren't designed for non-binary people, and for some, playing in gendered competitions rubs uncomfortably against their non-binary gender. They have to experience the situational misgendering that comes with the territory of playing in a men's or women's league. A non-binary athlete can be looked at as "woman-lite" or "man-lite" (terms meaning that they are like a lighter-weight category of a binary gender, though they don't identify with a binary gender) if they choose to compete in a gendered competition.

Similar feelings of dysphoria occurred when I was asked to write a poem commemorating a hundred years of women's football in Australia in 2021, on the anniversary of the 1921 match. I spoke to people beforehand and started to collect some ideas. In some ways I felt very proud to be asked; it was wonderful to be recognized as a football poet and a former player. In other ways I felt inadequate. I was nervous about standing up in front of the crowd, all impressive: players and coaches that had contributed to this hundred-year history. I knew they would all be encouraging, but this kind of performance made me feel shy. The commemorative match at the Gabba crept closer.

Are non-binary people seen as cis by association for playing in gendered competitions?

"Trans* people of a certain age can typically recall the moment they first saw an ambiguously gendered person," Jack Halberstam writes, using the asterisked umbrella term for people who aren't at the cis ends of the gender identity spectrum. Halberstam recalls his gaze on his gym teacher, describing her as "impressively muscular." My first memories of bodies that garnered second looks, weaving the artistry of femininity and masculinity and all in between in authentic and variable ways, also occurred in the sports setting, where these people shone translucent in the high sun, their bodysongs gnawing away at my own feelings. It felt like they were coded for no one but me.

I sat at the Gabba a few weeks before the date. Noisy, as traffic sped past, but birds came to sit beside me. Central to my feelings was the knowledge that this was a place from which mob had been driven off and excluded. I jotted down my thoughts, trying to come closer to a singular "we." I respected the women I was honoring and understood that they were part of the history that had led to me playing sport in an organized league. It was an important reflection too, though, that these women in the starting eleven had benefitted from a settler colony and White Australia that oppressed my people, and that we have been playing on Country for a lot longer.

When the day came, Dad was in hospital receiving chemo. I got to the ground and watched a re-enactment of the 1921 match, players from a local youth representative side taking up the New South Wales and Queensland colors, wearing the old-fashioned outfits down to the hats. We then moved inside to the function room. I was getting updates about Dad on my phone. When my former coach and the event MC, Rae, warmly introduced me to the crowd of familiar and unfamiliar faces, I felt my knees begin to shake. I stood tall and grounded myself through visualizing the earth underneath me. My voice faltered but got louder at the end of the poem. As soon as I had finished reading, I felt relief. It was done. I just wished Dad could have been there.

When I think of duality, I think of vigoro, a sport I've never played but always wanted to try. John George Grant invented vigoro (the name comes from the word "vigorous") in the year 1901 as a mix of tennis and cricket. Cricket was popular with men at the time and Grant wanted to capitalize on this to "masculinize" tennis. In the original version, tennis racquets were used, and the pitch was slightly shorter than a cricket pitch.

Interest in vigoro—or cricko, as it is also called—in England died down, but it became popular in Australia during World War I. Women participated in the sport in much larger numbers than men, and it was mandated in school in three states: Queensland, New South Wales and Tasmania. Vigoro is sometimes seen as synonymous with "women's cricket." Many First Nations women played. Oodgeroo Noonuccal founded a women's team, called the Brisbane All-Blacks, and represented Queensland twice.

Queensland is one of the only places in the world where it is still played. In its current form, it is more like T20 cricket or baseball. It's fascinating for me that this game that was created to "masculinize" tennis became a popular sport for women.

Perhaps I should return here, the bush near my home, a place where I feel validated, with the sun on my face, soft grass under my feet, and breathe deeply, from my belly. I remind myself, we are not shifting the ground by being who we are. This ground has already been grooved into; we have always been here. There are others that are moving towards us to understand our truth.

My Existence

*

I don't often tell you this, but I don't think shapeshifting is a private act. I think they teach us to hide our gifts.

Soon the curtain will fall from the face. Soon the rush will fall. Here, a sentence, a midden, a timeline, an existence. To connect me to those who caught waves.

Will I be haunted by everything I can't lift?

I don't know what to say until I'm saying it. I don't know what to do until I'm doing it. Words can be lungs. I love how alive I can feel when I'm writing. Dissociating is a strength in a writer because the imagined life and the real life are the same.

I exhaust myself through self-reflection. I constantly speculate on how I affect other people. Relationships are circular. I am constantly trying to do the work on myself to find the most harm-reductive way of engaging with people. I go overboard. Sometimes it means I am scared of making mistakes, to the point where I don't engage with people at all. Sometimes it means I can only engage with a few people at a time.

*

When I go to dress myself without much thought I can accidentally end up looking like the trans flag. Besides black, the two colors that I have a lot of in my wardrobe are blue and pink. I came to these colors separately. The blue as a watery color and pink as rock and roll. I have my clothes color-coded on a shelf; if I choose to grab one item from each pile, I end up looking like the flag.

Of course, I haven't mentioned white, the third color of the flag. It was designed by American trans woman Monica Helms in 1999, who describes the meaning as follows: "The stripes at the top and bottom are light blue, the traditional color for baby boys. The stripes next to them are pink, the traditional color for baby girls. The stripe in the middle is white, for those who are transitioning or consider themselves having a neutral or undefined gender."

Choosing the color white as neutral is problematic and why I feel uncomfortable wearing the full three colors of the flag. White is not my neutral. To quote the spoken word poet Laniyuk in her poem "March with Pride," "There's a reason why black and brown had to be added to the flag."

My garment, shield of choice, is the T-shirt. The fit becomes an obsession. It becomes my uniform. It's a work in progress. Will this one or that one accentuate my shoulders more?

I've been reading essa may ranapiri, a Ngāti Raukawa poet. "The nonbinary individual has full say over what they are," essa writes in *ransack* (2019). "The nonbinary individual need not exist within an in-between space."

*

Throughout my life, when I have been introduced as Ellen, I have had smug colleagues (cis, male) say, "Oh, Ellen, like Ellen DeGeneres. So are all lesbians called Ellen?" This has happened at least a dozen times. It is a snide comment meant to undermine me. As Ellen feels less and less like my name and more and more like someone else's, I unshackle myself from their attempt at intimidation.

EvN, in correspondence. El, in Brisbane. Evan, in Sydney. That's what my trans dude friends call me. The decision is made against a barrage of traffic outside the Seymour Centre. It was a name I used when I was eleven. Little Evan smiles back in recognition.

*

When a celebrity we grew up watching in movies comes out as trans, two of my best friends text me of the news. Cori writes, "Lemme tell u the HAPPINESS i felt reading their post." Rai writes, "brilliant news" with two purple hearts and the trans flag. It feels like everyone on the bus is talking about the announcement.

While I'm still on the bus, a blackfella writer calls out of the blue to tell me that she is considering removing me from her PhD cos I don't identify as a woman, is that right? (she asks)

Yes (I say) and then bring the question back to her. Are you including gender-diverse writers in your study?

We have a good chat after that. She has been reading the work of Wiradjuri person Dr Sandy O'sullivan on gender and the colonial project. Sandy asks who decides gender and exposes colonial bias in their article "The Colonial Project of Gender (and Everything Else)." Challenging gender binaries is anti-colonial, they say.

I'm sorry I misgendered you in my whole PhD, my friend says.

It's okay. It happens.

Apologies are an acknowledgement of harm and, in the best case, a promise. Her direct apology made the experience feel less surreal; I use surreal to describe dissociation. Like I use homesickness as a euphemism for dysphoria. Whether we're trans and/or non-binary or cis, we remember when we are misgendered as it interrupts us. They are splinters, but splinters can feel like stabs.

*

I tell people on the phone, as if the distance is necessary. I'm telling my cousin on the phone: I am genderfluid because my spirit flows like water. I am genderqueer because when I am my best self I don't care about making other people uncomfortable. Yet terms in English will never define me.

"Have you heard about Two-Spirit folks?" they ask.

"Yeah, I have," I say. "And TBH when I first heard about them I thought, 'This sounds like me.' But it has a very specific cultural, historical and political context in Turtle Island. Two-Spirit comes from 'Niizh Manidoog' in Anishinaabemowin (the Ojibwe language). The term 'Two-Spirit' [2S] is a pan-Native American term that came from a Native lesbian and gay international gathering in Winnipeg in 1990. It can't be applied here. Even though there is a natural exchange of ideas that happens in global Indigenous spaces, we would be pissed if they used our language and identities without permission or context."

Imported imposed colonial gender is a global issue, though our story is local. My cousin Jenny says it's important to go on the journey to find our own words, guided by the ancestors. We are creatives, we can come up with our own language. Just have a look at our community and you'll see we are a diverse mix of identity and sexual expression.

We can look at what we are to evidence what we were. Especially what we are together. It can feel like a patchwork journey for some, recovering what can be found, and what you feel. What other people share with you. Gender variance is not always marked in the way White people know. I have a multi-gendered identity to the people I'm in kinship with. I perform different roles when I'm with others.

"Indigenous uniqueness[es] separate to the coloniser were intentionally erased to make us same," Dr Sandy O'sullivan says.

We are not living in a post-colonial nation, and as such, the colonial gender complex has a strong influence on every aspect of our world: gender is medicalized, socialized, law-enforced, schooled and institutionalized. Indigenous gender identities can be influenced by imposed colonial gender and still be Indigenous.

*

My friend said they can't stand it when some Elders don't respect people's pronouns and the way they identify. I said, look, hopefully there'll be a shift. Things will get easier. Jenny reminds me that it wasn't too long ago we all had to hide. We struggle with the feeling of things not getting better quickly enough, but there's been so much progress.

Some community reckon all English pronouns are rude. It's hard to explain. Our old people think referring to someone as "they" is as rude as "she" is rude. "She's the cat's mother," Nana used to call out in a dry voice whenever my dad referred to my mum as "she" and not "Mum" or her name. In the words we chose, we were taught to carry respect for our old people. We were reprimanded for using a pronoun to refer to someone instead of a proper name, especially with inadequate reference; taught when we were younger to instead call someone by their name or how they were related to us. I'm not sure how this brushes up against kinship and/or the stuff our Elders had to put up with in the past, how their language and manners had to be in the way of the oppressor.

A Two-Spirit person I get to know through Knowledge of Wounds, a digital gathering, tells me they sometimes accidentally misgender themselves—I relate.

Speaking from my region, almost two hundred years of violent colonization and imported religious influence has had its effects. I remember that existing outside of the gender binary is existing outside the Western gender binary, and every time I fight transmisogyny I am fundamentally fighting anti-First Nations racism.

Often I miss Aunty. If she were still here—in the physical realm—I know she would understand. I wish I had the opportunity to tell her about my gender identity. I know she would accept me with open arms. There is a lot of strength and value in being able to talk to our Elders and expand our understanding, generosity and learnings. After all, there were always people like us. Colonization, Catholicism, misogyny and misunderstanding haven't made it easy for us to be together.

*

Am I more tolerant of FN folk getting it wrong than I am certain White folk? Disrespect goes beyond names and pronouns and you can only remain patient for so long. Who do you move from when they don't respect your identity? If they understand you in other ways? If you feel there is trust between you? It wasn't my friend Lisa's misgendering of me, which felt pointed. That was just the final straw. There was a dissonance before that between us. Whether it was our thoughts on politics or the world at large through the small details of a gathering, her anti-racism was unreliable. Why do our White friends react defensively when we are simply stating our reality? A dangerous White friend sees themselves as Black in their dreams. Their own trauma has rendered them into a feeling of not being able to be moved.

*

I do a reading on Yugambeh Country. Talking about my gender with intention in what feels like the first time on a public stage. The sound technician comes to me in tears afterwards. "My twelve-year-old is non-binary," she says. "And sometimes they get so angry and I don't know why."

When she says this, I recall sharp flashes, stabs. Sometimes the anger in my body has been directed at those I love, which has made me feel guilty. Sometimes it has been against the institutions and the systems that don't respect transness. The current culture does not like the oppressed to express anger, and sometimes that anger turns inward, for not standing up for the inner self. Anger can be useful in informing us what it is we need and what makes us feel unsafe.

Telling my parents, telling Laila and other friends, is not a simple semantic change: it is an experiencing of learning and making mistakes. For me, as well, there are things I learn. Patience. How to deal with the involuntary anger that flares up sometimes when someone misgenders me. I also start to experience a type of gratitude, maybe contentment, if this is a thing I can allow myself to feel. See, for me, the opposite of dysphoria is not euphoria; that's a privileged view. It is a freedom (or ease) that is everyday, not extraordinary. A relief, almost amusement—a letting go of the pressure valve I feel when my mum effortlessly switches her language.

I feel anger most keenly when young people—children—are in trouble. That's when I have to step up and be of use. Sometimes we are more protective of others than we are of ourselves.

Be glad you are sensitive to others, Laila tells me. It's your super-power. Not everyone has that. Those of us who genderflow, gender-queer, genderbend and genderdream, when we fight for others, we fight for ourselves. Tapping into sensitivity and acknowledging it as a gift not a burden is relatable to young people because they know there is not enough sensitivity in the world.

*

To exist: to have reality, to have being. To live, especially under adverse circumstances. People are starting to get it, family members, friends and colleagues are being more aware of the language they use for me. Though there is something about people not getting non-binary that feels like non-existence. To exist in the eyes of others, the first step is having a name (non-binary, they/them), but exis-tence is more than a noun, an adjective and pronouns. To exist is to be understood, and right now most people around me are still at the point of naming and haven't quite reached understanding, and maybe that's why sometimes I feel that I don't exist, because my existence is not understood (it is only just being acknowledged). To feel: you don't understand me, is crushing. Yet my urging. Don't turn away from me. See me for who I am. See me for how I exist.

GYM

I hadn't seen my shoulders and legs for weeks and actually they were okay. My pandemic body was wet newspaper. My pandemic body forwent the closing times. My pandemic body was unwritten. My pandemic body was its own shape. I learned to carry weights without fingers. Each time the gym shut down I took my problems elsewhere. When the rules reset and surfaces were freshly sprayed, I bounced on the treadmill till I reached the max exertion required to slip off my mask. My heart beat through my lips. Breathed in every variable. The forgotten fitness goals, scribbled-out promises. This was time and it was sensitive. Promise. I would be back again tomorrow in this body.

Invasion Day Spin Class

Australia does not exist
just a spray-painted picture
to try to paint a new painting
to evade the true identity of this land

DRMNGNOW

The days leading up to Invasion Day are slow stairs. Days that burn inside and outside. The weather's bright and muggy, but I keep away from the beach. I try to keep away from all the places where they have killed us.

Which is impossible, of course.

I keep my phone off, the television off and social media off.

In lots of ways, this time every year brings up the same sorts of feelings. Like Groundhog Day.

Every year right-wing commentators come out of the woodwork to defend their "sacred day."

Every year white Australians pool party on locations of attempted genocide and BBQ on sacred sites.

Every year astute web editors change the name of Margaret Court Arena to "Evonne Goolagong Cawley Arena" on Google Maps.

This year my gym is advertising an "Australia Day Spin Class," encouraging gym patrons to come dressed "in your best Aussie gear." I see the posters at the front desk and am tempted to pick up a pile and chuck them in the bin.

I'm kind of curious and at the same time already know what people who turn up to that 8:30 am class will be wearing. Is it really practical to wear White Australia flag flip-flops while riding the bikes? I imagine White Australia flag boardshorts would work. What songs will be on the "Killer Aussie Day Playlist"? I'm tempted to show up to the spin class and start filming and say it's for a project on white nationalism.

2021, a few days before the date, right on cue, Scott Morrison states his opinion.

I regret scanning the news for a second, but I'm doing it because of rumors the Tokyo Olympics have been canceled.

I see the headline. PM ScoMo criticizes the decision by some Big Bash League clubs to follow Cricket Australia guidelines and drop references to "Australia Day." The recommendations were made by Cricket Australia's National Aboriginal and Torres Strait Islander Cricket Advisory Committee, whose co-chairs are Mel Jones and Justin Mohamed, to create a safer and more inclusive environment for fans.

This was a "pretty ordinary" decision by the cricket clubs, according to Morrison, who claimed January 26, 1788, "wasn't a particularly flash day for the people on those [first fleet] vessels either."

To this false equivalence Cathy Freeman responds, "You can't compare the experiences of those 12 ships that first arrived to this country to what their arrival meant for all generations of Australia's First Nations people!" And Daniel James tweets, using the *IndigenousX* handle, "I'm not a doctor but sea sickness is not really the same as cultural genocide is it?"

Morrison's comments to "keep politics out of sport" were very reminiscent of Joh Bjelke-Petersen during the Springbok tour in 1971. Morrison, like many politicians before him, has weaponized sport on many occasions. Ian Chesterman, the new chair of the Australian Olympic Committee, told the world that it is important to use sport in Australia to change social "problems" like mental health and social cohesion. He did not mention racism or transphobia. Contradictory, considering ScoMo's comments on sport and politics. So sport is slippery—it can be political or apolitical in national discourse. Sport and religion are politics but people pretend otherwise. Whiteness is neutralized.

Professor Ghassan Hage writes,

> Seeing sport as a total social fact, and sportspeople as more than just sport performers is quite crucial in Australia. For there is still a willingness among the general population to approach sport and sportspeople with a sense of strategic purity. When people say "I am here for the sport" it does not mean that they are naive and can't see the sexism, racism and homophobia that are part of the sport's scene. Rather, they are stating that they strategically choose to bracket the total social fact so that they can enjoy the sport as a sport and nothing else. This strategic purification, while useful to enjoy a game, ends up being one of the key ways in which racism has continued to circulate in sport despite the many attempts at combating it.

Whiteness tries to hide in the dark. There are those I see in the corridors whose dissonance strikes me as frightening but familiar, those who wear red, blue and white with their lycra and sing a familiar false tune of freedom. Why is the ultranationalism so deeply entwined in facets of our society concentrated on the body? Why can't we go for a walk, swim or jog outside on this day? Do any of those things that promote wellness? Why are those spaces more theirs on this day?

I didn't make it to my gym to film the "Invasion Day Spin Class." I can't tell you what was worn or said or sung.

Water did not touch my back on that day.

To add salt to the wound, on Invasion Day, I find out the Coogee Women's Baths, on Gadigal land, where Laila and I went swimming a few times years ago, is explicitly excluding trans women who do not fit their definition of a trans woman.

Laila's reply email to me is riddled with expletives; basically, we're never going back there again.

Am I Public Space?

Am I Public Space? Am I physically and
socially accessible to all? Am I in your view
"fair game"? Am I a space controlled by
public actors, agents and agencies that act on
behalf of the state? Since colonization, are
my property and structures owned, leased
and controlled by government entities? Since
colonization, there are increased modes of
surveillance, as even our memories become
digitized. Take my photo if you want to and
post it without my consent. I didn't realize
I was high-profile until a friend told me.
Am I a space of education and discovery?
I am everywhere. Can't downplay it. I am
public. My movements are easy to trace.
Am I in my most mundane form a way of
getting from A to B? Can my boundaries
and borders be defined and shifted for your
convenience? These digital spaces are open.
No password. Wherever we went, they
followed. Whatever they needed, they got. It
was an easy transaction. The treatment has
become more hostile. I am a recommended
resource until Friday. There is no time left.
Am I part of your editorial approach? Can
my image be used as a placeholder? Am I

durable and sustainable? Am I conceptual or memorable? More than hostile. Who decides when knowledges become public and for whose benefit? Who decides what we don't know about Country? The digital resource is on Indigenous land. You can't feed your present. Have you found the central monument? Am I Public Space? Are we Public Space? If I am fragmentary to you, trace my movements and follow the patterns so you can find me. Now everyone knows my exit strategy. There are no guarantees. Are my family missing? The opposite of hostile is unhostile but more notably: flexible. Return my architecture to a language, a homogenized backdrop. Are we intimately involved? Are you watching me through the seams? Hoard my data as a collage, a common room, the fourth space. Am I by your design at risk of absorption and attack? Am I the violent public spectacle made digital? Am I safe in my own image? Am I Public Space? When did I become democratic space?

Tapestries of Poison

nyannum

Cuz and I are talking about how our
ancestors used poison to score a feed. I
have questions about nyannum. How
do you poison a fish and not be affected
when you eat it? Wouldn't it make you
sick? Stun sometimes, not kill, Cuz says,
and sometimes things are left to rise, to sit
in the water for a while so that toxins are
released. We both getting hungry, sitting
by the water, talking about fish. Nyannum
contains poison that only affects fish.
Stunned in a small rock pool. Perfect for a
grab bag. Nyannum leaves are heart-shaped
and shiny. Fish also stunned in a trap. Our
people are known for making beautiful
traps. Our architecture is destroyed for
other architecture. A light rail takes
precedence over the ancient traps that have
been there for thousands of years. Under
neo-colonial rule, they can't both co-exist.
The ghosts surface in the new city.

Is nature writing a white-settler literature? Perhaps you would think
so if you browsed the genre. It is only recently we've seen First
Nations names come up in discussions of the Australian canonistic

spectrum of nature writing, environmental literature and ecopoetics. A few names, cherrypicked to be on reading lists and citations. This inclusion seems to be a tokenistic gesture rather than a recognition of sovereignty, or a reading and writing ... and storytelling ... and a knowing ... that has always been present.

"Colonial lies have destroyed a very fragile ecosystem," Yamaji writer and art curator Stephen Gilchrist says. Colonial misinformation whitewashes crimes of the past committed by settlers. Literature is a valuable part of any colonial project. Vital to this colonial project is the fiction of terra nullius (land legally deemed to be unoccupied or uninhabited) and the fictions of conquest. The white-suprem acist view that settlers know more about the land and waters than Aboriginal and Torres Strait Islander people and are more deserving to benefit from the wealth of these places still holds weight in settler literature today. What would blackfellas know about nature?

arsenic

In the 1800s, the settlers got their hands
on poisons for agricultural purposes, and
soon used them for killing blackfellas,
lacing flour and damper with arsenic,
strychnine, prussic acid and others. They
sought to control the blacks just like they
did the native plants and animals; they were
encouraged to. I have a persistent memory
of being in a writers' room, on a TV drama
I had no passion for. I was young and naïve,
and this offered "a foot in the door" to one
day writing my own show. The series was
a late 1880s historical drama in the style
of *The Secret River*. The scene we were
workshopping involved a poisoning. The
scene was being pulled apart and tossed

around at a rate I couldn't keep up with
until the other blackfella in the room said,
"Why don't we get the Aboriginal character
to hand out the laced flour to the mob?"
and the room breathed, "That's too much!
That's so wrong ... but so right." And I
was left floating somewhere, I don't know
where. I was discombobulated—my body
had left the building. Blinking away tears, I
thought, what's wrong with you, you're too
soft, you're too sensitive, it's just a TV show,
an unwritten one at that, and these are just
characters. But the betrayal felt personal.
There was pressure to out-shock each other
with our ideas. I went to the bathroom to
hide. I was not going to write brutality.
The violence had already slashed my hands.
I quit before I could contribute to the
treatment of these characters and I ignored
the follow-up phone calls. I was living
between life and death and an old, white
male voice was saying in my head, "You're
not cut out for show business, sweetheart."
I did not want to recreate murder. I had
my people's dignity somewhere, and I did not
want them to die again, not for shock value,
not for edginess or whatever this story
factory was trying to manufacture. The
politics of imagining colonial landscapes
when there were real inheritors of trauma
on Country kept me up at night. Some
people saw this as a stepping stone, for
others it was a quick way to kill a big mob
of people.

Underneath each acknowledgement of Country is the pain that most First Nations people do not have legal recognition of their connection to their land and are denied access to their Country. This is at the heart of the black-green conflict, an unequal power dynamic and a difference in value systems about how to look after Country. We might disagree on what is "sustainable" or "sustainably sourced." We may have different cultural worldviews on ownership and property. We may have lores and laws that govern our relationships to water, earth, sky, plants and animals that have been historically oppressed and repressed. This contributes to the space we call nature writing, ecopoetics and environmental literature. First Nations knowledges of Country don't fit the Western definition of knowledge. First Nations writing, as decolonial writing, does not fit easily into preconceived notions of what nature writing is.

Acceptance into the nature writing club is conditional. These critical literary spaces can, from observation, be quite harmful for First Nations people writing in an anti-colonial way. First Nations writers are constantly being asked to prove their "authenticity" and at the same time their "credentials." Some settler writers go to great lengths to say they are "right" to defend the pillars of the genre and some of its colonial figures, and the First Nations writer is "wrong."

I recently watched the 2022 *Four Corners* special on the brumbies culture wars on Ngarigo and Djiringanj land, which so clearly shows the impact a singular poem, Paterson's "The Man from Snowy River," has on the Australian colonial mythology. The affective elements of the poem have been used by white Australians in the present day to justify horrific acts of violence and intimidation. The so-called "horse activists" see the wild horses not as feral pests that destroy native ecosystems but as heroic symbols of national heritage that must be protected above all else. The brumbies represent an idea that settlers thrive on—they believe they are free to do what they wish and do not have to respect the fact they are on Indigenous land. It's a microcosm of the war against Country going on across this continent. Colonists are not heroic adventurers that settled uninhabited new land; they are plunderers and destroyers and thieves.

Dr Jeanine Leane says, "much if not most of the built-up and over-built landscape that is the crime scene of post-Invasion Australia remains unmarked and/or over-written with visible signs of a 'settled space.'"

When I think of the British colonists I think of their strategies of deceit. The archetypal assassin wears a cloak to hide his identity or remain hidden from view and to obscure the presence or movement of the dagger. The British colonist is this figure, a vial of poison in the waistcoat.

The original deceitful act was to improperly apply the legal concept of terra nullius to Australia, disregarding First Nations presence and belonging to land, and regarding the land as empty for the taking without the need for a treaty. In 1770, Cook landed on Eora land and was greeted by Eora people, whom he and his party shot at, wounding one. After a few days there, he sailed up the coast to Bedhan Lag, one of the southernmost Torres Strait Islands, belonging to the Kaurareg people, which he renamed Possession Island, as this was where he claimed possession of the eastern coast of Australia on behalf of King George III.

The British colonists deliberately did not use any of the three "legal" pathways to possession. They acted as if Australia was uninhabited. And yet they stole and murdered in arrogance. In Cook's words, the First Nations people he dispossessed were "uncivilized inhabitants in a primitive state of society" and Country was "desert and uncultivated." They justified the Invasion by deeming First Nations people non-human beings. Eighteen years later the continent was claimed as a British penal settlement.

Deceit was in the weapons of biological warfare used, as the British soon figured out First Nations people had little immunity to their diseases. Smallpox was strategically passed on through innocent-looking items such as blankets, which were exchanged. Huge numbers of First Nations people lost their lives in the smallpox epidemic. Their deaths were seen by the colonists as deserved, as if it was meant to happen, a cleansing of the new land. Biological warfare was seen as justified.

In the 1820s, colonialists brought in the use of strong poisons to kill dingoes believed to be of threat to their sheep. Poisons were cheap and mandated by the state. The invaders used these poisons to massacre First Nations peoples. Mass poisoning events took place throughout the continent. These are just some examples, and no convictions against the perpetrators have ever been made: 1824, Bathurst, members of the Wiradjuri peoples are poisoned with arsenic-infused damper; 1833, Gangat, British give a large number of First Nations people poisoned flour in three separate incidents, killing them; 1846, Whiteside (sixteen kilometers from my house), at least three First Nations people are killed when arsenic-laced flour is placed out; 1856, Hornet Bank, a number of First Nations people are killed from eating strychnine-laced Christmas puddings they were given, in the lead-up to the Hornet Bank massacre; 1885, Florida cattle station, Yolngu people become ill and die after being given poisoned horse meat; 1895, Fernmount, six First Nations people are poisoned to death after being given aconite to drink by John Kelly. Poisoning was premeditated murder, seen as easier and more effective than killing by gun or other weapons.

bayoo

These seeds are beautiful red, as
captivating as embers from a fire. First
Nations people have complex methods
of detoxification. Soaking; leaching the
toxins out in water. Burning. Burying
and leaving in pits for months. Salting.
Fermenting in a specially made bag. These
methods were used to harvest and process
bayoo by the Noongar people. When the

seeds were eaten by invading Europeans,
they got very sick. De Vlamingh, the
Dutch botanist, and his crew poisoned
themselves eating what is for First Nations
people a rich food source. It is not just
transforming the inedible into the edible,
it's changing the poisonous into the
nourishing. The reward overtakes the risk.

Is it useful to expand the definition of nature writing to include us?
Certainly settler writer Kelsey Allen is right when she says, "There is
no environmental literature without Indigenous authors." Why does
society still see white writers as the experts in nature?

In recent times, other non-white racialized communities have
argued for their writing to be seen as nature writing, to expand the
authorship (and perhaps readership) of nature writing. I think here
of the anthology *Black Nature: Four centuries of African American
nature poetry* (2009) edited by Camille T Dungy, which is the first
and largest collection of African American nature poetry published.
This anthology came out of the anti-Black exclusion of African
Americans from nature poetry. This can't be easily compared to First
Nations literature, as African Americans are not Indigenous to the
land. They are not settlers either. Although they are beneficiaries of
the colonization of Turtle Island, they are descendants of forcibly
displaced Africans. This exclusion Dungy addresses is an anti-Black
exclusion rather than an anti-Indigenous exclusion.

I am not interested in how non-Indigenous Australians write
about connection to landscape and place. This is not my area of
interest. I am, however, interested in supporting and facilitating the
voices of First Nations writers and modes of writing with Country
that do not attempt to strip the voice of the land.

Some First Nations writers do not want to be seen as nature writers—it's an individual preference and they have their own reasons.
Many writers are against classification altogether. We deserve to call

our writing whatever we want to. I can't be so sure that, say, the late great Aunty Oodgeroo Noonuccal, who wrote often of nature, would want to be seen as a nature writer. I would love the opportunity to ask her. They say all roads are old roads created by First Nations people, already worn and measured and steadied. Noonuccal's work embodies how we as First Nations people read and write Country and have been doing so for thousands of years. Reading trees, for example, as Victor Steffensen writes about in *Fire Country* (2020).

First Nations people don't have a separate word for nature in our many languages. I am not aware either of any First Nations words for such things as environment or ecology, because it is all Country, which cannot be compartmentalized or labeled beyond what it is. In Indigenous worldviews, the concept of nature is a foreign one, a separation, separating ourselves from the environment we are related to. We see everything as connected.

I think of Kumeyaay writer Tommy Pico's book-length long-form poem, *Nature Poem*. Through a satirical lens, Tommy writes about his aversion to writing a poem about "nature"—that's because for Tommy, "nature" represents something that conflicts with his Kumeyaay heritage. The concept of nature has been cruel to native people, Tommy's work says. Social justice has been wrongfully related to nature, Tommy argues, while there is no justice for Native people. This is where the environmental white middle-class construction of pristine wilderness is exposed for its violence: see Germaine Greer's *White Beech* (2013).

"I can't write about nature," Ballardong Noongar writer Timmah Ball says, echoing Tommy. It reads as a confession, but it is a purposeful refusal. Timmah writes about the dugai consumption of nature, which sits in discomfort with her people's displacement off Country. She explains how the embedded networks in Country that are vital to our survival are rendered invisible by settlers.

To include First Nations writers in the genre of nature writing, we must ask, who is doing the classification? And for whose benefit? Who is doing the seeing, and the knowing?

bufotoxin

Every night I hear the cane toad in the
backyard. I rush downstairs to check on
Marta. I see her against the wall—her and
the cane toad are staring each other down.
Have I got there in time? Has contact been
made? I open her mouth for signs of poison.
The last few nights I've been distracted
by the tennis and it's wet, very moist. She
does not know—like I do—not to touch
the toad. Its surface. There's a cricket bat
somewhere in the shed—but I can't bring
myself to kill it. Instead I have to listen to
it—a sound that's been here for seventy-
three years. Marta as a border collie is
obsessive, wants to hunt it every night,
wants to find it, no matter where it is. I
take her for supervised bathroom breaks
with the torch shining. How do I teach her
about poison? I think I saw her touch the
toad. I watch her for signs of nausea and
confusion. I see seven toads on my nightly
walks with her—they are 98 percent
more densely populated in north-eastern
Australia than they are in their native South
America. Vague sensory childhood memory
of kicking or imagining I was kicking with
steel-capped boots. It's dark in our yard
and there's no moonlight. The yard backs
onto bush, creek, long grass; it's moist after
a storm. The toad's skin bulges. When
attacked, toads sit back and let it happen;
a learned pattern as they know their weapon
is their skin. It's been written a thousand

times before, but this animal is invasive,
its spotted skin, its breath. It connects to a
colonial history from Jamaica: sugar, slavery
and destruction. It's not the toad's fault it
has been made an invader. It wasn't very
good at catching the native cane beetle—it
couldn't climb or jump in the cane fields.
The sugarcane and then the cane toad
were uninvited and unwelcome guests to
Country. A so-called "biocontrol" attempt.
The toad's sound is familiar, almost as
familiar as rain, as I contemplate the
Indigenous uses for toad poison in South
America, and how crows here have learned
to flip them on their backs to feed from
their underbelly. Maybe there's hope in how
quolls (who became locally extinct after
the introduction of toads) can, through
humans, be taught to avoid the species, I
think, as I open Marta's mouth again.

I am not the first person to try to detach from nature writing's colonial implications. The Chicana writer Priscilla Solis Ybarra calls a grouping of Chincanx decolonial environmental writing "goodlife writing" in her book *Writing the Goodlife: Mexican American literature and the environment* (2016). There is a need to name our writing in ways that fully encapsulate where our writing is coming from.

Perhaps what I'm saying here is that I don't mind being called a nature writer, but it is not the way I identify myself, and I find alternative self-governing, self-sovereign terms more useful. I'm moving towards understanding myself as a nurture writer. It's a term that feels more appropriate for my own writing, and certainly other First Nations writers can use it as well, if they feel it is the right fit for them. It is situated in the active. Nurture is a doing word.

To make this distinction reminds me of Yuin designer Alison Page saying First Nations architecture is a verb, a doing, not a noun. Our cultures are active; our culture activates Country.

Nurture writing is writing that nurtures, that has nurturing in its essence. Nurture writing is a state of mind, an act of sovereignty and a form of resistance.

Is it useful to compile and weave a personal list—of course inexhaustive and still growing—of First Nations-authored writing that could fit into this camp? I do so here:

Oodgeroo Noonuccal "Reed Flute Cave"
Kirli Saunders *Bindi* Victor Steffensen *Fire Country* Warumpi Band "Waru"
Jeanine Leane "Native Grasses" John Mukky Burke "Point of View"

Sandra Phillips "Walking While Aboriginal"

Tony Birch "How Water Works"

Luke Patterson "Authority of Creeks"

Lisa Bellear "Beautiful Yuroke Red River Gum"
Samuel Wagan Watson "Brown Water Looting"
Jenny Fraser (ed.) *Plant Power Sisterhood*
Evelyn Araluen "Snugglepot and Cuddlepie in the Ghost Gum"
Alexis Wright *Tracker*

Jason De Santolo "Sun Showers and White Ochre"
Charmaine Papertalk Green "Walgajunmanha All Time"
David Unaipon "The Voice of the Great Spirit"
Patsy Cameron *Grease and Ochre*
Oral stories of Aunty Dawn Daylight

From 1837, the government forcefully bribed First Nations people to join the Native Police, taking them away from their communities and culture in exchange for food, money, housing and gifts. Our people received few hints that they would be required to track, battle and kill other First Nations people. For the British, it was a cost-effective military weapon that further aided in expanding the colony and killing off and dispossessing First Nations people.

White men and White women collaborated to commit rape against First Nations women and girls to display power and dominance. The growing number of children born with a Black mother and White father, and of a lighter skin tone, was to the white supremacists a "problem," but one that could be solved through state-sanctioned processes of "assimilation."

From the start of the twentieth century, based on the corrupt assumption that it would be for their own good, First Nations children were separated, often from birth, from their mothers and families. The aim of this was to break kinship connections, end First Nations culture, and meet demand for station workers and domestic servants. First Nations workers were often unpaid and overworked, their slave labor bolstering the economy. Authorities used the false guise of pretending First Nations parents were neglecting their children. At hospitals, babies were hidden from their mothers under blankets by cooperating nurses, taken far away, stripped of names and given numbers instead.

Deceit continued in the dark cloud that blew up over Maralinga, the traditional lands of the Maralinga Tjarutja of the southern Pitjantjatjara peoples in the 1950s. The Australian government knew enough about the potential effects of the blast to consider postponing the Melbourne Olympics, hundreds of kilometers from the site. Yet they agreed to the British nuclear testing that killed and made ill hundreds of First Nations people, leaving the community with poisoned land and health effects for generations to come. "People thought it was a wanampi, the serpent snake coming out and getting angry, but it was actually a mushroom cloud," Elder Jeremy LeBois said, illustrating that Anangu people were not warned about the test's dangers.

I could go on, but you have probably got the point. Nothing's fair in this country, which prides itself on false values of sportsmanship and mateship. First Nations people continue to get screwed over all the time, whether it's Juukan Gorge, or Dja Dja Wurrung trees. White people change the rules to suit themselves.

plutonium

Knocking softly on Yhonnie Scarce's
door in Wurundjeri country to interview
her for the newspaper. As nervous as
expected when meeting one of my favorite
artists. She lets me in and I have a cuppa
with her and her two nieces. We stop
and think about how acid rain traveled
from Yhonnie's Country as far as to my
Mununjali Country from a big, thick
cloud. Of what had been concealed but at
the same time was in the air, everywhere.
The 1950s and 1960s British atomic testing
that set fire to Country. The nuclear blasts
at Maralinga. The forced leaving of the
Spinifex people. I think about ground
zero and the mass poisoning event that
continues. Of Yhonnie's poisoned glass
yams and Ali Cobby Eckermann's poison-
tinged poems. When I visit Japan I meet
a teacher in Kumamoto who tells me my
writing about Country reminds him of a
friend of his, a woman warrior writer now
gone, who wrote about the poisoned land
and waters there. He urges me to keep
going, for her. Yhonnie spends hours in the
studio manipulating the hot glass with her
hands and mouth. The beaks of the yams in
the dead earth of the mass contamination
event. Not being able to grow anything,

life cut off. Children died, and the
intergenerational health effects continue.
The cancers spread. The clean-up botched.
How long will it take to break down the
toxins in the earth? It may never stop. The
ground is radioactive. No new shoots here,
no growth. The genocidal-ecocidal mindset
of not caring about mob and their land
has not been broken, yet. Yhonnie sees me
admiring (strange to admire, but I can't
think of a verb that carries both admiration
and fear) a yam and gives it to me as a gift.
In the hand-blown forms there is violence
and beauty. It sits on my desk while I write.

Pick your poison; Australia is known to be the deadliest place in
the world, and that's not in the Irish colloquialism adopted into
Aboriginal English. The continent contains some of the most poisonous plants, like the gympie-gympie, the stinging bush named by
the Gubbi Gubbi people. The venom is described as scorpion-like
and it's been claimed as the world's most dangerous plant; very fine
brittle hairs loaded with toxins cover the whole plant and para-
lyze. Horses who come into contact with the plant have to be shot
because they experience so much pain, though flying foxes camp in
the branches, and First Nations people extract the hairs to use as an
acupuncture-like treatment for arthritis.

We also have most of the world's top tier of venomous snakes.
The hundred and forty snake and thirty sea-snake species we have
today are all descended from one common ancestor, so they've
learned to outcompete each other in the environment. They had
strong evolutionary pressure to elevate the levels of venom in their
fangs.

So many poisons, and so many uses, on this beautiful continent
like no other. The Sydney funnel-web spider can kill a human in an

hour. Its K'gari version is known by Butchulla people as "mudjar nhiling guran," meaning "long-toothed spider." Scientists originally captured the spiders from this location due to their contrast—black against white sand—making them easier to spot. Its venom is even more dangerous and complex than that of the funnel-web. Only a handful of the 3000 peptide molecules are lethal, while some of the others have medical uses. Researchers have discovered one molecule with great potential to treat stroke and heart attack, and prolong the storage time of donor hearts for transplant.

Jellyfish, meanwhile, have more than 800,000 stinging organelles per square centimeter on their tentacles, which can only be seen under a microscope.

We often use the word "toxic" as a shorthand to describe social spaces that are not conducive to health and wellbeing, where things have become out of balance; where something has gone wrong, and efforts to alchemize the space have not helped. My cuz says she had to leave a blackfella Facebook group because it was "toxic." I notice we as blackfellas use this adjective a lot to describe unhealthy situations. We know that sometimes it's safer to disengage and disentangle. Of course, this is more complicated when it is our own families and our own Country. This requires complex responses, with care for ourselves and our legacy.

Ever walked into a room and known you had to leave? Ever felt like the walls were making you sick? What are the first signs that you are being poisoned? Behavioral changes. Loss of appetite. Feeling dizzy, drowsy and tired. A headache that spreads. Rapid heart rate. High blood pressure. Skin changes. Is it a slow poisoning or has it already happened? Is it already too late to reverse the effects?

anticoagulant

The anticoagulant is an important chemical
in the world of medicine. It is also used to
kill. Blood-thinning rat poison is designed

so the rat comes back to its location over
three days to get more and more poison
until they die. Wedge-tailed eagles, masked
owls, boobook owls and goannas eat the rats,
get the secondary poison and die. Goanna
is an important food source for some First
Nations people, meaning they risk their
health if they continue eating this cultural
food. The poison has made a network that is
widespread. I live under my parents' house,
a tiled room, and my dad wanted to do
some pest control. He wasn't going to go
with a safe option. I left the house for the
morning and went to do some work at the
library. When I came home the poison had
been sealed under the gaps in the tiles. I
had a blinding headache and a sore throat. I
vomited the first few days. My dad says I'm
just sensitive. I slept upstairs on the couch. I
couldn't work in my bedroom. Maybe we are
all living with the sickness. It's in our beds.
It's in our heads. It's in our blood.

Yamaji poet Charmaine Papertalk Green writes collaboratively with
dugai Anglo-Celtic poet John Kinsella about the destructive effects
of mining on her Country in mid-west Western Australia, and the
residue of past wrongs in *False Claims of Colonial Thieves* (2018).
The "colonial thieves" rob First Nations people and give permission
for a legacy of destruction in the mining state of Australia. The
book shows how agriculture and mining by-products directly and
indirectly poison the land and the people. Mining poisons the water.
Bores in the region are contaminated with arsenic, uranium and
nitrates. Unsafe levels of heavy metals and nitrates cause chronic

illness and early onset kidney disease in adults and sick babies. Where is the explicit consent to poison Country?

On Latje Latje land, on Barkindji land, on Dharug land, on many different lands, dead fish line the surface of the rivers. Lorikeets die from drinking from suburban-backyard bird baths. Sea eagles die from pesticides used on bananas. Once nutritious cultural foods have changed their properties and slowly start to kill. Can we take the harness off the land and just breathe?

Toxicity needs to be removed from the earth, water, sky and people. We need to be detoxified and restored to balance. Poison has its use, when used well, when targeted. Blackfellas know poison can be beautiful too, like the nyannum. Poison can sustain us when it's woven right, made proppa. The mode of creation of the harvesting basket and fermentation bag inspires the metaphor for the mode in which First Nations writers write. We have to know how to treat these plants and animals for them to treat us well, to nurture us, in return.

The Pain Game

Physical pain has no voice, but when it at last finds a voice, it begins to tell a story ...

Elaine Scarry

Pain is messy. I didn't like to complain, so I played injured, a lot. When I was young I could handle this okay, but it catches up with me later.

Waking up in pain, everything takes longer. Putting shoes on can elicit groans. Socks slip out of my hands. The shoe feels heavy and I have to sit down. This means I miss my bus to work and have to get the next one.

Sometimes there are moments on the massage table when a point is activated and the pain is relieved. I become ecstatic—I feel in those short moments great love for my friends, family and strangers, and perhaps gratitude to them for sticking with me. It's in those moments that I know who I love, and what I don't need. Pain makes that distinction blurry. Living in the pain is not being present. We are not our true selves when we are in pain.

My ancestral word for pain, burragull: an emotion, an expression, an experience, a collective memory.

I grew up hiding pain. At a certain point, I decided to be a bit more of my messy pain self around other people.

I persist in the overlap between illness and injury. The episodic nature of pain means that I experience life either in flare or in between flares, both without a sense of chronological time or logical structure. My friend Rai gives me practical materials about chronic pain and fatigue. How to see time differently and how to adjust my expectations of my body. I return to Lorde and hooks. Adrienne J Keene returns to me. Emezi is a constant burning presence. Laila brings me to Elaine Scarry, who has written about the unsharability of pain, how it resists language.

Everyone goes through pain, and when I get curious about my own, I start to get curious about other people's. How do they communicate it? How do they hide or reveal it? Our whole basis for understanding health and illness is cultural.

We must not compare pain, as our pains come from history and presence.

I am interested in the representation of pain in creative works. How does it translate onto the page and stage? There's something raw and real and human about a person revealing their pain to others. The yarning circle.

I am asked to keep a pain diary. It is not the type of writing I am used to performing. For one, I've never kept a diary. Writing feels like a transgression, or a flex, not a routine or daily activity, like how you might brush your teeth or take the dog for a walk.

My pain diary can be counted in the times I grab a part of my body. Feel my brain constrict. Pain colors experiences—my pain colors are a blazing orange and red that I can see like a cloud behind my eyes. It bursts during certain movements.

A self-reported measure, the McGill Pain Questionnaire has seventy-eight words that act as descriptors of pain. Words like "prickling," "crushing," "tingling," "tender" and "cool." The users mark the words that best fit.

Standard pain questions have never been adapted for Indigenous communities, Dr Manasi Murthy Mittinty writes. Some experiences of pain are unique. A spiritual connection with pain perceives a health issue as being more than just a biological one.

"What is it trying to show me?"

My dad has two favorite players who he believes to be on par: Johan Cruyff and Marco van Basten. Van Basten has glass ankles that forced him to retire at the age of thirty after years on the sidelines. His last professional match was when he was twenty-eight. He was known for his close ball control, attacking intelligence, stylish headers and spectacular strikes, including an absolute peach of a volley in the 1988 Euro final.

My first ankle injury came at the age of twenty-four. I did not seek treatment.

What gave?

A shadow event at the time. My defenses struck. The ankle, a pivot. Holds the weight of the whole body. On it, we spin, we jump, we land, we go down.

This was the last time I moved pain-free. My posture changed. I went from an easy, steady gait to shuffling along with short steps. Doing anything on one leg was an SOS to my body. The type of attacking football I played as a striker no longer worked: the quick, sharp change of pace; the power in the shot. I felt like a shadow of the player I was. Sometimes even watching people doing activities can make my ankle twinge in pain.

I quit football at the age of twenty-nine during a COVID-19-ravaged season, after repeated attempts to come back from this recurrent injury. After trying many Western and non-Western treatments, the only option that presented itself was to press pause for an indefinite amount of time.

My body was finally giving me some relief. The physio I went to see at Dulwich Hill suggested it was due to my sedentary lifestyle as a writer and said I needed to move every thirty minutes, recommending I take ibuprofen three times a day for three days to see if it helped. It seemed to. It was amazing. Would it have gone differently had I not offered the last six years of my life to writing and editing? Sedentary lifestyle, the physio said. Stiff and sore and hard to repair. No longer plastic and bendy.

They say that stress is the biggest factor in chronic health issues, and I've picked the wrong profession. Writing is stressful, and so is editing other people's work, and so is teaching, and presenting. But I think any job will be stressful. Living in today's world is hazardous. I try to tap out when I can. When I feel run-down and anxious, I sing and hum to stimulate the vagus nerve.

The body buckles under stress. I wake up for what by necessity will be a busy day. It's a Sunday, but I plan on working most of the day. I have deadlines.

I have set my alarm for 7:00 am. I eat something for brekkie, cuppa tea. I go to a yoga class to try and start the day with some movement, as I know I will have little time later. While at yoga I feel stress, all the things I need to get done going around my mind but also determination. I am going to get everything done today.

But half an hour after I get back from yoga, just after I help Mum with something and just before I'm about to get started on work, I feel pain come on me sharply. My back buckles. Over three hours I have painful spasms that leave me bedridden. The spasms at their worst last about four minutes. They come as frequently as every twenty minutes. The shock of the pain is bad enough to make me think I should go to hospital. But I learn to just breathe, to stay as still as possible and to get through those four minutes.

As the pain starts to ease, I'm tired. My nerves are pinching. By the time I start to test the waters of the pain I am in anticipation of the next bout. The soft band of my boxer briefs feels like a tight rubber band. While the pain eases, my mind does not allow itself to rest. I don't know where this pain has come from. I don't know how I could have prevented it.

Shortly after quitting playing for good, I took up fantasy football. This was a way to transfer my obsession with the sport into something I could do behind a screen. There was no risk of injury, but that doesn't mean that there wasn't anxiety.

I play A-League men's fantasy football. Currently, I am ranked first in Queensland, but don't read too much into that; the interest in this game is not high, and an extremely small number play it. I wonder why there is an absence of women's sports in fantasy leagues and what that means.

There are my go-to players every season, players who are guaranteed cash cows: Goodwin, Maclaren. These players will get consistent scores all season long. Then there are the experiments. Gambling on players unknown to the league. Looking up their stats on Wikipedia, their goals-per-game ratio. Goal-scoring defenders are gold, but you have to look at how many goals their team is likely to concede and whether it's worth it. A bit of research (including watching a lot of games) will determine which players take their team's penalties, corners and free kicks. These players are guaranteed to bolster points.

Looking at the team sheet just before the game is also a trick that can guarantee you have a team where all players are in the starting eleven. An up-and-coming youngster who will get minutes when senior players are away can increase your team's value.

There is a bleak side to fantasy football. Yes, you feel elated when you're winning, but you also feel shithouse when you have a bad week. Most people who play report feelings of anxiety due to the out-of-control nature of the competition. It is a soft form of gambling, as no money is exchanged, but it has mental engagement.

Playing fantasy football during a pandemic year was even more precarious. Matches were canceled at short notice, players were out because of COVID-19 protocols, match schedules had numerous changes. Keeping up with international selections required effort. I bemoaned selections—why hadn't I trusted my instinct and chosen that player as captain, which would have doubled their points? Watching real games was colored by the expectations of the fantasy game. I couldn't enjoy it. I was becoming like my dad, who can only watch sport if he bets on it. It felt demoralizing. I knew I would feel a lot more relaxed watching a game I didn't have a stake in. It was a type of consumption that was not always healthy.

As much as I convinced myself I was some sort of informed genius, football is luck. That's why we love it so much. The statistics can mean nothing on the day. Last game's most effective player who scored a hat-trick and an assist could get sent off in the first minute or put the ball in their own net. I still play because I became connected to these players through their successes and their failures. It's a way to escape, something to do, something to be invested in. Most of us don't know how to engage with games without investing a lot of ourselves in them.

If I don't finish first in Queensland it won't matter. There are minimal prizes.

Starting English Premier League fantasy football in my teens was a way to prove myself. I could prove I knew just as much about the game as the mostly cis men I competed against. This sense of wanting to prove myself is still there. There was safety in participating in a community that was fully online, with limited individual engagements (the website doesn't have a chat function, so mostly it occurs at arm's length of others). In some ways it's a competition against yourself.

When I return to fantasy football as an adult I know exactly what I've signed up for. Fantasy football is a type of fanfiction. I'll admit, the loneliness might be necessary to write.

My rep coach noticed me clutching my back when playing the year of my first period. I remember bouts of excruciating back pain between the ages of twelve and seventeen. I got a scan that showed scoliosis. My parents took me to the chiropractor and the physio who gave me scoliosis-specific exercises while I was reaching skeletal maturity. This is when I was first introduced to my core. When I try to engage my core now, I think of Tommy Pico, who once wrote about it in a nature poem. First time I had ovulation pain I was seventeen. I thought I had to go to the hospital. I thought it was my appendix. Still, my inquiry, what is lodged in?

A laparoscopy at the age of thirty confirms I have been living with endometriosis, a chronic menstrual disorder that affects at least one in nine people who are assigned female at birth. The median length of time from symptom onset to diagnosis is seven years. Trans and non-binary people often suffer in silence and the medical system can be a scary place to navigate if you're not cis. I have been living with symptoms—pain in back, stomach, pelvis and hips; aggravated periods; painful ovulation; muscle spasms; fatigue—since my teens. I am told I need to address all aspects of these issues.

Pain is racialized. Folks die or spend lifetimes in heightened pain due to the medical system not taking their pain seriously. Medical racism erases traditional forms of healing. Why is some pain more important than others? Why are women, queer people, trans people and non-white people not allowed to be in pain? How much of what is ours do we minimize? When I voice my pain I think I am indulging too much. Indulging in what? I don't know.

(This is for those of you whose enjoyment of a sport has been marred by pain)
I am more than a pile of prescriptions and a foam roller in my bed
I am more than my endo apps
I am more than a history of doctors, a line of opinions that curls
    around the door
Sometimes I am scared of surgery. Because pain has never failed to
    be a belonging and place.
I have not been taught how to be in pain, but I am learning
Sometimes I wonder what I'm doing, living with my family, keeping
    my bedroom under the house untidy like my mind, going to the
    gym and bush and
trying to do things around the home, on my good days
watching telly with my legs propped up on my bad days,
bickering with Mum or Dad, always going to bed
with the feeling of something unfinished
Whole weeks and months and years pass like this
until I decide to find a circuit-breaker

What football has taught me about writing (a question two people, Joe and Sam, have asked me that I have not yet answered well enough).

I spend some of those hours in which I used to practice football at the desk practicing putting words together. I am a slow writer. Like many writers, I go through many drafts before I feel okay enough to show a friend or an editor. My process sometimes involves picking up a sentence, putting it back down, then picking it up again, which reminds me of repeatedly placing the ball in the same spot to practice a free kick. If I could get three in a row, in which the ball went where I wanted it to, I would be happy and able to move on to the next thing. If I couldn't, if the hits kept coming up sloppy, I would stay till darkness began to descend on the park, which was enough motivation to finally hit some sweet form. Going home in the complete dark, sometimes my feet would be red and aching, as I'd taken off my boots or joggers to connect more with the ball.

I am struggling very much to find a new way of living when it used to be so much part of my identity.

Why are we in certain company silent about tenderness in narrating experiences of sport?

I think it's complicated.

When I was thirteen, my coach used to say that contact with the chest in football causes breast cancer. I wasn't sure if that was true.

Corinne says the ball hurts her every time it hits her. It wasn't until I started the pill that I knew what she meant. The soreness was full on. I couldn't lie down on my front. Certain positions in Pilates were uncomfortable. I was extra conscious about how I moved in the world. Trying not to make contact with anything.

N texts me. They have just started taking the pill too. The very-present soreness and having none of their bras or binders fit them and having to size up elicits strong feelings of dysphoria. They are a few months behind me and I say it should get better, don't worry.

I would always tell lovers no sleepovers before a game. But I lost my strict routine with my girlfriend. We were so into each other.

My pregame ritual of:

Eat nutritious carb-loading meal of fish and rice and leafy vegetables before 7:00 pm

Sleep by 10:00 pm

Wake 8:00 am coffee

9:00 am start hydrating and eat healthy breakfast of yoghurt and muesli

10:00 am do yoga and stretching with TheraBand

11:00 am eat half a banana

12:00 pm pack bag and change into match kit

12:30 pm do team pick-up

1:00 pm warm-up and team talk

2:00 pm game

goes out the window.

I'm on my back, telling her about my rule of no sex before matches so as not to affect my performance. I must have read about how orgasms could make you docile or something and stuck to it. I have been trying to keep these two pleasures separate for so long now. I realize how rigid I sound when I say it, and she convinces me to try another way.

I'm on my stomach and her warm mouth and hands are all over me and my nerve endings and this proves too pleasurable. We've slept in like usual and then woken up and got busy. We are addicted to each other's bodies and the new experiences possible with each other. Somehow I let her try anal on me a few hours before a game. Tongue, fingers, opening me up. It's a fantastic new feeling and I have no idea what to do with it.

I lose track of time.

When we finally pause to take a breath, to take a sip of water and glance at our phones, the game is two hours away, one hour before I have to be there to warm up. I get up and I'm walking funny. She goes downstairs to make us coffee and I realize another hard rule, a meal three hours before the game, has slipped away. Bread, fresh from a bakery on her side of town, with ricotta and honey. My mate comes to pick us up for the game. I hope we don't stink like sex in the car. I get out on the pitch, still seeing stars, still walking funny, score not one but three spectacular goals: a half-volley from a ridiculous angle, a lightning bolt from outside the box, and an amazing run from my own half, with my girlfriend cheering from the sidelines. My teammates attribute her presence to my first hat-trick for the club. We win 3–0.

Postgame she joins me in the bath to prepare for sex again, and we talk about the goals and the new match-day routine we've created together.

It was much more than one thing. Something had happened, but it was what had happened those years ago.

The original injury. And the event that had allowed it to happen. The person who had shattered my defense. It gave. My legs buckling like a horse's.

Spiraling on the tram to practice. Only a few stops to go, and I told myself to hold off. Melbourne's crowded public transport was itself a trigger. I tapped my foot obsessively while standing and holding the rail. My legs were shaking. I wasn't sure if I could make it those few stops, but I did. I got off at Dawson Street and walked the fifteen minutes to our artificial-pitch training ground.

Once there I met my teammates. Stripped off my two layers. Ran around the park a few times. I was that wound up that it took the whole ninety-minute training session for my anxiety to ease and for me to even catch a breath. I remember collapsing on the cold artificial turf during our cool-down stretches, glancing at the city lights behind us and being very glad for my own heartbeat, the patterns of my brain rewired during the cardio.

Early in the season, Kath did her anterior cruciate ligament. A few weeks later, Jill did hers too playing that same position, right-wing. Both at wide spaces on the field—running to the ball. Soon the coach was calling this position cursed.

On average, one teammate would succumb to an ACL injury per year in my team. It would be horrible to watch—to witness the injury, which mostly happened in games rather than training. They'd get the scan a few days later, but most of the time they knew and we knew that it would be their ACL. Someone would have heard the pop.

Then they would be out for the rest of the season and we would be low on numbers. They would be hobbling around at the team break-up, and we'd say, hope to see you again next year, but we'd know it was unlikely they would rehab in time. And everyone would be nervous because we didn't want it to happen to us.

I haven't been through it myself, but I've seen it enough times that it feels like a sad inevitability. Statistics show that people who are assigned female at birth are two to ten times more likely to experience an injury to the ACL than men, and Australia has some of the highest rates in the world. When we were younger, we were told it was because our bodies are different, because of a weak pelvis. When the inevitable did occur, it was normalized. It was as if it was another reason why we shouldn't be playing, or should only be playing with caution.

This misrepresents the contributing factors, cultural and environmental, that cause ACL injuries. A study in the AFLW, where ACL injuries occurred at rates up to 9.2 times higher in the women's first two seasons compared with the men's, determined that relative infancy of leagues and reduced access to facilities, training opportunities and medical/athletic development staff were potential environmental and sociocultural drivers for differences in ACL injury rates. This makes sense to me, from what I've observed. Even while I've been playing in the top women's team at the club, our facilities, access to medical staff and financial incentives have been incredibly limited compared to the men's teams.

In 2017, an ACL prevention program was implemented in clubs in Victoria. We went through a routine before every training session and game where we activated the knee joint correctly. It gave me a sense of security, but unfortunately we still had ACL injuries that season.

When I hear someone say, "Well, AFAB bodies are just built differently," I say: invest in women's sport, give AFAB people equal standing in sport and in every aspect of life, then run the statistics on knee injuries again.

The bearer of injury and pain can often dwell on a sense of self-blame that is unhelpful. You think that the persistent injuries are somehow your fault—that you didn't train enough, didn't stretch enough, weren't mindful enough, when it's just how our bodies are made and the luck of the draw. I know how hard I worked to try to play again.

There is shame in injury.

The ankle, a bridge. Between the feet, which touch earth, and the body. It wasn't my fault.

There's a feeling of either being highly visible, like when you have to be stretchered off the pitch, or invisible, like when you're on the sidelines for a game and everyone knows you're off the list. The mental aspect can be the hardest. My mum told me to just quit and hang up my boots. She saw the pain I was in. For a while, I was stubborn, but then, in my last match, tears on Yuggera Country, I knew.

Feb 25

Remembered to stretch out my psoas when I came home from work tonight

I dream about coming back to play all the time. I have no aspirations to play at a high level again. I want to be able to play on a team with people I love and not feel that pinch in my ankle. To feel lighter. To feel free. I'm scared.

Feb 24

Listening to hypnotic music. The melodic sound of a wave crashing. The trickling of rain. This music helps me manage my nervous system.

I remember reading an article about older women playing footy for the first time, never having had the opportunity to do so earlier. One of the women mapped out the geography of her doubts on a whiteboard: letting the team down, making a fool of herself, not being able to get through a match etc. It was a powerful visual for how we sometimes get in our own way, or at least worsen problems through negative thinking. If it does happen, I will chart my return to sport like a journey of vulnerability and doubt.

Feb 23

Thought I was better. But I woke up with the same pain.

I have taken to telling people who ask me what my goals are that my aim is to live relatively pain-free, not to return to sport. I don't want to get my hopes up. Every time I dream again, I have nightmares.

A new pain. Teeth, especially at night. I keep going back to my dentist thinking I have a hole in my tooth, until they tell me my pain is from TMJ disorder, a jaw joint problem. My endo physio, who shares my name, says jaw pain is common with people who have chronic pelvic pain. Once again, she kindly shows me how to breathe through discomfort.

Mum goes to a Healer. Healing comes from old traditions. Sometimes the spirit gets stuck. Realigning the spirit gives pain and stress reason to leave. Touch is fear leaving the body.

I go to the ocean to float. Ankle. Pelvis. I feel sun.

I hug my mum in the kitchen.

What would you do without me? she says.

Rai sends care packages through the mail: two types of bakhor, for clarity of thought, safety and good health. I burn.

Johanna Hedva: "the most anti-capitalist protest is to care for an other."

Why does pain linger when the threat is gone?

I feel like dribbling, mucking around in the backyard.

But I must admit, there are occasional days where I do not think of football at all. Then I am reminded that, even though it has meant failure and pain for me in the past, it has also meant life.

I miss the old me, the person with the football at their feet. But I guess no matter what happens, the football is still there, beside me, even if I can't touch it.

As Country

There is a common misconception that "caring for Country" means humans looking after land, water, trees, animals and anything else that is non-human. But we are Country, we are the land, water and sky, so caring for Country is "caring as Country," as Ngarrindjeri person Daryle Rigney says. It includes caring for ourselves. It's a relational concept and these relationships are the basis of everything. We all know that if our rivers, and our waterways, and our air, and our trees, and our animals are all well, then we are well too.

This continent was invaded and colonized without consent and no treaty was signed nor has been signed since. There are active discussions in Queensland, Victoria and the Northern Territory to enter into a treaty process with the First Nations that fall within those colonial borders. I speak about the absence of treaty in my writing because it means that anything I write is on shaky ground. And I feel until there is a treaty in place between the colonial state and Country, there can be no full commitment to climate justice.

Land and water need Indigenous Knowledges. These knowledges have been accumulated over hundreds of thousands of years and remain committed to adapting, sharing and cross-pollinating, and are inherently interdisciplinary.

We can look at the way that First Nations literature addresses space and time as a site to embody past, present and future all in one. A story does not exist in a static time or space. We look at what our ancestors left for us and we carry what we want our descendants to bring forward. Any actions we make today, anything that we start, anything we continue, is for the thrival of generations hundreds of years into the future.

I use this word a lot, "thrival." It comes from a text I sent my Aunty, "we have survived," and she said, "no, honey, we have survived, and we have thrived." It's informed by a critical term in First Nations circles on Turtle Island, "survivance," an active word. Anishinaabe person Gerald Vizenor says, "an active sense of presence." Thrival is in opposition to victimhood. It is a knowing that we are continuing. Like the butterfly that just attached itself to my last word.

First Nations writing is Country. If you want to know about the Country you're on, read the works of its writers. Find out what happened here. And don't forget it. This is part of our learning. Learn from the past so it doesn't happen again. My poetry and prose is my Country. Wiradjuri person Jeanine Leane says, "Indigenous writing is all anchored in a landscape that is both imposed and which has always been here." The place where I live is embodied in the slick whispers to river by Samuel Wagan Watson, the powerful truth of lore by Oodgeroo Noonuccal and the vivid calls to the original tongue(s) by Lionel Fogarty. Writing about Country is writing about change.

We are the first artists, we are the first writers and the first scientists. We read Country—that is the most important literacy.

The way I make sense of the world is through going back to the stories I was told when I was a child. These stories were about knowing where I come from—a building-up, a shaping of self—and being proud of who I am.

I think about the first time I, as a young person, knew that I was on Country. Our Mununjali ancestral land. I would have been about ten years old. I was in the backseat of a car. My Uncles and Aunties were telling me and my cousins that this—where we were—was our Country. I remember that it was a hot day. I remember the heat. I remember the car seats. I remember the color of the dust and the space and the way we moved on Country. I don't know where we were in colonial spatial terms. I can't pin it on a map. I really just know the feeling of that moment. And I could trace it for you with my hands.

That was a powerful moment for me. And it was one that I tried to bring back to my classroom. I was so excited to share with my peers some of the history of my people and my ancestors that I had learned that weekend. Saturday morning I was floating on air like Mibunn the wedge-tailed eagle from the strength of being around family and on Country. Monday morning I was crashing back down to earth. I was flat on my face because my classmates didn't believe me and they discredited me when I told them our story of the land. Worse, they laughed at me, and told me that I—and my family—was worth nothing. The teachers were uncaring, indifferent, ambivalent. I think I carry both emotions from that childhood memory, the rightness and the hurt, in me at all times.

We can see everything we do as an opportunity to support and platform First Nations knowledge keepers, and to be in solidarity with people of other First Nations. Knowledge keepers—storytell- ers—hold the solutions to the problems we are facing. To be passive is not a response. The land and waterways need active attention to recover, to come to life, to diversify, to thrive, a management of fire and water and a relational understanding that you will find nowhere else but within Country, within Country-people. Actively listening is amplifying the voice of Country.

Too often we forget the "why" in what we do. Why are we trying to save what many say is doomed, is lost, is losing? The answer is we do what we do because it connects us to what we've always done, what's in our blood: we practice good relations, we employ as many tools as we need, and we get to work, because there's work to be done.

When I'm on Mununjali Country I have a powerful sense of being who I need to be—a wedge-tailed eagle person—a Mibunn—a being that collides with the sky—that sees—and reads—laterally and through the reflection of yalnun—light from the sun.

HOME

Thirty-two, two years of no season, no club, no
home ground. Almost forgotten the taste of wet
grass and the wind chill on my shins through
thin socks, the weight of a goal when it's carried to the sheds after training. My mum says I
still have the appetite of when I was fourteen.
My dad still talks to me for hours about sport
until Mum tells them to give it a break. I give my
brother my pair of shinnies, no longer used, and
watch his back VAN NEERVEN spin in sky
and floodlights near hoop pines. I trace my lips
across the wet promise of caring for my body.
Where am I? Playing is the way I learned to be.
This was my grounding and connection. At the
gap of knowing there is still so much more to
learn. I am more in my body than ever before. I
have met mob who have called me a north star.
Not a dislocation. It is them I know. The ways I
have always connected fused with this new way
of moving as Country.

How to Play Sport on Indigenous Land

1. Acknowledge Country

Always was, always will be Aboriginal land is attributed to Uncle Jim Bates's explanation, in the 1980s, of his unbroken connection to his Barkandji Country.

This football field, sporting ground, park, swimming pool, beach, gym—anywhere we play, train and exercise—is on unceded Indigenous land.

Biripi man Jade North, chair of the Football Australia National Indigenous Advisory Group, explains, "Protocols for welcoming visitors on country have always been part of Aboriginal and Torres Strait Islander cultures. It has been long used by our People to convey safe passage and protection of visitors' spiritual being during their journey on country, as well as a sign of respect for the country of another."

Through the land rights movement, the Mabo decision and the reconciliation movement, things have shifted societally in the last few decades so more people understand the meaning of Country. Acknowledgements and welcomes have been widespread the last fifteen years. The first time I remember hearing an acknowledgement or Welcome to Country at a sports match was at the 2011 Indigenous All Stars rugby league match on Yugambeh Land. I was there with my girlfriend and my cousins. But it wasn't until the 2020s that I saw widespread acknowledgements and welcomes at mainstream (with non-Indigenous involvement) sporting events. It is always the right way to start.

It is my understanding, from anecdotal information and a decade traveling abroad, that First Nations Australians have been instrumental in the adoption of land acknowledgements in countries like the United States and Canada.

I was part of two groups that traveled to the United States in 2015: one went to Austin, Texas, in springtime, and the other to New York City plus Charlottesville, Virginia, in the fall. Acknowledgements in Turtle Island were not normalized at the time, and we faced puzzlement from non-Indigenous locals. As part of the First Nations Australia Writers Network (FNAWN) contingent, we had a responsibility to the First Peoples of the land we were traveling on.

When traveling to Texas, I was with my esteemed non-Indigenous mentor, Sue Abbey. We did our research and when we did meet First Nations people, they were grateful for our acknowledgement. The common understanding led to a rich connection.

Don't modify an acknowledgement significantly so that it deviates from its original purpose.

I remember being in a yoga studio in Kurilpa and being surprised by an awkward acknowledgement of Country before a two-hour intensive class. I wondered: is any gesture better that no gesture at all? The next time I attended the instructor's class, a year later, I noted the acknowledgement had improved and now felt like a genuine, grounding and seamless transition into connecting with the place we were on.

2. Recognize sovereignty

The book *Aboriginal Camp Sites of Greater Brisbane: An historical guide* (2015) by Ray Kerkhove in consultation with the Turrbal and Yagera people speaks about how most parks and sporting grounds in Brisbane were originally Aboriginal camps. Think about what this place was before Invasion; not just the ground but what is in the sky and what's under the earth.

There is grief attached to some of these places. Loss. Pain. Violence. No matter how changed, urbanized or controlled, Country remains Country. Think about this place as continuing First Nations presence and think about how to facilitate this.

Let the athlete dually be an Australian athlete and an Indigenous athlete (if they want to be). They don't have to choose. They don't need to participate in militant nationalism that denies the diversity of identities on the continent.

3. Allow equitable access to sport

Make sport—both competitive and recreational—available for everyone. This includes refugees; migrant populations; Indigenous people from remote, regional and urban localities; people with disabilities; LGBTIQSB+ people; people without housing; and people of all classes and all ages.

Go beyond the tokenism of an Indigenous round. Indigenous rounds without Indigenous players or cultural safety are a bad look. Some of our most talented sports stars have been plucked from relative obscurity, so to speak—from parks, from remote communities—and given a so-called golden ticket. These people are not lucky to have sport. Sport is lucky to have them.

Allow a multitude of leagues and teams and individuals to co-exist. Don't monopolize the space for profit-chasing. Sport is fair game. This was always our way as First Nations people; everyone gets to play a role.

4. Practice ceremony

What Indigenous-run sporting events do best is create the right atmosphere to reflect the *why*. Every action is meaningful and goes beyond mere performativity. Expectations are challenged; for example, why do we always play the current national anthem before events when it is offensive to First Nations sovereignty?

A smoking ceremony (albeit not during a heatwave) can vitalize the start of a game and make players feel like they are supposed to be there. Dancing the ground can put the spirit into the place. Speaking in local language (using protocols and respectful practice) can harmonize with the trees and the birds and surroundings.

Sometimes sport goes through the motions, the monotonous same old, same old. Indigenous perspectives can help shake this off.

Our ancestors have been practicing ceremony for thousands of years, and that has kept land and culture thriving. Through sport, we have the opportunity to continue and extend on ceremony in the twenty-first century.

5. Reward kindness

Reward kindness on the pitch—in sport, in leisure, in the pursuit of fitness. Encourage children to be empathic with the bodies they interact with, with the earth, animals, plants. Choose leaders who will bring out this spirit of kindness and reciprocity in sporting communities. Remember, there is no "win at any cost": that's not winning. Remember, there are no losers. Everyone can gain something from wellness and exercising on Country.

6. Care for water

Water is central to all life. Rising water temperatures leads to blue algae in lakes and rivers, making watersport participants sick, while worsening droughts cause heavier falls and more serious injuries. Implement water-neutral policies. Try not to drink up all the water. Don't overwater grass. Recycle water. Don't poison it. Limit your use of plastic. Conserve coastal areas. Look after life underwater too.

7. Give back to the earth

With 80 percent of athletes worried about climate change, we have reached a critical point of consciousness that is presenting in a shifting of power dynamics and an increased focus on relationships with Country.

As we enter an era of "climate-positive" Olympics and Paralympics, achieving "carbon negative" through limiting personal travel, using zero-emissions vehicles, running on renewable energies and using existing venues, will there be scrutiny of all aspects of sport?

Consider the environmental impact of synthetic clothing. Polyester is made from fossil fuels, can't be recycled and isn't biodegradable. Sport encourages overproduction of polyester and clothing waste. It must be all those years at school wearing jerseys and tracksuits, but I can't wear them anymore—I can't stand the effect on my skin. I often think of buying a Matildas jersey, but I just can't do it.

Think of the lifetime of the object. Consume responsibly. Apply sustainable best practice, but interrogate who is determining it is sustainable. Don't mine community. Consent must be explicit and in fair terms in all engagements with community. Don't take without giving. Don't use sport sponsorship to offset extraction of land.

Give back what was taken. Don't take more than you need. Love the ground you're playing on. Every inch of it.

8. Tread carefully

"A child was born here," Uncle Archie Roach sings in his song of the same name. Indigenous people have this regard for the land because we come from it. There were no hospitals or maternity wards or morgues. We didn't have that separation. I think about the ancestors every day. I know they warm my bones because our blood is on this place. If we think about the ground we stand on as activating life and death, then perhaps we think about walking life and death when we place our feet on Country.

When I first had problems with my feet, my osteopath suggested walking barefoot on the sand every day. This felt like a very middle-class suggestion. Barefoot running has been a trend for the last little while; it releases tension, it's corrective. When we are jetlagged, we take off our shoes. It's a grounding. It's a rhythm.

Something happens when a foot touches Country: it makes a print. How long that print will remain is up to Country. Whether the print is a mindful one is up to us. Tread carefully on what has been stolen underneath you.

One day in 2019, taking advantage of a break during two weeks of play development, a friend, Phoebe from North Queensland, and I lay in the middle of a park in Newtown, Gadigal land, shoes off, heads down. We watched the sky and I relaxed so much I almost fell asleep. I never thought I could feel so calm in such an unfamiliar urban area, but Phoebe made it look easy.

9. Travel mindfully

When you travel to another place for sport and leisure, travel mindfully and with the utmost of care. Do not bring any unnecessary burdens to the place. Know you are a visitor and frame your stay as a visitor. Respect the Country you are on. Give as much as you can. Facilitate mutual cultural exchange. Share something, from one community to another; that's our cultural way. Respectfully learn stories from the place, and carry those stories with you.

10. Protect heritage

Never forget the possum-skin ball and the first sports that were played here. There's a legacy and heritage that goes back over 65,000 years. Anniversaries of one or two hundred years, although important to mark, pale in comparison to the timeline of Indigenous life.

11. Recognize other sentient beings

Since the Invasion, sport and leisure have contributed to the extinction of many hundreds of animals and plants. When I was growing up, watching the senior men's team at our football club, someone would yell ironically, "Watch out for the koalas!" whenever a player kicked a ball towards the trees behind the goals. In reality, the koalas were long gone from that area because of habitat erasure and disease from chemical-related cancer.

I was raised to be respectful of "pitch-invaders": snakes and birds. In reality, we are the invading force and if we are in the way of these beings, if we put them in danger, we do not deserve to be there.

Centering humans as the supreme race, and the only race whose sports and games matter, is damaging. Dismantle horseracing and dog racing; these are cruel games.

Have you ever watched crows play? Dolphins surf? Please then try telling me that humans invented sport. Our people hunt with dolphins and work sophisticatedly with them in the waters.

12. Promote gender equality

Return female power to the land. Respect women and gender-diverse people.

Increase opportunities for women and gender-diverse people to play sport, and in other underrepresented roles such as coaching, officiating and senior administration.

Don't discount personal experience. We've been taught to be humble, but we need to tell our stories, no matter how minor we think they are. It's not vain to center ourselves in our stories along with what we love—it's necessary.

13. Support human rights on a global level

There was no slavery on this continent pre-colonization. When the settler-colonists came to Australia, thousands of First Nations women, men and children were enslaved, as well as South Sea Islanders who were "blackbirded" and other indentured laborers who were forced into a violent system.

As Jackie Huggins writes,

> Young Aboriginal women were taken from country reserves and missions; the majority of interviewees went to white homes that wanted maids. White women considered such help essential to the running of the household, especially in the tropics. In more isolated areas, Black women performed a wider range of jobs than their European counterparts: they mustered cattle, went droving, served as shepherds, worked at road and fence building and repairing. … They worked as hard as their men and possibly harder, since men often passed over disagreeable jobs to the women and sat back to watch them work.

A tournament is not worth it if it's based on suffering—then we all suffer.

When I woke up on February 2, 2022, to the news that the Socceroos had drawn 2–2 with Oman, hampering their bid for a fourth straight World Cup appearance, meaning that they would have to compete for one of the last play-off spots, I thought maybe it was for the best. The Qatar 2022 World Cup was marred by human rights issues. Craig Foster said each goal scored at the Qatar World Cup would be stained with the blood of around forty deceased workers whose plight the Qatari government has attempted to remove from history. The World Cups in Russia and Brazil were marred by similar human rights abuses.

A few months later, Australia qualified for the Qatar World Cup the hard way through a play-off against Peru. I remained unsure if I would watch or boycott. These tournaments raise serious ethical questions for players and fans. We can't separate our pleasure in consuming sport from the horror that enables it.

14. Honor materiality

Tokenism hurts. An example: using Indigenous language or design without mention of where it comes from, and not compensating Indigenous people.

Alison Page says the most distinguishing feature of Indigenous design is storytelling: "The story and the art that represents it have a function that in turn imbues an object with preciousness, which makes it more sustainable. So all of the design principles—functionality, sustainability, storytelling—are interrelated and work together to define Indigenous design."

Indigenous design doesn't need air-conditioning because it knows how to create buildings that naturally keep cool. I often think about that as we swelter through another heatwave, our houses not built for these temperatures. They trap in the heat.

Australian international netballer turned climate change activist and analyst Amy Steel was forced to quit her career due to permanent damage suffered from heat stroke in a game played in extreme conditions on Yorta Yorta Country in March 2016. Athletes are praised for "getting through it," whereas in Amy's case pushing through had dire consequences.

Why is the Australian Open, a tournament for tennis, one of the sports with the most heat exposure, played at the hottest time of year in Melbourne? Are the images of athletes routinely collapsing and spectators falling ill part and parcel of the game? They don't want to change it because that would mean admitting that climate change is a real thing.

15. Prioritize health and wellbeing

Play in tandem with the seasons. Don't fight the body. Know its limits. Be mindful of burnout in volunteers, staff and athletes. Refusals are powerful, such as tennis player Naomi Osaka refusing to do media conferences—situations largely controlled by white men that negatively affected her mental health. Or gymnast Simone Biles voluntarily withdrawing from several events at the Tokyo Olympics, prioritizing her wellbeing.

Encourage and support others to put their health and wellbeing above any other commitment. Set an example. Be vulnerable to be strong. Don't abandon yourself. Reveal yourself.

Postgame

My first football club: the grounds are in a new place now, brand-new fields, closer to the village center. The old grounds hold memories that resurface and resonate in my sister-cousin's voice many years later. Two cousins on a warm day, both eleven, running onto the field, swimming in baggy blue jerseys. One of us with darker skin.

"You remember when I lived with youse when we were eleven? We went to your soccer training together and I borrowed some clothes off you. Remember how many pairs of socks you had? Like a whole drawer," my cousin is saying.

I nod in recognition. I did have a lot of socks. Many of them were hand-me-downs from my dad.

"We played a game, girls against boys. They were much bigger than us and played rough. They called me names, 'abo' and 'blackie,' and kicked me without the ball. Nobody did anything, not even your dad. Maybe he didn't see. Except you. You stood up and wanted to fight. They had to pull you apart from this boy! And on the way home, we got a lecture about fighting and I never got taken there again. You look shocked to hear that, cuz. But you did that. You stood up for me. That's the only time I seen you wild."

It takes a while for this to sink in, before I offer an apology to my cousin for not remembering that day until now. In some ways I feel like the child version of me was more self-knowing than the person I have become. When I was a child I was much more in tune with my surroundings.

Sport is such a big part of Australian identity, but we only see a certain layer, which is often highly curated and clean. My passion for examining the race, gender, sexual and social politics of the game reveal that real sport is dirty and complicated. When I started playing, it was hard to find a club in metropolitan Brisbane that had a "girls' team." Now women's sport has exploded, yet the gender inequalities are still stark.

A writer fears once they write about something they love, their relationship with it will be forever changed. It is a good problem to have. Arts and sports are entwined: each have taught me about the other.

I started thinking about this book in 2015. Compiling writing and thinking over a long period culminated in a process of carving that has been unlike any other book-forming process I've done. There's still so much I'm uncertain about. But there's beauty in these questions and transitioning thoughts.

One of the more interesting things about this writing-carving process is that some of this work was created when I was gender-questioning and didn't know how to represent myself on the page in a way that felt comfortable. Self-realization of gender identity deepened my relationship with myself, and the writing changed.

In 2018, working with State Library of Queensland, I had the honor of profiling five Queensland Aboriginal and Torres Strait Islander sportspeople, some who played alternative sports to those usually associated with Indigenous sportspeople, for an exhibition called *Our Sporting Greats*. Under the banner of "unsung heroes," these people included Rhonda Purcell, Quandamooka woman and international bodybuilding gold medalist; Danny Morseu, two-time Olympian and Uncle of Patty Mills and Nathan Jawai, representing Indigenous basketball past, present and future; Uncle Charlie King, president of the Brisbane Natives Rugby League team and a driving force behind the Boathouse Dances social scene of the 1950s and 1960s, as remembered by his daughter Aunty Sandra King; Aunty Lesley Williams, member of the recently reunited "Imparas" Cherbourg Marching Girls team, a nationally renowned marching troupe that traveled the country during an era of restricted movement for Aboriginal people; and Uncle Willie Prince, Cherbourg man and Queensland track and field champion, 2000 Sydney Paralympics torchbearer and 2018 Gold Coast Commonwealth Games baton carrier. The sports stories in our community are endless.

Settler-colonists' views of our bodies from the start of the occupation rendered us as "very athletic people," and every aspect of our bodies and behaviors was examined through a racist binary lens. The gifts of talented sportspeople were taken advantage of. For example, some men were coerced to be part of the Native Police for their tracking abilities and bush skills, and Palawa women and girls were taken for their diving and swimming ability. This view of our bodies has contemporary echoes in decisions around who participates in sport and how this is received. Gifted athletes are viewed as connected to the orientalist trope of "black magic," whereas those who are not conventionally athletic can feel at odds with a mainstream culture that perpetuates racist myths.

Playing sports can sometimes be a demoralizing experience for blackfellas. Celeste Carnegie wrote in her piece for *IndigenousX* that despite growing up in a netball-obsessed household, racism experienced in a team environment contributed negatively to her body image and self-esteem and forced her to quit the sport. Netball is well-loved by blackfellas, but only three Indigenous women have represented the national team in one hundred years. For Celeste, the psychological injuries are so deep she still can't bear to watch the sport.

We can use those athletic qualities on our own terms. People who are not "sporty" or do not have your stereotypical athletic body can participate in fitness and active wellbeing in ways that do not body-shame or exclude. After all, in our way, sport is not about humiliation but enjoyment, community and Country.

With the whole world watching and the pressure to perform, "I'm Black and I'm the best!" was Cathy Freeman's proud inner monologue during her 2000 Sydney Olympics win. She explained that she not only believed she was the best, she got that belief from her family and community. "Belief is something other people give you," she said.

I take inspiration from those who possess that kind of Blak belief. It is an act of defiance, as colonization has given us many reasons to doubt ourselves; the settler state does not believe in us. Yet belief, for us, is a driving force. An armor. An ancestral anchor. Believing in ourselves is not tooting our own horns or showboating. We are, in general, not ones to call attention to ourselves from our mob. But we are known to use belief when we need it, in those moments we are called into action. This is where we find our personal best.

ACKNOWLEDGEMENTS

Earlier versions of several pieces in *Personal Score* appeared previously in the following publications and outlets: *Griffith Review, Sydney Review of Books, Australian Poetry Journal, Right Now, Overland, Swamphen, Ytali, Island*'s Nature Writing seminar series, Digital Writers' Festival's *Wormhole*, Queerstories, SBS's *True Stories* podcast, UQP's *Extraordinary Voices for Extraordinary Times* podcast, *Reading Like an Australian Writer* (NewSouth), *Balancing Acts: Women in sport* (Brow Books), *It Happened Off the Leash* (Affirm Press), *Living with the Anthropocene: Love, loss and hope in the face of environmental crisis* (NewSouth) and *New Directions in Contemporary Australian Poetry* (Palgrave Macmillan). Thank you to the editors for supporting my work.

The development of this book was supported by an Australia Council for the Arts grant in 2016, a Peter Blazey Fellowship in 2019, a Sidney Myer Creative Fellowship in 2022–23 and an Arts Queensland UQ Writer in Residence in 2022.

For your time and generosity, thank you to Leonie Young (née Yow-Yeh), Lee Sheppard, Arlie Alizzi, Zaky Shahruddin and Louis Blake.

Thanks to my editors Dr Jeanine Leane, Margot Lloyd and publisher Aviva Tuffield, as well as Felicity, Paula, Jacinta and Trâm, who gave important feedback on specific sections.

For your support on and off the pitch, thanks to my teammates and coaches throughout the years.

I reserve the last note of appreciation to my family and friends.

Thanks for supporting me during this journey.

References

PREGAME

Crenshaw, K. 1989, "Demarginalizing the Intersection of Race and Sex: A Black feminist critique of antidiscrimination doctrine, feminist theory and antiracist politics," *University of Chicago Legal Forum*, vol. 1989, no. 1, available online.

Graham, M (interviewee) & Fidler, R (interviewer). 2013, "Indigenous Elder Mary Graham Describes the Essence of Indigenous Perception," *Conversations*, ABC Radio National, January 22, available online.

Kerkhove, R. 2015, *Aboriginal Camp Sites of Greater Brisbane: An historical guide*, Boolarong Press, Brisbane.

Part One

I WANT TO PLAY

brown, am (interviewee) & Watson, SK (interviewer). 2020, "The Mecca," *HBO's Between the World and Me*, podcast, November 30, available online.

VERY ATHLETIC PEOPLE

Cunningham, A, papers 1814–1839 (as filmed by the AJCP), microform, National Library of Australia digitized item.

Edwards, K & Meston, T. 2008, "Yulunga Traditional Indigenous Games," *Australian Sports Commission*, available online.

Evans, R. 2007, *A History of Queensland*, Cambridge University Press, Port Melbourne.

Foley, F. 2020, *Biting the Clouds: A Badtjala perspective on the Aboriginals Protection and Restriction of the Sale of Opium Act, 1897*, UQP, St Lucia.

Fraser, J. 2022, "Na'bulela," *Ngoonjook, Australian First Nations' Journal*, no. 36, pp. 52–63.

Graham, M (interviewee) & Fidler, R (interviewer). 2013, "Indigenous Elder Mary Graham Describes the Essence of Indigenous Perception," *Conversations*, ABC Radio National, January 22, available online.

Lewis, N (ed.). 1978, *The New Roget's Thesaurus of the English Language in Dictionary Form*, GP Putnam's Sons, New York.

Maynard, J. 2011, *The Aboriginal Soccer Tribe: A history of Aboriginal involvement with the world game*, Magabala, Broome.

McGregor, CA. 2019, "Art of the Skins: Un-silencing and remembering," PhD thesis, Griffith University, Brisbane.

McGregor, C & Watson, J. 2021, *djillong dumularra*, exhibition, January 16 to April 5, Artspace, Sydney.

Watson, J & Perkins, H. 2019, "HEARTSTRING," *NETS Victoria*, available online.

SUGAR FIELDS

Bugeja, T. 2015, "Meeting Uncle Jim," *WWF Australia*, February 20, available online.

Kwai, I. 2020, "'No slavery in Australia'? These Pacific Islanders tell a different story," *The New York Times*, August 12, available online.

GENDER POLICE

Shamir [@ShamirBailey]. 2015, *Twitter*, March 24, available online at https://twitter.com/shamirbailey/status/580175617192169473

PROTEST IN SPORT (A SMALL SELECTION, 1957–2023)

Cheetham, D. 2015, "Young and Free? Why I declined to sing the national anthem at the 2015 AFL Grand Final," *The Conversation*, October 20, available online.

Foley, D & Read, P. 2020, *What the Colonists Never Knew: A history of Aboriginal Sydney*, National Museum of Australia Press, Canberra.

State of Emergency, exhibition, September 30, 2012, to April 19, 2013, State Library of Queensland, Brisbane.

Taltz, C & Taltz, P. 2018, *Black Pearls: The Aboriginal and Islander Sports Hall of Fame*, Aboriginal Studies Press, Canberra.

Taranto, C. 2003, "Go Home Springboks," *Hindsight*, ABC Radio National, September 7.

THE BIKE PATH

Australian Human Rights Commission. 2021, *Change the Routine: Report on the Independent Review into Gymnastics in Australia*, May 3, available online.

Leahy, T, Pretty, G & Tenenbaum, G. 2002, "Prevalence of Sexual Abuse in Organised Competitive Sport in Australia," *Journal of Sexual Aggression*, vol. 8, no. 2, pp. 16–36.

SKILLS

Davies, C. 2012, "FWA Interview: Antonín Panenka," *Football Writers' Association*, June 26, available online.

LESBIAN MAFIA

Duncan, P. 2017, "Gay Relationships Are Still Criminalised in 72 Countries, Report Finds," *The Guardian*, July 27, available online.

Football Federation Australia. 2019, *Independent Review of Football Federation Australia Limited ("FFA") National Teams' Management*, October, available online.

Hogshead-Makar, N [@Hogshead3Au]. 2019, *Twitter*, February 4, available online at https://twitter.com/Hogshead3Au/status/1092235323424280576

Kemp, E. 2020, "Alex Blackwell: 'I have felt profiled as a predator because I'm a lesbian,'" *The Guardian*, December 20, available online.

Mark, D. 2019, "Independent Review Says No Lesbian Mafia in Matildas, Alen Stajcic Removal Not Personal," *ABC News*, December 19, available online.

McKay, B [@benmackey]. 2019, *Twitter*, December 19, available online at https://twitter.com/benmackey/status/1207468549104529408

Mendes S (interviewee) & Shepard, D (interviewer). 2020, "Shawn Mendes," *Armchair Expert with Dax Shepard*, podcast, December 14, available online.

Parkinson, C. 2017, *100 Women: Rugby for lesbians in South Africa*, film, BBC News Africa.

Plan International Australia. 2019, *Snapshot Analysis: Social media commentary of women athletes and male athletes*, Plan International, April 18, available online.

Sanchez, AA. 2017, "The Whiteness of 'Coming Out': Culture and identity in the disclosure narrative," *Archer Magazine*, July 7, available online.

Singh, J. 2018, *No Archive Will Restore You*, Punctum books, Santa Barbara.

Solomon, A. 1997, "Sneakers," in J Sandoz & J Winans (eds) *Whatever It Takes: Women on women's sport*, Farrar, Straus and Giroux, New York, pp. 243–251.

Symons, CM, O'sullivan, GA & Polman, R. 2017, "The Impacts of Discriminatory Experiences on Lesbian, Gay and Bisexual People in Sport," *Annals of Leisure Research*, vol. 20, no. 4, pp. 467–489.

Part Two

BOOKMARKS

Rudd, K. 2008, *National Apology to the Stolen Generations*, February 13, Parliament House, Canberra.

Watson, SW. 2004, *Smoke Encrypted Whispers*, UQP, St Lucia.

Winch, TJ. 2006, *Swallow the Air*, UQP, St Lucia.

FLOODING MY SENTENCES

Cook, M. 2016, "Damming the 'Flood Evil' on the Brisbane River," *History Australia*, vol. 13, no. 4, pp. 540–556.

Cook, M. 2019, *A River with a City Problem: A history of Brisbane floods*, UQP, St Lucia.

Gela, F. 2011, "Torres Strait Warning of Grave Threat," *Koori Mail*, no. 506, p. 9.

Gorman, J. 2015, "Cyclone-hit Nerimbera Soccer Club Menaced by Another Storm," *The Guardian*, March 24, available online.

COUNTRY IS LIKE THE BODY

Australian Human Rights Commission. 2009, *Native Title Report 2008— Community Guide: Climate change, water and Indigenous knowledge*, Australian Human Rights Commission, February 18, available online.

Birch, T. 2015, "It's Been, It's Here: Tony Birch on climate change's past and present," *The Wheeler Centre Blog*, March 24, available online.

Birch, T. 2014, "Trust and Our Children: Tony Birch reflects on the story of Bunjil the Eagle," *The Wheeler Centre Blog*, September 2, available online.

Dow, S. 2007, "Eden's Lost Horizons," *The Sydney Morning Herald*, November 28, available online.

Kolbert, E. 2014, *The Sixth Extinction: An unnatural history*, Henry Holt and Company, New York.

Mathiesen, K. 2015, "Losing Paradise: The people displaced by atomic bombs, and now climate change," *The Guardian*, March 10, available online.

Memmott, P, Reser, J, Head, B, Davidson, J, Nash, D, O'Rourke, T, Gamage, H, Suliman, S, Lowry, A & Marshall, K. 2013, *Aboriginal Responses to Climate Change in Arid Zone Australia*, National Climate Change Adaptation Research Facility, Gold Coast.

Mitchell, K & Ross, A. 2017, "Navratilova Brands Court a Racist and Homophobe in Arena Row," *The Guardian*, June 2, available online.

Mooney, M, Walsh, F, Hill, R, Davies, J, Sparrow, A & Central Land Council Lytentye Apurte Rangers. 2014, *Climate Change: Learning about what is happening with the weather in Central Australia*, CSIRO with Central Land Council, August 14, available online.

O'Brien, L & Watson, I. 2014, "In Conversation with Uncle Lewis: Bushfires, weather-makers, collective management," *AlterNative*, vol. 10, no. 5, pp. 450–461.

United Nations Economic and Social Council. 2008, *Permanent Forum on Indigenous Issues: Report on the seventh session (April 21 to May 2, 2008)*, United Nations, available online.

TAKING A STAND AGAINST A NAME

Fox Sports. 2021, "Carlton Urged to Change Theme Song as Tune's Racist Origins Surface," *Fox Sports Australia*, April 10, available online.

Graham, M (interviewee) & Fidler, R (interviewer). 2013, "Indigenous Elder Mary Graham Describes the Essence of Indigenous Perception," *Conversations*, ABC Radio National, January 22, available online.

Hagan, S. 2005, *The N Word: One man's stand*, Magabala Books, Broome.

Robertson, J. 2017, "'A Blot on the Landscape': Queensland calls time on racist place names," *The Guardian*, August 30, available online.

Unfinished Business: The art of Gordon Bennett, exhibition, November 7, 2020, to March 21, 2021, QAGOMA, Brisbane.

Webb, C. 2021, "Indigenous People 'Should Have Been' Consulted on New Coon Cheese Name," *The Age*, January 13, available online.

PERSONAL SCORE

Freeman, E. 2010, *Time Binds: Queer temporalities, queer histories*, Duke University Press, Durham and London.

Halberstam, JJ. 2005, *In a Queer Time and Place: Transgender bodies, subcultural lives*, NYU Press, New York.

Nelson, MB. 1999, "My Mother, My Rival" in J Sandoz & J Winans (eds) *Whatever It Takes: Women on women's sport*, Farrar, Straus and Giroux, New York, pp. 109–112.

AUSTRALIA IS OPEN (TO HOLD! RECEIVE! TAKE!)

A.B. Original. 2016, *Reclaim Australia*, Golden Era Records.

Phillips, S. 2022, "Walking While Aboriginal," *Qualitative Inquiry*, vol. 28, no. 2, pp. 198–199.

Rankine, C. 2014, *Citizen: An American lyric*, Graywolf Press, Minneapolis.

Part Three

WHAT I WANT WHEN I WANT YOU

Akbar, A. 2016, "What Belongs to You by Garth Greenwell, Book Review: Repression and rent boys," *Independent*, March 24, available online.

Als, H. 2013, *White Girls*, McSweeney's, San Francisco.

Badu, E. 2003, "I Want You," *Worldwide Underground*, Motown.

Feinberg, L. 1993, *Stone Butch Blues: A novel*, Firebrand Books, Ithaca.

FAMILY IS A STADIUM

Antinoro, M, Bernstein, Shapiro, M & Staeger, W (executive producers). 2018, *Being Serena*, TV series, HBO.

Barty, A [@ashbarty]. 2022, *Instagram*, March 23, available online at www.instagram.com/p/Cbbbr7xBX7N/?hl=en

Carayol, T. 2022, "Ash Barty Built a Near-Perfect Game but Never Lost Sight of the No 1 Priority: Herself," *The Guardian*, March 24, available online.

Cooney, S. 2017, "Serena Williams Joins Long List of Athletes Who Have Competed While Pregnant," *Time*, April 28, available online.

Crawford, F & McGowan, L. 2019, *Never Say Die: The hundred-year overnight success of Australian women's football*, NewSouth, Sydney.

Dellacqua, C, Fuller, R, Hinds, R & Underwood, K (host). 2020, *Offsiders*, television broadcast, February 2, ABC, Sydney.

Emezi, A. 2018, *Freshwater*, Grove Press, New York.

Glover, B. 2020, "Australian Tennis Legend Mark Woodforde Calls Out Ash Barty's Press Conference Stunt," *Wide World of Sports*, January 31, available online

Kleyn, B. 2021, "Australian-First Study Paves Way for Professional Athletes to Return to Elite Sport After Having Children," *ABC News*, November 13, available online.

Leane, J. 2018, *Walk Back Over*, Cordite Books, Melbourne.

Leavy, J. 1978, "Bringing up Baby, Goolagong Style," *The New York Times*, April 30.

Mesic, D. 2022, "Tatjana Maria Calls Out WTA for Not Having 'Pregnancy Rule,'" *Tennis World USA*, March 23, available online.

Play On: The art of sport—10 years of the Basil Sellers Art Prize, 2017. [Exhibition catalogue]. National Exhibitions Touring Support Victoria c/-National Gallery of Victoria and the Ian Potter Museum of Art, University of Melbourne.

Sheppard, LK, Rynne, SB & Willis, JM. 2021, "Sport as a Cultural Offset in Aboriginal Australia?" *Annals of Leisure Research*, vol. 24, no.1, pp. 29–50.

Sheppard, L. (unpublished), "Sport for Development: Privatised aid and Aboriginal sport in Australia," PhD thesis, University of Queensland, Brisbane.

Skerritt, HF. 2011, "Preview: Josie Kunoth Petyarre: Sugarbags," *Artist Profile Magazine*, vol. 15, pp. 122–123.

Sport Australia. 2019, "Sport Australia Thanks Volunteers: 'Backbone of our industry,'" *Australian Sports Commission*, May 20, available online.

Whitaker, C, Law, D & Roberts, M (host). 2020, "Aus Open Day 11—Did Barty Blow It?" *The Tennis Podcast*, January 30, available online.

OUR DESCENDANTS ARE WATCHING

Behrendt L. 2016, *Finding Eliza: Power and colonial storytelling*, UQP, St Lucia.

Gibran, K. 1995, *The Prophet*, pocket edition, Knopf, New York.

Lorde, A. 2018, *The Master's Tools Will Never Dismantle the Master's House*, Penguin Classics, London.

Mokak, G. 2017, "Cannibals and Savages: The power of colonial storytelling," *NITV*, August 29, available online.

White, M. (undated), "The Master's Tools: The wisdom of Audre Lorde," blog, available online at www.activistgraduateschool.org/on-the-masters-tools

STORYING CARE

Bonson, D. 2018, "Closing the Indigenous LGBQTI Health Gap," *IndigenousX*, February 12, available online.

Belcourt, B-R. 2017, "The Body Remembers When the World Broke Open," *artseverywhere*, August 2, available online.

Darwin, L. 2017, "Vital Voices Are Missing in the Discussion to Reduce Indigenous Suicide Rates," *HuffPost*, May 25, available online.

Kelaher, M, Luke, J, Ferdinand, A, Chamravi, D, Ewen, S & Paradies, Y. 2018, *An Evaluation Framework to Improve Aboriginal and Torres Strait Islander Health*, Lowitja Institute, Melbourne.

Lavelle, C. 2017, "Death by Racism: Bigotry in the health system is harming Indigenous patients," *IndigenousX*, February 6, available online.

Fogarty, W, Bulloch, H, McDonnell, S & Davis, M. 2018, *Deficit Discourse and Indigenous Health: How narrative framings of Aboriginal and Torres Strait Islander people are reproduced in policy*, Lowitja Institute, Melbourne.

National Aboriginal Community Controlled Health Organisation. (undated), "Aboriginal Community Controlled Health Organisations (ACCHOs)," *NACCHO*, available online at www.naccho.org.au/ acchos/

Pearson, L. 2018, "Is the National Indigenous Health Survey Ethical?" *IndigenousX*, November 10, available online.

Walter, M & Kukutai, T. 2015, "Recognition and Indigenizing Official Statistics: Reflections from Aotearoa New Zealand and Australia," *Statistical Journal of the IAOS*, vol. 31, no, 2, pp. 317–326.

Watego, C. 2018, "Moving Beyond the Frontline: The power and promise of an Indigenous health workforce," *IndigenousX*, October 29, available online.

FRANCE 2019

Armstrong, K. 2019, "The US Women's Soccer Team Is Suing for Equal Pay," *yahoo!finance*, March 9, available online.

Department of Prime Minister and Cabinet, "Australian National Colours," available online at www.pmc.gov.au/government/australian-national-symbols/australian-national-colours

VIRUS IN A SCORCHED LAND

Allam, L. 2020, "Grave Fears Held for Hundreds of Important NSW South Coast Indigenous Sites," *The Guardian*, January 16, available online.

Burton, N. 2020, "Invasion Day Is a Day of Mourning for Indigenous Australians. The Bushfires Make This Year Extra Poignant," *Vox*, January 24, available online.

Commonwealth of Australia. 2020, *Royal Commission into National Natural Disaster Arrangements Report*, October 28, available online.

RMIT ABC Fact Check Unit. 2020, "Does Australia Have the Highest Food Security in the World?" *Crikey*, May 19, available online.

Williamson, B, Markham, F & Weir, J. 2020, "1 in 10 Children Affected by Bushfires Is Indigenous. We've Been Ignoring Them for Too Long," *The Conversation*, April 2, available online.

WHAT SURVIVAL FEELS LIKE

Agbabi, P. 1995, *R.A.W.*, Gecko Press, Wellington.

Harkin, N. 2021, "REFUSE/RETURN/REMAIN," in Disney, D & Hall, M (eds), *New Directions in Contemporary Australian Poetry*, Palgrave Macmillan, p. 26.

Lorde, A. 2018, *The Master's Tools Will Never Dismantle the Master's House*, Penguin Classics, London.

Part Four

2023

Saadlou, S. 2019, "Sahar Khodayari—Football's Most Unlikely Heroine," *Medium*, September 11, available online.

Cave, N. 2018, *UNTIL*, exhibition, November 23, 2018, to March 3, 2019, Carriageworks, Sydney.

TRANS SPORTING UTOPIAS

Adams, WL. 2009, "Could This Women's World Champ Be a Man?" *Time*, August 21, available online.

Adetiba, E. 2020, "Caster Semenya and the Cruel History of Contested Black Femininity," *SB Nation*, April 20, available online.

Australian Human Rights Commission. 2019, *Guidelines for the Inclusion of Transgender and Gender Diverse People in Sport*, June 13, available online.

Faatau'uu-Satiu, G. 2020, "Football's First Fa'afafine: Trans rights trailblazer Jaiyah Saelua on stardom and sisterhood," *The Guardian*, August 1, available online.

Hyndal, P. 2016, "Inclusion of Transgender and Intersex People in Sport," Diversity and Inclusion in Sport Forum, *Play by the Rules*, available online at www.playbytherules.net.au/resources/videos/peter-hyndal

Kirkbright, W. 2015, "Queer Utopias, Art Practices and Worldmaking," panel, Queer Provocations, Red Rattler Theatre, Sydney.

Law, S [@siufung_law]. 2019, *Instagram*, September 5, available online at www.instagram.com/p/B2BBxSAnHLA/?hl=en

O'Halloran, K. 2017, "AFL Cannot Play Equality Card When Denying Transgender Footballer Hannah Mouncey," *The Guardian*, October 17, available online.

ranapiri, em. 2021, "Ellen van Neerven, (untitled) Commentator: Essa Ranapiri," *Australian Poetry Journal*, vol. 10, no. 2, p. 80.

CHALLENGING THE BINARY

Adcock, B. 2013, "Is It Hard to Surf with Boobs?" *Griffith Review 40: Women & Power*, available online.

Aeria, G, Darling, A & Pearce, D. 2022, "AFL Grants Exemption to 14-year-old Victorian Girl to Play Footy with Boys in Mixed Comp," *ABC News*, May 13, available online.

Crawford, F & McGowan, L. 2019, *Never Say Die: The hundred-year overnight success of Australian women's football*, NewSouth, Sydney.

de la Cretaz, F. 2021, "Living Nonbinary in a Binary Sports World," *Sports Illustrated*, April 16, available online.

Halberstam, J. 2018, *Trans: A quick and quirky account of gender variability*, University of California Press, Oakland.

O'Halloran, K. 2022, "Gold Coast Sun Tori Groves-Little on Coming Out as Non-Binary Ahead of AFLW Pride Round," *ABC News*, January 21, available online.

Tuohy, W. 2021, "'Absolutely Huge': AFLW star Vescio changes the game on gender diversity," *The Age*, December 30, available online.

Quinn [@TheQuinny5]. 2020, *Twitter*, September 12, available online at https://twitter.com/thequinny5/status/1304757113986732032

MY EXISTENCE

FOLX Health. 2022, "A Conversation with Living Legend Monica Helms, Creator of the Transgender Flag," *FOLX Health*, February 28, available online.

Laniyuk [laniyuk]. 2021, *Instagram*, May 23, available online at www.instagram.com/tv/CPMldYQA3Y7/

O'sullivan, S. 2021, "The Colonial Project of Gender (and Everything Else)," *Genealogy*, vol. 5, no. 3, available online.

ranapiri, em. 2019, *ransack*, Victoria University Press, Wellington.

INVASION DAY SPIN CLASS

DRMNGNOW ft. Philly, Adrian Eagle & Culture Evolves. 2018, "Australia Does Not Exist," Pataphysics.

Freeman, C. [@CathyFreeman] 2021, *Twitter*, January 22, available online at https://twitter.com/cathyfreeman/status/1352421660893175810

Hage, G. 2021, "In Honouring Those Who Are Prejudiced, the Australia Day Awards Perpetuate Bigotry," *The Guardian*, January 24, available online.

James, D [as @IndigenousX]. 2021, *Twitter*, January 23, available online at https://twitter.com/indigenousx/status/1352785242520621056

McLennen, A. 2022, "Finding Next Cathy Freeman, Ian Thorpe the Mission of Ian Chesterman as Australian Olympic Committee President," *ABC News*, May 2, available online.

TAPESTRIES OF POISON

Allen, K. 2021, "There Is No Environmental Literature Without Indigenous Authors," *Book Riot*, August 5, available online.

Ball, T. 2021, "Unfollow the Map," *Sydney Review of Books*, November 8, available online.

Cobby Eckermann, A. 2016, "Thunder Raining Poison," *Poetry Magazine*, May, available online.

Dungy, CT (ed.). 2009, *Black Nature: Four centuries of African American nature poetry*, University of Georgia Press, Athens.

"Feral: The bitter clash of culture over Australia's wild horses," 2022, *Four Corners*, television broadcast, February 21, ABC, available online.

Gilchrist, S. 2022, "Unbelonging to Australia: Asserting Indigenous sovereignty," online webinar, February 12, Artspace, Sydney.

Greer, G. 2014, *White Beech: The rainforest years*, Bloomsbury, London.

Jonscher, S & Lysaght, G-J. 2019, "Maralinga Story to Be Told Through the Eyes of Traditional Owners Affected by Britain's Atomic Bomb Testing," *ABC News*, July 1, available online.

Page, A & Memmott, P. 2021, *Design: Building on country*, Thames & Hudson, Port Melbourne.

Papertalk Green, C & Kinsella, J. 2018, *False Claims of Colonial Thieves*, Magabala Books, Broome.

Pico, T. 2017, *Nature Poem*, Tin House, New York.

Scarce, Y. 2015, *Thunder Raining Poison*, exhibition, October 8, 2015, to January 17, 2016, Art Gallery of South Australia, Adelaide.

Steffensen, V. 2020, *Fire Country: How Indigenous fire management could help save Australia*, Hardie Grant, Melbourne.

Ybarra, PS. 2016, *Writing the Goodlife: Mexican American literature and the environment*, University of Arizona Press, Tucson.

THE PAIN GAME

Hedva, J. 2016, "Sick Woman Theory," *Mask Magazine*, January, available online.

John, W. 2022, "Why Standard Pain Questions Don't Work for Indigenous Australians," *Rheumatology Republic*, May 26, available online.

O'Halloran, K. 2022, "Why AFLW Players Are Up to Six Times More Likely to Injure Their ACLs than Men," *ABC News*, March 20, available online.

Pico, T. 2017, *Nature Poem*, Tin House, New York.

Scarry, E. 1985, *The Body in Pain: The making and unmaking of the world*, Oxford University Press, New York.

AS COUNTRY

Leane, J. 2017, "Gathering: The politics of memory and contemporary Aboriginal women's writing," *Antipodes*, vol. 31, no. 2, pp. 242–251.

Rigney, D, Bell, D & Vivian, A. 2021, "Talking Treaty: A conversation on how Indigenous Nations can become Treaty ready," in A Whittaker, H Hobbs & L Coombs (eds) *Treaty-making: 250 years later*, The Federation Press, Sydney.

Vizenor, G. 1999, *Manifest Manners: Narratives on postindian survivance*. University of Nebraska Press, Lincoln.

HOW TO PLAY SPORT ON INDIGENOUS LAND

Foster, C. 2022, "Writing with Purpose," panel, Football Writers Festival, March 25–27, Johnny Warren Football Museum, Jamberoo.

Huggins, J. 2022, *Sister Girl: Reflections on tiddaism, identity and reconciliation*, UQP, St Lucia.

Kerkhove, R. 2015, *Aboriginal Camp Sites of Greater Brisbane: An historical guide*, Boolarong Press, Brisbane.

North, J. 2022, "Statement from Chair of National Indigenous Advisory Group, Jade North," October 2, *Football Australia*, available online.

Page, A & Memmott, P. 2021, *Design: Building on country*, Thames & Hudson, Port Melbourne.

Rice, M, Weisbrot, E, Bradshaw, S, Steffen, W, Hughes, L, Bambrick, H, Charlesworth, K, Hutley, N & Upton, L. 2021, *Game, Set, Match: Calling time on climate inaction*, Climate Council of Australia Limited.

Roach, A. 1997, "A Child Was Born Here," *Looking for Butterboy*, Mushroom Records.

POSTGAME

Carnegie, C. 2020, "Racism Ended My Netball Career Before It Even Began," *IndigenousX*, September 22, available online.

Two Dollar Radio
Books too loud to Ignore

ALSO AVAILABLE Here are some other titles you might want to dig into.

A HISTORY OF MY BRIEF BODY
ESSAYS BY **BILLY-RAY BELCOURT**

→ **2021 Lambda Literary Award for Gay Memoir/Biography, Finalist.**
→ **"A Best Book of 2020"** —*Kirkus Reviews, Book Riot, CBC, Globe and Mail*

← "Stunning." —Michelle Hart, *O, The Oprah Magazine*

A BRAVE, RAW, AND fiercely intelligent collection of essays and vignettes on grief, colonial violence, joy, love, and queerness.

THEY CAN'T KILL US UNTIL THEY KILL US
ESSAYS BY **HANIF ABDURRAQIB**

→ **Best Books 2017:** NPR, *Buzzfeed, Paste Magazine, Esquire, Chicago Tribune, Vol. 1 Brooklyn, CBC* (Canada), *Stereogum, National Post* (Canada), *Entropy, Heavy, Book Riot, Chicago Review of Books* (November), *The Los Angeles Review, Michigan Daily*

← "Funny, painful, precise, desperate, and loving throughout. Not a day has sounded the same since I read him." —Greil Marcus, *Village Voice*

NIGHT ROOMS ESSAYS BY **GINA NUTT**

→ **"A Best Book of 2021"** —NPR

← "In writing both revelatory and intimate, Nutt probes the most frightening aspects of life in such a way that she manages to shed light and offer understanding even about those things that lurk in the deepest and darkest of shadows." —Kristin Iversen, *Refinery29*

← "A hallucinatory experience that doesn't obscure but instead deepens the subjects that Nutt explores." —Jeannie Vanasco, *The Believer*

SOME OF US ARE VERY HUNGRY NOW
ESSAYS BY **ANDRE PERRY**

← "A complete, deep, satisfying read." —Gabino Iglesias, NPR

ANDRE PERRY'S DEBUT COLLECTION of personal essays travels from Washington DC to Iowa City to Hong Kong in search of both individual and national identity while displaying tenderness and a disarming honesty.

808S & OTHERWORLDS ESSAYS BY **SEAN AVERY MEDLIN**

→ **"September's Most Anticipated LGBTQIA+ Literature"** —*Lambda Literary*

← An elegant mash of memoir, poetry, tales of appropriation, thoughts on Black masculinity, Hulk, Kanye." —Christopher Borrelli, *Chicago Tribune*

← "Purrs with variety and energy, with riffs on Black masculinity, anime, gaming, rap, gender identity, and dislocation in Phoenix's western suburbs." —Michelle Beaver, *The Los Angeles Review of Books*

← "Gives a voice to queer Black rap enthusiasts." —*Teen Vogue*